Julie Taboulie's
Lebanese Kitchen

Julie Taboulie's
Lebanese Kitchen

Authentic Recipes for Fresh and Flavorful
Mediterranean Home Cooking

Julie Ann Sageer

with

LEAH BHABHA

PHOTOGRAPHS BY ALEXANDRA GRABLEWSKI

ST. MARTIN'S GRIFFIN
NEW YORK

To my mentor, master chef, and miraculous mother, Mama.
I would not be here without you. I could not do this without you.
I wouldn't be the woman and chef that I am today without you.

Because you believed in me, I believed in me. I believe in you. I am blessed to have
you as my mother. I love you with all of my heart and soul forever more.

CONTENTS

INTRODUCTION

I AM SIX YEARS OLD, A BOUNCY TANNED KID WITH LONG BROWN HAIR AND lots of energy. On this sunny afternoon, I am completely and totally focused on the task at hand: picking na'na (fresh mint) from our garden. I carefully select the largest, greenest leaves, slowly running my fingers around their outer ridges. I am surrounded by the plant's heady, refreshing scent, and I can't wait to return to the kitchen and show the spoils to Mama, who is preparing one of my absolute favorite dishes—and one that accompanies most of our meals: taboulie.

When I enter the kitchen, Mama has an enormous wooden bowl in front of her—the biggest bowl I can imagine. I perch myself on a kitchen stool and watch carefully as she finely dices the vine-ripe tomatoes—also from our garden and hand-picked by yours truly—and meticulously chops up the fragrant parsley, always with a sharp knife so the leaves don't bruise. She inspects the na'na with approval, and I'm on to my next task: lemons. My small hands grasp each lemon wedge, squeezing as hard as my little palms let me, and carefully picking out any pips that fall into the bowl. When my hands can squeeze no more, I pluck each mint leaf off the stem, so it, too, can be added to this enormous bowl of flavor. After a thorough chopping, in goes the mint, followed by the fine beige grains of soaked bulgur wheat, and then the rest of the diced vegetables and remaining herbs.

I watch closely as Mama's hands slide up and down the side of the bowl, as she weaves her fingers in and out of the mixture, so that every bite contains a morsel of each ingredient. Now it's time for the olive oil, and I hold the slippery bottle carefully, pouring a thin, steady stream into the bowl, before Mama instructs me to stop, and I add some of my hand-squeezed lemon juice. "A little more lemon juice, Joule" she tells me, and I pour it in, before grinding the pepper and salt into the mixture, because few dishes are complete without these two star ingredients. After a final mix comes my favorite part: taste testing. Mama's hands are slick with oil as she reaches for a crisp romaine lettuce leaf, into which she scoops some of the fresh taboulie. I open my mouth as wide as possible, and take in the tastes and textures—the crunchy salad, firm beads of wheat, and an avalanche of refreshing flavors with a tang of lemon juice at the end. "How is that, habibi?" she asks me, and I nod vigorously, trying to smile with my mouth full, my eyes open wide with excitement. With my seal of approval, the taboulie joins the rest of Mama's dishes on our table, each more delicious than the last.

I may no longer be six years old, but my love of preparing and eating taboulie—this essential Middle Eastern dish—has never waned, not even for a second. It's no accident, then, that the grain salad has become an irreplaceable part of my identity. When I meet the wonderful fans of my TV show *Cooking with Julie Taboulie*, the first question I'm always asked is "Is Julie Taboulie your real name?" The answer is no, not legally, but it might as well be! Growing up in Utica, a small industrial town in upstate New York, I was constantly surrounded by the many members of my tight-knit family and the town's large Lebanese community. When I was just six or seven years old, my uncles gave me the nickname "Julie Taboulie" after noticing my obsession with the dish, and food in general. Like *hummus to pita*, the name stuck and continues to stick—it's even shaped my entire career!

But how did I turn a family nickname into a cooking show watched by audiences throughout North America? Well, like every good story, it's a long one, so take a seat and a sticky square of *baklawa* and hear me out. In 2007, I was living in New York City hosting, writing, and producing television segments for Bloomberg's NYCTV. I found that as fun as the red-carpet segments and charitable event coverage were, I was always especially drawn to the food-focused pieces. Not that I don't love flowing gowns and fancy events, but food, now that, I could sink my teeth into. When I wasn't on TV, I was watching TV—food TV. I soon noticed that there weren't any Lebanese or Middle Eastern cooking shows and that whenever an American TV chef was creating Lebanese food I was yelling—yes, yelling—at the TV. "You're not supposed to bake those" and "that's not what that's called!" I would scream at the television, knowing that none of their dishes and concoctions could compare with the magical tastes that I enjoyed in my Mama's kitchen.

In the summer of 2007, a fantastic opportunity presented itself to me: a month-long trip back to the old country, Lebanon, a place which had deeply impacted my identity even though I'd never visited. Growing up I had heard so much about my Lebanese family, as my mother had come to the U.S. with only her brothers—leaving her four sisters and parents behind. On the rare occasions that my *Sitto* (maternal grandmother) visited us, I relished her stories and company, and wished I could return with her to experience the country of my parents' youth. I had spent so long as a child wondering what Lebanon was like—how it looked and smelled, how it was different from our home in upstate New York, and, of course, how the food tasted compared with ours. Politically, Lebanon has often been a place of turmoil, but my family had always spoken of it with so much affection and nostalgia—I had to see for myself.

On August 1, 2007, after thirteen hours of travel and a distance of six thousand miles, I found myself on my Sitto's doorstep, where a crowd of family members was waiting for me. I stepped out of my uncle's car, and into my grandmother's outstretched arms—arms I hadn't encountered in more than ten years—bringing tears to both of our eyes. After the many hugs and kisses, we shared my "welcome" meal—which was fit for a queen. For the rest of the month, I explored my Lebanese roots with my eyes wide open, sleeping in the bed my mother had slept in during her childhood, and embracing my beloved culture. My Arabic flourished in Lebanon, as I improved my speaking and comprehension skills encouraged by my loving (and patient!) family. With each day, I saw more and more of myself in my relatives: my love of cooking and feeding people and my endless capacity for conversation and curiosity.

Since one of my cousins was getting married, the house was constantly filled with magnificent bouquets of flowers and stacked boxes of sweets. I noticed that all of the sweets were wrapped the same—and all of them seemed to come from one particular place: Abdul Rahman

and Sons in Tripoli. Eager to examine the place where these heavenly sweet treats were prepared, I proposed a visit to Tripoli. The moment I walked in, I was entranced by a flurry of activity. The many-floored building featured ice cream makers, chocolatiers, savory chefs and, of course, the pastry bakers. After persuading my cousins (and one of the store's employees) to take a tour, I luxuriated in the experience—a kid in a literal candy shop—snapping pictures (especially after my video camera was banned!). Finally, I had seen where these magical sweets were being made!

Although the food in Lebanon was mostly very similar to the dishes on my mother's table, the varieties of produce, meat, and dairy (and the lack of preservatives) provided even more flavor. As I bonded with my cousins—all of whom are around my age—we went on more food adventures, including a visit to see where *bizzar*—the deliciously spicy nut mix on every Lebanese table—was roasted. I examined the many different kinds of roasted nuts, selecting my favorites to make a homemade mix—feeling very far away from the States, where the mixes are premade and packaged. As the days drew to a close, I dreaded leaving my family, with whom I had forged a very close bond. Lebanese hospitality was more than I ever could have imagined with every visit, even to a clothing store, involving a cup of strong Arabic coffee, sweets, and conversation. In my last few days, I held my family even closer, and took care to remember the little things: the friendly man shaving shawarma near our house, and the way my grandmother looked at me, as I so closely resembled my mother at a young age. I left with a full, heavy heart, knowing that this experience would change me for a lifetime.

Returning to New York was bittersweet, as I had experienced such a feeling of belonging and fulfillment in Lebanon. I continued watching my food TV shows, and thinking more and more of my connection with the cuisine of my childhood and heritage. I'm not sure exactly when it happened, but I had soon written down—scribbled into my trusty notebook—the words "Julie Taboulie, Lebanese Cuisine." It dawned on me that what I most wanted was to popularize Lebanese cuisine and culture and continue my family's culinary legacy.

From Julie Taboulie, young impressionable kid, to Lebanese cooking authority! I returned to my family again, but this time in the Finger Lakes region of New York State. Invigorated by my experience in Lebanon, I immersed myself in the cooking of my heritage, logging countless hours in my Mama's kitchen and trying to soak up all her culinary skills. I watched her rolling out *ajeen* (a traditional non-yeasted bread), pickling vegetables for a medley called *kabees,* and blending chickpeas for hummus. I was immediately transported back to my childhood, where the scents of rose water and orange blossom signaled the arrival of the holidays, and Sundays brought with them the smell of Mama baking bread.

After lots of culinary practice, I launched my brand, "Julie Taboulie, Lebanese Cuisine" and created a month-long introductory Lebanese cooking course at a local library. My first course sold out very quickly, and I soon became a sought-after instructor in the area, teaching my hands-on classes at institutions like the Syracuse Test Kitchen, Wegmans School of Culinary Arts, and the New York Wine and Culinary Center. I was right—people *did* want to learn about the delicious foods of the old country, and how to cook them! I received calls from various organizations in the area, and returned to TV—this time with my own weekly Lebanese cooking segment "Cooking with Julie Taboulie"—written, produced, and created by Ms. Taboulie, herself!

I was on the local ABC and PBS networks, and soon started my own cooking show, which aired on PBS in March 2012. Soon, the show was picked up by the regional district programmers, and within a year, *Cooking with Julie Taboulie* was distributed nationally.

The stunning Finger Lakes region of upstate New York serves as the backdrop and setting for my show—a one-of-a-kind experience for my viewers featuring local farms, markets, wineries, and, of course, lots of time with my Mama in her gorgeous vegetable garden. My goal is to introduce the viewers to the food of my culture, and show that they, too, can prepare all of these fabulous delicacies with ease, finesse, and fresh, easy-to-find ingredients. Using my experience and cultural heritage, I craft authentic Lebanese recipes passed down through the generations, teaching viewers my own tips, tricks, and shortcuts along the way. In February 2013, I received an Emmy nomination for best informational/instructional program. In addition to numerous television and radio appearances, I am a media spokesperson for two wonderful food companies: Sabra dip company and Toufayan Pita bakery. I am a frequent presence at local and nationwide Lebanese and Middle Eastern culinary events where I get to meet (and feed!) many of my lovely, devoted fans.

My passion for Lebanon and its cuisine and culture has led me to a career in educating and enlightening a whole new group of Middle Eastern food enthusiasts! With its emphasis on fresh, seasonal ingredients, whole grains and simple, healthy cooking techniques, Lebanese cuisine could not be a better complement to the wellness and health-conscious approach to life today, and I thank my lucky Lebanese stars every day that this is the food of my family and heritage. Lebanese food is generally served all at once—not coursed out like many other cuisines. This ensures that everyone is together at the table throughout the meal—leaving more time for conversation and shared eating—just another thing I love about my food heritage! Much awaited by viewers of my show and my cooking students and fans, this cookbook will use the same easy techniques and effervescent enthusiasm I display on my TV show to illuminate Lebanese cuisine for the masses.

Each Julie-tested, Mama-approved recipe will provide readers with hands-on instructions, tips, and tricks—as if I was cooking beside them! I want Lebanese food to become second nature to my readers and fans—something you can whip up time and time again and even pass on to the next generation! I use heaps of fresh, seasonal ingredients in my recipes and my motto is: "fresh is best." The recipes range from classics such as falafel, shawarma, and (of course) taboulie, to warming *bazilla*—a stew of tomato, green peas, and lamb—and rose water–infused sweet treats. In these 125 recipes, you'll learn how easy it is to make fresh *labneh* (strained yogurt), and how simply you can put together your own delicious, multipurpose spice mixes. In addition to our flavorful meat and chicken dishes, Lebanese cuisine offers a wide variety of vegetarian, pescatarian, vegan, and gluten-free dishes—usually with no substitutions whatsoever! Every chapter here includes a multitude of main dishes for eaters of all kinds and preferences, from meat lovers to veggie heads and everything in between! Welcome, *Ahla Wou Sahla*, ترحيب!

MEZZA

small plates

hummus b tahini . . . 11
CLASSIC CHICKPEA AND SESAME SEED SPREAD

khoudra wa kabis . . . 15
LEBANESE VEGETABLE CRUDITÉ

baba ghanouj . . . 17
ROASTED EGGPLANT DIP

mouhamarah . . . 18
ROASTED RED PEPPER–WALNUT SPREAD

fatteh hummus . . . 21
WARM CHICKPEA-PITA-CHIP-DIP BOWL

kibbeh batata . . . 25
POTATO, BULGUR, AND HERB SPREAD

kibbeh nayeh . . . 27
LEBANESE STEAK AND BULGUR WHEAT TARTARE

MEZZA, PRONOUNCED MAH-ZAH, IS A UNIQUELY MIDDLE EASTERN course, and the way every Lebanese meal begins: with a variety of small dishes and bites—we were doing "small plates" way before it was a trend! My favorite thing about mezza is the many tastes you experience at the same time, from luscious, flavorful dips like Hummus b Tahini (Classic Chickpea and Sesame Seed Spread), Mouhamarah, (Roasted Red Pepper–Walnut Spread), and Kibbeh Batata (Potato-Bulgur-Herb Spread) to crunchy pickled veggies, Khoudra wa Kabis, and our unique take on steak tartare, Kibbeh Nayeh. Served with heaps of fresh baked pocket bread, mezza is the perfect start to a meal; with everyone gathered around the many plates, swapping news, conversation, and mouthfuls. Mezza is just as much a course as a social hour in our culture—we Lebanese love to linger over many hours of colorful conversation, good company, and, of course, food! In my selection of Taboulie-approved mezza, there's something for absolutely everyone, no matter your age, hunger level, or dietary preferences! Santein! To your health and happiness!

Hummus b Tahini

classic chickpea and sesame seed spread

Hummus *translates literally as "chickpea" in Arabic, and my recipe is a simple, purist's version—creamy and nutty with some lemon and garlic weaved in. If you're scared to try homemade hummus, don't be! It's only a little more work than opening a container, and the flavor is heavenly. Since the chickpeas (also called garbanzo beans) need to be soaked overnight, make sure to start this process the day before! I always stick true to tradition and use dried chickpeas instead of canned because of their vibrant fresh flavor.*

I like to serve my hummus warm (the Lebanese way!), with a drizzle of extra-virgin olive oil, chopped fresh parsley, and a sprinkling of paprika and toasted pine nuts. It's the perfect spread for toasty Khebez Arabi, *or "pita bread" (page 205), or sliced raw veggies. If you're looking for more variety—for a party or gathering—check out my "I Heart Heavenly Hummus Bar," (page 14).* ❖ **MAKES 4 TO 6 SERVINGS**

1 cup dried whole chickpeas

½ teaspoon baking soda

3 garlic cloves

⅓ cup tahini (see page 280), thoroughly stirred

½ cup freshly squeezed lemon juice

1 teaspoon sea salt

1 tablespoon unsalted butter, for toasting the pine nuts

¼ cup pine nuts, for garnish

2 tablespoons extra-virgin olive oil, for garnish

2 pinches sweet paprika, for garnish

1 tablespoon fresh flat-leaf parsley, finely chopped, for garnish

6 large pita bread pockets, warmed and sliced into wedges, for serving

One day before you plan to serve the hummus, spread the dried chickpeas evenly into one single layer on a clean surface and discard any that are discolored. Place the chickpeas in a large bowl, cover with 6 cups of cold water, and stir in the baking soda. Cover the bowl and set aside at room temperature to soak overnight.

The next day, drain the chickpeas and thoroughly rinse with cold water. Place the chickpeas in a large, heavy-bottomed pot and fill with 8 cups of cold water. Cover the pot and place over high heat. When the water comes to a rolling boil, remove the lid, and skim off any foam that has collected on top of the water. Continue to boil the chickpeas for another 10 to 15 minutes, watching carefully to prevent boiling over, and skimming the foam about four or five times.

After the chickpeas have boiled for the additional 10 to 15 minutes, test a chickpea by squeezing it in between your finger, it should be somewhat squishy. Reduce the heat to a simmer, cover the pot, and continue to simmer for 25 to 30 minutes until the chickpeas are very soft but still hold their shape, and the skin begins to come off. Taste a chickpea: it should melt in your mouth, with no crunch at all. If needed, continue to cook until the chickpeas are very soft. Drain the chickpeas, reserving ¼ cup of the cooking liquid and ¼ cup of the cooked chickpeas for garnish.

continued

Using a food processor, add the garlic, the cooked chickpeas, and process until smooth, pausing periodically to scrape down the sides and bottom of the bowl. If the mixture is too thick and the chickpeas aren't breaking down, add the reserved cooking liquid. When the paste is smooth, add the tahini and fully incorporate into the paste. Add the lemon juice and salt, and process several times until the mixture is silky and a light beige color. You should be able to taste all the ingredients; a lemony taste first and foremost with a subtle hint of garlic and a nutty tahini aftertaste.

In a small pot, melt the unsalted butter on medium-high heat. Once it begins to froth, add the pine nuts and toast for a minute or two, just until fragrant. Remove from the heat and set aside in a small bowl.

Transfer the hummus from the food processor and, using a spatula, spread the hummus onto a large serving plate or bowl and drizzle with the olive oil. Sprinkle with the paprika, chopped parsley, and toasted pine nuts and place the reserved whole chickpeas in the center of the hummus or make one of the variations below. Serve warm with the warmed bread.

I Heart Heavenly Hummus Bar

Housemade. Homemade. Handmade. With lots of Lebanese love from my Lebanese kitchen to yours, each of these incredible culinary combinations are drizzled with extra-virgin olive oil

HEAVENLY HUMMUS & HESHWI ❖ Add Heshwi (page 123) a mouthwatering meat mixture of sautéed onions, luscious lamb meat, freshly chopped mint leaves, and toasted-to-perfection pine nuts spiked with allspice and seven spice.

FEELING FRESH HERB & SPRING ONION ❖ Finish with fresh and finely chopped flat-leaf parsley, mint leaves, spring onions (scallions), and chives.

SIMPLY SMOOTH STYLE ❖ Add extra-virgin olive oil, a little bit of freshly squeezed lemon juice, and lightly sprinkle with sea salt.

SELMA STYLE ❖ This one is for my vegetarian sister, Selma! My own version of a vegetarian heshwi. Add finely diced and sautéed Vidalia onions, baby bella mushrooms mixed with freshly minced mint leaves and flat-leaf parsley seasoned with sea salt, allspice, and seven spice topped with toasted-to-perfection pine nuts.

SOME LIKE IT HOT HUMMUS ❖ Add spicy and smoky concoction of cayenne pepper, Aleppo crushed red pepper flakes, and sweet and smoky paprika for a "some like it hot hummus!"

Khoudra wa Kabis

lebanese vegetable crudités

In Arabic, khoudra *means "produce," while* kabis *translates to "pickled."* Khoudra wa Kabis *always accompany a mezza platter, and is one of my favorite ways of showcasing the seasonal vegetables from my Mama's* jinah, *or "garden." During the winter months, you'll find even more pickles that we've prepared and stored in our* mouneh *(pantry). Feel free to experiment with your favorite vegetables, herbs, onions, and olives, and make sure to beautifully arrange all of your seasonal bounty!* ❖ **MAKES 4 TO 6 SERVINGS**

1 cup Zaytoun olives, left whole (see page 184)

4 bell peppers (1 each of red, orange, yellow, and green), cored, seeded, and sliced into spears

3 ripe garden tomatoes, 2 cut into thick wedges and 1 left whole

3 Persian cucumbers (or other seedless cucumbers), sliced into long spears

6 pickled Persian cucumbers *(Kabis Khyar)*, left whole (see page 190)

6 radishes, trimmed and halved

1 small white onion, quartered

1 cup pickled turnips *(Kabis Lefet)*, left whole (page 193)

6 pickled baby Indian eggplants *(Kabis Batanjan)*, left whole (see page 187)

4 scallions, ends trimmed, 2 sliced in half, and 2 left whole

1 small bunch fresh flat-leaf parsley sprigs, left whole

1 small bunch fresh chives, left whole

3 fresh thyme sprigs

3 long hot red and green peppers (see page 281) or Hungarian wax hot peppers

Select a medium to large serving platter. Place the olives in a small bowl in the center of the platter, with another small bowl on the side for the pits. Arrange the bell peppers in a circular pattern around the olive bowl, starting with red, then orange, then yellow, and ending with green. Continue arranging in a circular pattern with the tomato wedges and cucumber spears followed by the radishes and onions around the tomato and cucumber. Place the pickled cucumbers, turnips, and eggplants around the other ingredients, and circle those with the scallions, parsley, chives, and thyme. Finish by placing the long hot peppers all around the other ingredients. Serve cold with other mezza.

بابا غنوج

Baba Ghanouj
roasted eggplant dip

Baba ghanouj, *meaning "father of pestle," is always seen as a sidekick to hummus. The eggplants are charred until silky soft and lightly smoky and then blended with nutty tahini, garlic, fresh lemon juice, and herbs. This earthy eggplant spread is rich and robust and makes a terrific appetizer with warm pita or* Khebez Arabi *(page 205)*, Khebez Muhamas *(crispy pita chips, page 206), or as a topping for grilled vegetables or meat.* ✣ **MAKES 4 TO 6 SERVINGS**

3 meduim Italian eggplants
   (see page 280)

3 garlic cloves

1 small bunch fresh flat-leaf parsley
   leaves, finely minced

⅓ cup tahini (see page 280), thoroughly
   stirred

2½ to 3 tablespoons freshly squeezed
   lemon juice

1 teaspoon sea salt

2 tablespoons good-quality extra-virgin
   olive oil, for garnish

2 pinches crushed red pepper flakes,
   for garnish

6 large pita bread pockets, warmed and
   sliced into wedges, for serving

Preheat the oven to 450°F. Using a sharp paring knife, pierce small slits all over through the skin of each eggplant, so they will release air and roast evenly. Place the eggplants on a baking sheet and roast on the center rack of the preheated oven for 40 to 45 minutes, turning over halfway through the roasting time, until they are soft and visibly deflated. Remove the eggplants from the oven and transfer from the baking sheet to a cutting board to cool slightly, or until they are still warm to the touch, but can be handled.

Once they have cooled, slice each eggplant in half lengthwise, split apart with your fingers, and scoop out the roasted pulp; discard the peels. Place the pulp in a fine-mesh sieve over a bowl, and press down with a spatula to release as much excess liquid as possible. Set aside.

While the eggplant drains, place the garlic and parsley in a food processor and process until finely minced. Add the tahini, 2 tablespoons of cold water, lemon juice, and salt, and process until well incorporated, scraping down the sides and bottom of the bowl periodically; the consistency should be smooth and silky without being too thick or too thin. Add the roasted eggplant pulp to the food processor and pulse a few times, just enough to incorporate; do not overprocess.

Transfer the baba ghanouj to a large serving bowl. Drizzle with the olive oil, and sprinkle with the red pepper flakes. Serve at room temperature with the warm pita bread.

Mouhamarah

roasted red pepper–walnut spread

Mouhamarah, pronounced "Moo-hum-moo-rah," means "reddened," referring to this savory spread's bright crimson color. Mouhamarah originated in Aleppo, Syria, and is served throughout the Middle East, usually as a part of the mezza. Smoky-sweet roasted red peppers take the stage, combined with sweet roasted garlic cloves and caramelized onions. Toasted walnuts, pomegranate molasses, a hint of fresh lemon juice, and crushed Aleppo red pepper flakes add even more flavor to my mouhamarah, which you can make using an outdoor grill or in the oven.

Mouhamarah is a perfect spread for my Sumac and Sesame Seed Pita Crisps *(see variation on page 206) and is also delicious with grilled vegetables, steak, shrimp, and scallops.* ❖ **MAKES 4 TO 6 SERVINGS**

1 head garlic (about 10 cloves)

1 ½ cups whole walnuts, unsalted and toasted

3 medium red bell peppers

⅔ cup plus 2 teaspoons extra-virgin olive oil

1 ¼ teaspoons sea salt

1 medium yellow onion, finely diced

2 tablespoons freshly squeezed lemon juice

1 tablespoon pomegranate molasses (see page 280)

1 ½ teaspoons Aleppo crushed red pepper flakes (see page 279)

Preheat the oven to 375°F.

Wrap the head of garlic in aluminum foil and place on the middle rack of the preheated oven for approximately 30 minutes, or until the garlic is completely softened. When roasted, remove from the oven, unwrap the foil (wearing mitts!), and set aside slightly to cool.

While the garlic is roasting, spread out the walnuts in an even layer on a baking sheet and toast in the oven for 5 to 7 minutes until lightly browned and fragrant. Remove from the oven and transfer to a small mixing bowl to cool.

Preheat a grill, or set the oven to broil. Lightly oil the bell peppers with 1 tablespoon of the olive oil and sprinkle with ¼ teaspoon of the sea salt. Place on the hot grill (if using) or on a baking sheet under the broiler for 10 to 15 minutes, turning them occasionally, until all sides are evenly charred, the peppers are slightly deflated, and the skin is blistered; this will facilitate peeling off the skins later. Transfer the peppers to a large mixing bowl, cover tightly with plastic wrap, and set aside for 10 to 15 minutes to steam.

continued

While the peppers steam, heat ¼ cup of the olive oil in a medium pan over medium heat. Add the diced onion, season with ½ teaspoon of the sea salt and toss to coat with the oil. Cook until softened, and lightly golden, about 10 minutes, stirring occasionally, then transfer to a food processor.

By now, the bell peppers should be softened and cool enough to peel. With a small paring knife, scrape the charred skins off the flesh, then slice the roasted peppers down the center and discard the stems and seeds. Transfer all the peppers to the food processor.

Squeeze the roasted garlic cloves from their skins into the food processor. Pulse this mixture a few times, just enough to incorporate all the ingredients. Add the toasted walnuts and with the food processor running, stream in ¼ cup olive oil until a thick texture forms. Pour in the lemon juice and pomegranate molasses and season with the remaining 1 teaspoon salt and ½ teaspoon Aleppo pepper. Pulse the mixture a few more times to combine and create a thick-textured spread with small pieces of walnuts throughout.

To serve, spread out on a plate, drizzle with the remaining 1 tablespoon olive oil, and sprinkle with the remaining ½ teaspoon Aleppo pepper flakes. Serve with pita chips

Fatteh Hummus
warm chickpea pita chip dip bowl

In Lebanon, this peasant-style layered chickpea dish is often eaten for breakfast, and is a favorite morning meal of my Uncle Dominick. Every time he visits my Sitto (grandmother) in our village in Northern Lebanon, he dives into a big serving of this. I've found, though, that this meatless meal is perfect for breakfast, brunch, lunch, or dinner. Warm chickpeas are smashed with garlic cloves and covered with luscious tahini-spiked laban (yogurt) sauce and topped with fresh herbs, toasted pine nuts and—my favorite part— baked pita chips. While the pita is often fried, I prefer to bake mine for a healthier but still crispy-crunchy version.

Even though using soaked dried chickpeas is more time-intensive, I really recommend it—the flavor makes all the difference to this tasty bowl! ❖ **MAKES 4 TO 6 SERVINGS**

1 cup dried chickpeas or 2 cups canned chickpeas

1 teaspoon baking powder

2 large pita pockets, cut into triangular wedges

6 tablespoons extra-virgin olive oil

2 teaspoons sea salt

2 tablespoons sesame seeds

2½ to 3 tablespoons freshly squeezed lemon juice

6 garlic cloves, mashed into a smooth paste

2 cups Laban (homemade Lebanese yogurt, page 223) or whole milk yogurt

½ cup tahini (see page 280), thoroughly stirred

2 tablespoons unsalted butter

⅓ cup pine nuts

2 tablespoons fresh mint leaves, finely minced

2 tablespoons fresh flat-leaf parsley leaves, finely minced

¼ teaspoon sweet paprika, for sprinkling

If using dried chickpeas: The day before you plan to make the layered dip, place the dried chickpeas in a large bowl, completely submerge them in 6 cups cold water, and stir in the baking soda, which will help to accelerate the softening process. Cover the bowl and let soak overnight at room temperature.

The following day, drain and rinse the soaked chickpeas in cold water. Transfer the chickpeas to a large, heavy-bottomed pot over high heat and cover with 8 cups of cold water. Bring the chickpeas to a boil, skimming off any foam that rises to the surface. Once the water is boiling, reduce the heat and simmer for 30 to 45 minutes until the chickpeas are completely cooked through and tender. Turn off the heat and leave the chickpeas in the hot cooking liquid until ready to use.

continued

If using canned chickpeas: Drain and rinse the chickpeas in cold water. Place the chickpeas in a small saucepan, pour 3 cups of cold water over the chickpeas over medium heat and heat through for approximately 5 to 7 minutes, until warm. Turn off the heat and leave the chickpeas in the hot water until ready to use.

Preheat the oven to 450°F. Divide the pita wedges between two baking sheets, placing them in a single layer. Lightly drizzle the pita wedges with about 4 tablespoons of the olive oil, 1 teaspoon of the sea salt, and 2 tablespoons of the sesame seeds. Bake the pita on the center rack of the preheated oven for 10 to 15 minutes until crispy, slightly curled-up on the sides, and lightly golden brown, flipping them over halfway through the baking time. Remove the pita wedges from the oven and set aside to cool slightly.

Drain the chickpeas from the water, reserving ⅓ cup of the cooking liquid. Place the chickpeas and reserved liquid in a medium bowl, along with the remaining 2 tablespoons olive oil, the lemon juice, half the garlic paste, and ½ teaspoon of the sea salt. Using a fork, smash the chickpeas slightly, then toss together thoroughly.

In a medium mixing bowl, combine the laban with the tahini and the remaining garlic paste and mint and whisk together until smooth and creamy and all the ingredients are incorporated. Pour this mixture into a small pot over medium-low heat and whisk continously until warmed. Remove from the heat and set aside.

In a small sauté pan over medium-low heat, melt the butter and add the pine nuts. Cook, stirring continuously, until toasted, fragrant, and light golden brown. Immediately remove from the heat.

In a serving bowl or medium casserole dish, layer half the pita pieces on the bottom, then spoon half the chickpea mixture over it. Ladle the warm laban sauce over all. Add the remaining chickpea mixture over the sauce and sprinkle with the minced parsley, paprika, and toasted pine nuts. Finish by arranging the rest of the pita chips around the serving bowl or casserole dish. Enjoy warm.

––––––––––

taboulie tip! It is key to continuously whisk the yogurt tahini sauce to achieve the correct creamy consistency, otherwise it will likely curdle.

كبة بطاطا

Kibbeh Batata
potato, bulgur, and herb spread

I'm not a vegetarian, but one thing I love about Lebanese food is how many dishes are naturally meatless or just as delicious prepared without meat. Kibbeh Batata comes from my Sitto (grandmother), who would make this each spring during Lent, when we abstain from meat. I love the springtime, not only because it's a gorgeous full-of-life moment after the harsh winter here in Upstate New York, but also because I get to delve into the vault of vegetarian recipes from my mother and grandmother.

The combination of bulgur wheat, creamy potatoes, scallions, and herbs makes for a silky, substantial spread that I like to serve with crunchy Bibb lettuce and radishes. If you're looking for a gluten-free alternative, simply swap the bulgur out for quinoa. ❖ **MAKES 4 TO 6 SERVINGS**

3 medium Yukon Gold potatoes, scrubbed

½ cup fine #1 bulgur wheat (see page 279)

1 teaspoon sea salt

3 garlic cloves, smashed into a smooth paste

2½ to 3 tablespoons freshly squeezed lemon juice

¼ cup extra-virgin olive oil, plus 2 tablespoons for garnish

1 small bunch fresh chives, finely minced

1 small bunch fresh flat-leaf parsley leaves, finely minced

1 small bunch fresh mint leaves, finely minced

4 scallions, ends trimmed, 2 thinly sliced, for serving, 2 finely minced

1 head Bibb lettuce, leaves separated, for serving

1 medium white onion, thinly sliced

2 Persian cucumbers, sliced into spears, for serving

6 radishes, sliced in half, for serving

⅓ cup Zaytoun olives (see page 184) or mixed olives, for serving

Place the potatoes in a medium pot, fill with cold water, and bring to a rolling boil, uncovered over high heat. Once the water comes to a boil, reduce the heat to maintain a steady simmer and cook the potatoes until they are fork-tender, 20 to 25 minutes.

Fill a large bowl with ice and cold water. Once cooked, drain the potatoes and place them in the ice bath to cool. Drain and refrigerate until they are completely cold.

Place the bulgur wheat into a bowl and cover with 3 cups of cold water. Set aside to soak and soften, about 20 minutes.

Remove the potatoes from the refrigerator, peel them, and cut them into quarters. Put the potatoes in a large mixing bowl and, using the back of a fork or a potato masher, mash into a smooth mixture with no lumps.

continued

Once the bulgur has softened and a grain squishes between your fingers, gently squeeze the excess water out of the wheat, working handful by handful, and sprinkle it into the potato mixture. Stir the potato-bulgur mixture to incorporate, season with the sea salt, and mix in the garlic paste, lemon juice, and the ¼ cup of the olive oil. Add the minced herbs and finely minced scallions and stir to distribute thoroughly.

Spread the potato mixture in a circular pattern in the center of a medium serving platter, then make small half-moon indentations in the mixture with the back of a spoon. Pour the remaining 2 tablespoons olive oil into the indentations. Serve with lettuce leaves, sliced scallions, thinly sliced onions, cucumber spears, radishes, and olives.

For the perfect bite, scoop the spread onto a lettuce leaf and top with the raw vegetables and olives.

VARIATION ❖ Replace the bulgur wheat with ½ cup cold cooked quinoa for a gluten-free version.

taboulie tip! It is key that the potatoes are completely cold before smashing otherwise you will end up with mashed potatoes!

كبة نيّة

Kibbeh Nayeh

lebanese steak and bulgur wheat tartare

If there's one quintessentially Lebanese dish, it is Kibbeh Nayeh. *It is the national dish of Lebanon, and Lebanon is internationally known for this dish, so much so, that when someone asks me if I make (or more importantly eat) Kibbeh Nayeh, I know that they're immediately sizing up* how *Lebanese I am. But I have to respect this, because our version of steak tartare is a must-try item, and the king of any mezza table. While many American children weren't fed raw meat on a regular basis (unless by mistake!), my siblings and I looked forward to savoring the taste of Kibbeh Nayeh, which was always present at special occasions and summer barbecues.*

In my family, we approach this dish as purists: high-quality meat, minimal spices, and fine bulgur wheat. We serve it with warm pita, hot peppers, fresh herbs, and a spicy olive oil. Although it has traditionally been (and often still is) prepared by pounding the meat in an large stone jidan *(morter and pestle) I've provided a more streamlined preparation method. As a last tip, make sure that you purchase very high-quality, freshly ground lean meat, as you'll be eating it raw. Let the butcher know that you'll be preparing it tartare-style, so it should be ground in front of you on the cleanest blade possible to avoid contamination. Request a small bag of ice to place on top of the meat so it remains very cold. Use it the same day it is purchased.* ❖ **MAKES 4 TO 6 SERVINGS**

1½ pounds lean sirloin (95 to 99 percent lean), freshly triple ground to order

1 teaspoon sea salt

1 medium yellow onion

½ cup fine #1 bulgur wheat, rinsed (see page 279)

½ teaspoon freshly ground black pepper

2 tablespoons extra-virgin olive oil, for serving

6 fresh mint sprigs, for serving

3 scallions, ends trimmed, green and white parts thinly sliced, for serving

1 large white onion, sliced into wedges, for serving

3 green and red long hot peppers, sliced, for serving

⅓ cup hot pepper–infused olive oil (see page 280), for serving

6 large pita pockets, warmed and cut into wedges, for serving

Season the ground meat with salt and place it in a food processor with about 3 ice cubes. Process for 2 to 3 minutes until the meat has formed a large, smooth ball. Immediately transfer the meat to a large resealable freezer bag, and press down to release all of the air from the bag. Seal the bag, and flatten the meat from the outside so that it forms a 2- to 3-inch-thick rectangle. Keeping the bag flat, place it into the freezer, and chill it for 20 minutes, until ice-cold but not frozen.

While the meat is chilling, grate the onion into fine shreds and put in a large mixing bowl. Set up a small bowl of ice cold water for dampening your hands.

continued

Just before you remove the meat from the freezer, rinse the bulgur wheat in ice-cold water and squeeze the grains to remove any excess water. Add the bulgur to the grated onions and mix together, seasoning with the black pepper. Dip both of your hands into the small bowl of ice-cold water, then knead the bulgur wheat into the onions with your knuckles until the two ingredients are bound together, keeping your hands ice-cold at all times.

Next, remove the meat from the freezer and the bag and place it into the mixing bowl with the onions and bulgur. Combine the mixture and the meat with your hands until the ingredients are entirely incorporated. Then, dip your hands into the ice-cold water (you may need to add more ice or cold water to the bowl at this point or replace the water entirely), and knead the mixture together so that it is well blended. Continue to dip your hands into the cold water, and knead and pound the mixture so it binds together and creates a smooth, moist, spreadable consistency. If the mixture is too thick or dry, add ice-cold water by the tablespoon and knead until you achieve the correct consistency. Do not add too much water, or the mixture will become soggy and stringy.

To serve, spread the Kibbeh Nayeh into a thickness of 2 to 3 inches on a large circular platter. Using the ends of a fork, make small indentations around the dish. Drizzle with 2 tablespoons of the olive oil so that it nestles into the small marks. Place the mint leaves on top and arrange around the mixture. Serve the scallions and white onion wedges and hot pepper slices in side bowls along with a heaping plate of warm pita bread. Set out bottles of extra-virgin olive oil and hot pepper–infused oil near the serving area for guests to add more as needed.

Kibbeh Nayeh should be served immediately, or within 30 minutes of being prepared. If you're not serving it immediately, tightly cover the bowl with plastic wrap and place in the refrigerator until you are ready to plate.

VARIATION ❖ Replace the bulgur wheat with ½ cup cold cooked quinoa for a gluten-free version.

---

taboulie tip! Kibbeh Nayeh should not be eaten the next day, you can simply bake or grill any leftovers. (That is, if there are any!).

SALATA

salads

SALADS (*SALATA*) ARE ONE OF MY ABSOLUTE FAVORITE THINGS TO MAKE and eat—no surprise, since my motto is "Fresh Is Best!" With our love for seasonal produce, lean meats, and wholesome grains, Lebanese cuisine is not only absolutely delicious, it's naturally nutritious as well. In my show and cooking classes, I'm known for my obsession with salads, from my namesake Taboulie to crunchy and refreshing Fattoush and luxurious Khyar b Laban (Cucumber, Yogurt, and Mint Salad). I have to say I'm lucky, though, with my Mama's bountiful garden as a resource, I'm never without salad inspiration or ingredients! Unlike American salads, we Lebanese use heaps of fresh herbs in ours, and you may find yourself sneaking mint, parsley, and scallions into your crunchy greens from now on!

Khyar wa Banadoura

cucumber, tomato, and fresh herb salad

In the summertime, when the produce is at the height of ripeness, I love to make Khyar wa Banadoura—*a simple, flavorful medley of sweet tomatoes, cooling cucumber, and a mass of fragrant chopped herbs. Simply tossed with a classic lemon-infused vinaigrette, it's the ideal accompaniment to any warm-weather meal, especially my* Stuffed Kousa Squash *(page 95).*

Make sure you select tender, thin-skinned Persian cucumbers—they will provide the best texture and flavor for the salad, as they are sweeter and suppler, with fewer small seeds than other varieties.

✤ MAKES 6 SERVINGS

3 Persian cucumbers, ends trimmed and sliced ½ inch thick on the diagonal

3 tomatoes, cut into ½-inch-thick slices

3 sprigs fresh flat-leaf parsley leaves, coarsely chopped

3 sprigs fresh mint leaves, coarsely chopped

3 scallions, ends trimmed, green and white parts finely sliced on the diagonal

3 sprigs fresh oregano, picked and leaves left whole

3 sprigs fresh thyme, picked and leaves left whole

3 garlic cloves

1 teaspoon plus 1 pinch sea salt

⅓ cup extra-virgin olive oil

2 to 3 tablespoons freshly squeezed lemon juice

Combine the cucumbers, tomatoes, and herbs in a large shallow serving bowl and toss together lightly with your hands.

Using a mortar and pestle or garlic press, mash the garlic cloves to a smooth paste, then mash in a pinch of salt. Drizzle the olive oil and fresh lemon juice into the garlic paste and mix until all the ingredients are well incorporated. Set aside.

Evenly sprinkle the remaining 1 teaspoon salt over the salad and evenly distribute the vinaigrette, pouring from the outer edge of the bowl inwards. Lightly toss the salad together.

Serve immediately or cover with plastic wrap and refrigerate for up to an hour before serving.

———————

taboulie tip! Serve this salad in a large but shallow bowl so that the vegetables don't get soggy sitting in the dressing.

taboulie tip! THE CUT MATTERS: Make sure the cucumbers are sliced on the diagonal and slightly large and thick, and that the tomato wedges are also thick.

Fattoush

lebanese peasant bread salad

The Arabic word fattoush *means "little bread crumbs," which refers to the crispy pieces of pita that top this favorite Levantine salad of mine. In Lebanese cuisine, as in many others, we are very conscious of using leftovers, and have a whole family of dishes known as* fattat, *which features day-old bread. Romaine and purslane* (Bakleh), *are combined with vegetables and herbs then topped with the crunchy pita croutons. If you can't find purslane, baby arugula or watercress are a great substitute.* ✣ **MAKES 4 TO 6 SERVINGS**

1 large pita pocket or 2 small pita
    pockets, split into halves

2 tablespoons extra-virgin olive oil

½ teaspoon sea salt

1 teaspoon sumac spice (see page 280)

2 romaine lettuce hearts, coarsely
    chopped

½ each green, red, orange, yellow bell
    peppers, cored, seeded, and thinly
    sliced

3 Persian cucumbers, ends trimmed,
    quartered, cut into ¼-inch-thick slices
    on the diagonal

6 radishes, cut into ¼-inch-thick slices

3 scallions, ends trimmed, green and
    white parts cut into thin strips on the
    diagonal

3 tablespoons fresh flat-leaf parsley
    leaves, coarsely chopped

3 tablespoons fresh mint leaves,
    coarsely chopped

1 tablespoon fresh thyme leaves, picked
    and left whole

1 cup purslane, watercress, or baby
    arugula leaves

3 tomatoes, cut into thick wedges

DRESSING

3 garlic cloves, mashed into a
    smooth paste

⅓ cup extra-virgin olive oil

⅓ cup freshly squeezed lemon juice

¼ cup red or white wine vinegar

1 teaspoon sea salt

½ teaspoon freshly ground black pepper

1 teaspoon sumac spice (see page 280)

1 teaspoon fresh mint leaves, minced

1 teaspoon fresh thyme leaves,
    picked and left whole

Preheat the oven to 400°F. Drizzle both sides of the halved pitas with olive oil and sprinkle with the sea salt and sumac spice. Place on a large baking sheet on the center rack and bake for about 12 to 15 minutes, turning halfway through, until the bread is crispy and golden brown. Immediately remove from oven and set aside.

Layer all the other salad ingredients in a large serving bowl in the order in which they are listed. In a small bowl, whisk together the garlic paste and slowly stream in the olive oil, lemon juice, and vinegar. Season with the salt, black pepper, sumac, mint, and thyme leaves.

Before serving, break the toasted pita halves into small pieces over the vegetables. Pour in the dressing, and toss the salad thoroughly. Serve immediately so that pita pieces remain crunchy.

تبولة

Taboulie

finely chopped herb, tomato, and bulgur wheat salad

It's no surprise that taboulie is one of my absolute favorite things to make and eat—it's a part of my TV name and identity! This refreshing salad of finely chopped vegetables, herbs, and bulgur wheat originated in the area around Mount Lebanon and is an iconic Lebanese dish throughout the world—there's even a National Taboulie Day celebrated on the first Saturday of July.

In Lebanese culture, there is no gathering or meal that doesn't feature a big bowl of taboulie on the table. Although you can eat it with a spoon or fork, I always serve taboulie the traditional way: with fresh romaine hearts to scoop it up. ✦ **MAKES 6 SERVINGS**

3 bunches fresh flat-leaf parsley leaves, finely chopped

⅓ cup fresh mint leaves, finely chopped

½ cup #1 fine bulgur wheat (see page 279), or 1 cup cooked, chilled quinoa

4 firm, ripe tomatoes, finely diced

6 scallions, ends trimmed, green and white parts thinly sliced

¾ cup to 1 cup freshly squeezed lemon juice

½ cup extra-virgin olive oil

1½ teaspoons sea salt

Hearts of romaine leaves, for serving

At least 30 minutes before preparing the taboulie, thoroughly wash the parsley and mint leaves in cold water to remove dirt or debris. Shake out any excess water and drain in a colander, stem sides down. If you have a salad spinner, you can dry the herbs in that way or lay out on paper towels or a clean kitchen cloth to air dry; just make sure they are very dry before you chop them.

Place the bulgur wheat into a bowl and cover with 3 cups of cold water. Set aside to soak and soften, about 20 minutes.

Combine the tomatoes, scallions, and herbs in that order in a large mixing bowl. By now, the bulgur wheat should have softened. To test, squeeze some of the grains between your fingertips, it should squish and be completely soft. Soak the bulgur longer if needed.

Using your hands, squeeze out the soaked bulgur, removing as much excess water as possible. Sprinkle the bulgur on top of the fresh herbs and vegetables in the bowl. Pour in the lemon juice and olive oil, and season with the salt. Toss all the ingredients together (preferably with your hands); it should be juicy but not soggy. Taste and add salt as needed.

Serve the salad as soon as possible with fresh, crisp romaine lettuce hearts for scooping.

---

taboulie tip! The cut matters! Use a sharp serrated knife for best results. Finely chop.

Sitto's Batata Salata

my grandmother's lebanese potato salad

Lebanese people love potatoes—so much so that when my grandmother visited us many years ago, she included potatoes in almost every meal she cooked! My mother and I have carried on the tradition, and we love making Batata Salata *(potato salad). Unlike many American potato salads, this one contains no mayonnaise—just fresh herbs, lemon juice, garlic, and a bit of olive oil.* ❖ **MAKES 6 SERVINGS**

6 gold "creamer" (small size) potatoes

6 red "creamer" (small size) potatoes

6 purple (small size) potatoes

1 teaspoon sea salt

3 scallions, ends trimmed, green and white parts thinly sliced

1 small bunch fresh chives, finely sliced

½ bunch fresh flat-leaf parsley leaves, finely chopped

1 small bunch fresh mint leaves, sliced into thin strips

VINAIGRETTE

6 garlic cloves

Pinch of sea salt, plus more as needed

⅓ cup extra-virgin olive oil

⅓ cup freshly squeezed lemon juice

Put the gold and red potatoes in a large pot with cold water to cover and place over high heat, leaving the pot uncovered. Put the purple potatoes in a separate medium pot, so that their natural color does not dye the other potato varieties. Cover with cold water and place over high heat, uncovered. When both pots come to a rolling boil, immediately reduce the heat and simmer the potatoes for 10 to 15 minutes just until they are fork-tender; do not overcook!

Drain the potatoes and set aside until they are cool enough to handle.

Meanwhile, make the vinaigrette: Mash the garlic cloves and the pinch of salt in a mortar and pestle until it forms a smooth paste. Slowly stream in the olive oil and lemon juice and whisk or stir vigorously until all the ingredients are well combined. Set aside.

Once the potatoes have cooled slightly but are still warm, remove the skins using a small, sharp knife, then slice the potatoes into quarters. Place in a large mixing bowl, and season with 1 teaspoon of salt. Pour the dressing over the potatoes and thoroughly toss to coat entirely.

Sprinkle the scallions, chives, parsley, and mint over the potatoes, taste and season with additional salt, if needed. Serve warm immediately, or make ahead, chill and serve cold.

———————

taboulie tip! The potatoes will better absorb the dressing when they are still warm, so do not let them cool completely.

Khyar b Laban

cucumber, yogurt, and mint salad

My favorite thing about **Khyar b Laban** *is its versatility. Combining three simple ingredients with some garlic and sea salt, you have a dish that is perfect as a stand-alone summer salad, a wonderful complement to other dishes like* **Stuffed Grape Leaves** *(page 99), and even makes for a delightful chilled soup! I usually enjoy it as a soup, but Mama insists that it makes the ideal summer salad—a constant (but friendly) debate between the two of us.* ✣ **MAKES 6 SERVINGS**

6 cups unstrained Laban (page 223), or store-bought, full-fat plain yogurt, chilled

3 garlic cloves

1 teaspoon plus 1 pinch sea salt

3 Persian cucumbers, ends trimmed and cut into ½-inch cubes

6 fresh mint leaves, finely minced, 1 tablespoon reserved for garnish

Ladle the yogurt into a large mixing bowl (if possible, use a stainless-steel bowl and spoon to keep yogurt cold). Thoroughly whisk until silky smooth.

Using a mortar and pestle or a garlic press, pound or purée the garlic cloves into a smooth paste then mash in a pinch of salt and stir into the yogurt.

Add the cucumbers, mint, and remaining 1 teaspoon salt. Stir to incorporate all the ingredients thoroughly. Taste, and add additional salt, if needed.

Cover with plastic wrap and refrigerate for 30 to 60 minutes until chilled. If chilling serving bowls for an extra-refreshing salad (see Taboulie Tip!), place them in the refrigerator as well.

Just before serving, spoon the salad into the bowls and sprinkle with the reserved 1 tablespoon minced mint leaves.

———————

taboulie tip! Since I like to serve this ice-cold, I usually put the bowls in the refrigerator beforehand to chill, but you can also use room-temperature bowls if you prefer.

Sitto's Malfouf Salata

my grandmother's cabbage salad

One of the biggest influences in my life is my Sitto (grandmother) who still lives in Lebanon. Spending the summer with her in 2007 is a time I will always cherish, and although I miss her terribly, making her recipes brings me closer to her. Malfouf Salata, *which literally means "cabbage salad" is one of her (and now my) go-to autumn salads.*

Whenever a recipe calls for cabbage, I usually choose Savoy because I find the leaves sweeter, tenderer, and far less acidic than some of the other varieties. ❖ **MAKES 6 SERVINGS**

1 head Savoy cabbage, thoroughly washed, thick outer leaves removed and discarded

6 scallions, ends trimmed, green and white parts thinly sliced on the diagonal

½ bunch fresh flat-leaf parsley leaves, coarsely chopped

1 small bunch fresh mint leaves, coarsely chopped

6 radishes, cut into thin matchsticks

2 to 3 tablespoons freshly squeezed lemon juice

DRESSING

1 head garlic (about 10 cloves)

1 teaspoon sea salt

1 cup extra-virgin olive oil

2 to 3 tablespoons freshly squeezed lemon juice

Using a sharp serrated knife, cut the cabbage in half down the center. Working with one half at a time, finely shred through the tender leaves (see Taboulie Tip!), working toward the core. Discard any tough sections. Place the shreds in a large bowl and loosen the leaves with your fingers.

Add the scallions, herbs, and radishes to the bowl, and pour the lemon juice over the ingredients. Set aside while you make the dressing.

Using a food processor or mortar and pestle, pound the garlic cloves into a smooth paste along with the sea salt. Then, with the processor running, slowly stream the lemon juice and then the olive oil into the garlic until the mixture thickens, allowing the mixture to blend after each addition, and making sure the olive oil doesn't break. After all the lemon juice and olive oil is added, keep blending for a few minutes until the mixture is light and airy, and pale yellow.

Spoon the dressing over the salad, and lightly toss so that the vegetables are all coated. Serve immediately.

---

taboulie tip! **THE CUT MATTERS:** Make sure to thinly shred the cabbage leaves so that the dressing can completely coat the shreds.

Jarjir Salata

watercress and radish salad

Whenever Mama and I make Jarjir Salata, *she remembers picking* jarjir *(watercress) from the streams and rivers near our* Bustan *(farmland) in Lebanon. In the Finger Lakes region of Upstate New York where we live now, there is much freshwater surrounding us, and my mother always points out the tiny watercress growing all around us. I wouldn't recommend using the watercress you find for cooking, but I love the experience of seeing the plant growing in the water, and then purchasing it at the farmers' market for my salad!*

We traditionally serve this salad with all of our freshwater fish dishes such as Siyediyeh *(page 138) and* Samak Harrah *(page 143), as the spicy, crunchy watercress and peppery* fajel *(radish) accentuate the flaky softness of the fish. For a final flourish, I coat the salata in a tangy lemon-thyme dressing that is totally divine.* ❖ **MAKES 6 SERVINGS**

2 bunches watercress, tough stems trimmed

6 radishes, sliced thinly

6 sprigs fresh lemon thyme (or regular thyme if you can't find it), leaves picked and left whole

2 to 3 tablespoons freshly squeezed lemon juice

DRESSING

1 teaspoon sea salt

1 head garlic (about 10 cloves), mashed into a smooth paste

1 cup extra-virgin olive oil

2 to 3 tablespoons freshly squeezed lemon juice

Fan out the watercress leaves on a large, flat serving platter. Layer the radish slices evenly over the watercress. Run your fingers top to bottom on 3 of the lemon thyme sprigs, and sprinkle the leaves on top of the radish slices. Pour the lemon juice over the salad and set aside.

Prepare the dressing: Add the sea salt to the minced garlic or garlic paste, and then slowly stream the olive oil into the mixture, mixing until all of the oil is incorporated, and a creamy consistency is formed. Pour the lemon juice into the mixture and blend well. Add the leaves from the remaining 3 sprigs of lemon thyme, stir and set aside.

Serve the dressing in a small bowl alongside the salad.

سلطة بصل و بندورة

Basal wa Banadoura Salata

onion and tomato salad

This salad combines two very important ingredients in Lebanese cuisine, basal *(onion) and* banadoura *(tomato) in one of our favorite forms: a salad! Basal wa Banadoura Salata is one of my go-to salads for harvest time, as summer transitions to fall, and the gold and bright red cherry tomatoes mirror the changing colors of the trees. This salad is a celebration of color, taste, and texture, with sweet tomatoes and tangy red onions coated in a bright garlic-lemon vinaigrette spiked with sumac spice that you make right in the salad bowl. I like to serve this salad at room temperature, as the tomatoes taste more vibrant to me when they aren't chilled. Feel free to let this salad sit for a while, as the flavors will develop and become even stronger and more delicious.* ✧ **MAKES 6 SERVINGS**

3 medium vine-ripened tomatoes, cored and sliced into thick wedges

1 pint yellow cherry tomatoes (1½ to 2 cups), stemmed and left whole

1 pint (1½ to 2 cups) heirloom cherry tomatoes, stemmed and left whole

1 medium red onion, thinly sliced

3 garlic cloves, mashed into a smooth paste (using a garlic press or mortar and pestle)

2½ to 3 tablespoons freshly squeezed lemon juice

⅓ cup extra-virgin olive oil

1 teaspoon sea salt

1 teaspoon sumac spice (see page 280)

Place the tomato wedges on the bottom of a large, shallow salad bowl. Layer the cherry tomatoes on top of the tomato wedges, and toss the red onion slices all over the tomatoes, separating the slices with your fingertips.

Add the garlic paste on top of the tomatoes and onions and pour the lemon juice and then the olive oil over all the ingredients, starting in the center of the bowl. Season with the salt and sumac, and lightly toss the salad together. Serve at room temperature.

Hummus Salata
chickpea salad

While you may think of of hummus exclusively as a chickpea spread, the word hummus *actually translates to "chickpea" in Arabic. In this protein-rich salad, whole chickpeas meld beautifully with crunchy Persian cucumbers, radishes, scallions, and a host of fragrant fresh herbs. I make* Hummus Salata *throughout the year, and often serve it with my chickpea-stuffed* Swiss Chard Leaves *(page 102)—because you can never have enough chickpeas!*

For this salad, I highly recommend starting off with dried chickpeas, and soaking them overnight before cooking them. Canned chickpeas really won't deliver the same taste in this delicate and bright salad. I promise, the overnight soak is well worth it!

This salad keeps very well—in fact the flavors will become even stronger, so feel free to prepare it one day ahead, or save some for the following day. ❖ **MAKES 6 SERVINGS**

2 cups dried chickpeas

1 teaspoon baking soda

3 Persian cucumbers, diced

6 radishes, thinly sliced into half-moons

3 scallions, ends trimmed, green and white parts finely diced

1 small bunch fresh flat-leaf parsley leaves, coarsely chopped

1 small bunch fresh mint leaves, finely sliced into thin strips

DRESSING

3 garlic cloves, finely mashed into a smooth paste

⅓ cup extra-virgin olive oil

2½ to 3 tablespoons freshly squeezed lemon juice

1 teaspoon sea salt

One day ahead, place the dried chickpeas in a large mixing bowl and cover with 8 cups of cold water. Stir in the baking soda so that it dissolves, cover the bowl, and set aside to soak overnight at room temperature.

The next day, the beans will have doubled in size, yielding about 4½ cups of chickpeas. Drain in a colander or strainer and thoroughly rinse under cold running water.

Place the soaked beans in a large, heavy-bottomed pot, cover with 8 cups of cold water, and bring to a boil over high heat, uncovered. When the beans come to a rolling boil, after about 10 minutes, skim off any foam and chickpea skins that rise to the top of the pot. Boil for about 15 minutes total, skimming at least twice during the process.

Reduce the heat to medium-low and simmer for about 30 minutes, or until the chickpeas are completely cooked through and tender but not mushy. Drain the beans and rinse under cold

running water to stop the cooking process. Transfer to a large mixing bowl. Add the diced cucumbers to the bowl, and layer the radish pieces over them. Spread the scallion slices all over the radishes and top with the parsley and mint.

Add the garlic paste over the herbs, and drizzle the olive oil starting from the center of the bowl and working your way out. Then evenly pour the lemon juice over the salad, and sprinkle with the sea salt. Toss the salad so all ingredients are coated with the dressing. Serve cold or at room temperature.

Julie Taboulie's Signature Salata

chopped salad with tangy tahini dressing

I created this salad, which has since become my signature, during one of my first Lebanese cooking classes in Skaneateles, New York. The students ended up falling in love with this salad, which includes crunchy pickled turnips, Zaytoun olives, and Persian cucumbers—all toppings for falafel. Feel free to add some of my fresh Falafel Fritters (page 75) on top, or just serve this salad by itself. I hope it leaves you smiling with each and every bite, just like it did for my cooking students! ❖ **MAKES 6 SERVINGS**

3 medium tomatoes, cored and diced into
½-inch cubes

3 Persian cucumbers, diced into
½-inch cubes

6 radishes, thinly sliced into half-moons

6 pickled turnips (page 193), cut into
bite-size pieces

3 scallions, ends trimmed, green and
white parts sliced thinly on the
diagonal

1 bunch fresh flat-leaf parsley leaves,
coarsely chopped

1 small bunch fresh mint leaves,
sliced finely into strips

½ cup Zaytoun olives (see page 281),
pitted and coarsely chopped

TAHINI DRESSING

3 garlic cloves

1 cup tahini (see page 280)

1 cup freshly squeezed lemon juice

1 teaspoon sea salt

First prepare the dressing: In a food processor, finely mince the garlic cloves. Vigorously shake the container of tahini and then allow it to settle. Stir the oil and tahini paste together so they are completely incorporated and blended together.

Pour 1 cup of the tahini into the food processor over the garlic, and add ⅓ cup of cold water. Blend all the ingredients together, then add the lemon juice and salt. Run the processor for a few minutes, pausing to scrape down the sides and bottom of the bowl. The dressing should be a creamy consistency and not too thick.

Spread the tomato slices on the bottom of a large flat serving platter. Place the cucumbers on top followed by the radishes and the pickled turnips. Spread the scallions all over the ingredients and cover with parsley and mint. Add the chopped olives in the center of the salad. Drizzle with the Tahini Dressing and serve immediately.

If you are preparing the salad ahead, refrigerate it, undressed and covered with plastic wrap until you serve it, but not for longer than 2 hours or the tomatoes will get soggy. Dress the salad just before serving.

SHAWRABA

soups and stews

THIS SECTION IS ALL ABOUT SOOTHING THE SOUL FROM THE INSIDE out. And what's more soothing than a big pot of steaming soup? The winters are very cold and very long both in Upstate New York and in Lebanon. Since childhood, one of my favorite ways of shaking off the finger-tingling chill has been a bowl of bubbling soup or stew. Walking home from school in the knee-high mounds of snow, I knew my Mama would have a big pot of soup steaming on the stovetop, whether Bemyeh b Lahem, a baby okra, lamb, and tomato stew, Mjadrah, a hearty lentil soup, or Djej wa Rez, our aromatic Lebanese-style chicken soup. In Lebanese cuisine, though, we don't limit our enjoyment of soup just to the wintertime: I love to make lemony Kibbet Raheb swimming with hearty bulgur bites in the spring, and to showcase summer squash, my Makbouseh squash stew in summer. One of my family's favorite celebratory soups is Shish Barak, a luscious, silky yogurt-base soup packed with succulent lamb dumplings. Whether you're thawing out your friends or family after a freezing day, or embracing fresh vegetables sprouting from the ground, your soup options are endless in this chapter!

مجدرة

Mjadrah

lentil, brown rice, and caramelized onion stew

Originating from the area around Mount Lebanon, Mjadrah *is a very traditional and simple stew often served during Lent, as it is a meatless dish. Even though* Mjadrah *contains only three main ingredients, it has a complex, satisfying flavor, thanks to the deeply caramelized onions. Make sure that your onions are very caramelized (probably darker than you've seen before) to ensure the most flavorful stew possible. I've swapped in brown rice for white rice here, to make it even more wholesome and healthy. I often serve this stew with* Fattoush *(page 34), or* Khoudra wa Kabis *(Lebanese vegetable crudites, page 15).*

✤ MAKES 8 TO 10 SERVINGS

2 cups Pardina or green lentils
   (see page 279)

½ cup extra-virgin olive oil

2 medium yellow onions, finely diced

1 tablespoon sea salt

1 cup whole-grain brown or
   long-grain rice

Spread the lentils out onto a clean kitchen towel or paper towels, and run your fingers through the lentils to ensure that there are no small stones or impurities, and discard any. Rinse the lentils in a fine-mesh sieve under cold running water and drain. Put the lentils in a heavy-bottomed pot on the stovetop but *do not* turn on the heat. Cover with 8 cups of cold water.

Heat the olive oil in a medium sauté pan over medium-high heat. Add the onions and cook, stirring continuously, until they turn from translucent to golden brown to very dark brown, almost black, about 15 minutes. After 7 or 8 minutes (when the onions are light brown), turn on the heat under the pot of lentils to medium, keeping the pot uncovered.

Once the onions are blackish, turn off the heat, and strain the onions over the pot of lentils, allowing the hot onion oil to drip into the pot, and stir into the lentils. Immediately return the caramelized onions to the sauté pan over medium heat, add 2 cups of cold water and the salt and stir. Bring the onions to a rolling boil, then reduce the heat to low and simmer for 5 to 7 minutes until the onions have softened. Turn off the heat and strain the onion liquid through a fine-mesh sieve into the pot of lentils and stir in. Add the rice and stir to distribute evenly throughout the lentils.

Return the caramelized onions to the unheated sauté pan and mash them into a smooth paste. You can also use a food processor to create the onion paste. Add the paste to the lentils and rice, and stir to incorporate thoroughly. When the lentils and rice begin to boil, reduce the heat to medium-low and simmer, uncovered, for 15 to 20 minutes until most of the liquid has been absorbed and the lentils and rice are tender and soft but not mushy. Remove from the heat and serve immediately.

Bemyeh b Lahem

baby okra, lamb, and tomato stew

Bemyeh b Lahem *will always have a special place in my soul, because it's the dish I always ask Mama to make when I've been away from home. The savory combination of aromatic lamb, rich tomato sauce, and baby okra cooked to perfection is the most wonderful way to be welcomed home, and I can always smell it bubbling on the stovetop when I enter the house.*

For many people, okra is not a go-to vegetable, but this recipe will change that! Make sure you select the smallest okra you can find, and it will turn into a smooth, succulent veggie with not an ounce of sliminess (I promise!). For an authentic Arabic meal, spoon the Bemyeh b Lahem *over my* Rez b Shayriyeh, *a rice and vermicelli pilaf (page 165).* ❖ **MAKES 8 TO 10 SERVINGS**

3 tablespoons pure olive oil

3 tablespoons unsalted butter

1 pound boneless leg or shoulder of lamb, cut into 1½-inch cubes

1 large yellow onion, finely diced

2 small shallots, finely diced

2 whole heads garlic (about 20 cloves) peeled, cloves from 1 head left whole and cloves from 1 head finely minced

6 to 8 medium tomatoes on the vine, cored and finely diced

1 cinnamon stick

1 tablespoon sea salt

1 pound fresh baby okra (whole, not halved, or one thawed 16-ounce bag frozen baby whole okra, not cut okra)

1 tablespoon freshly squeezed lemon juice

½ teaspoon freshly ground black pepper

1 teaspoon ground allspice

In a large, heavy-bottomed pot, heat 3 tablespoons of the olive oil and 3 tablespoons of the butter over high heat until the butter sizzles and the pot starts to smoke slightly. Add the cubes of lamb and sear in small batches, making sure not to overcrowd the pan, until the meat is evenly browned on all sides, 2 to 3 minutes per side; the meat should be caramel colored and have a crisp crust.

Once all the meat is seared, add the cubes with the lamb's natural juices back into the pot, stir, and reduce the heat to medium. Stir the onion and shallots into the pot with the lamb cubes, along with the whole and minced garlic cloves and sauté until the onion and shallots are translucent and have slightly caramelized, about 5 to 7 minutes.

Stir in the diced tomatoes along with 2 cups of cold water, the cinnamon stick, and 1 tablespoon of the salt. Increase the heat to high, cover the pot and bring to a boil. Once the stew begins to boil, reduce the heat to low and partially cover the pot with the lid. Simmer for about 45 to 60 minutes, or until the meat becomes very tender and the stew thickens.

continued

While the stew is simmering, gently wipe the outside of the okra with a clean kitchen towel or paper towel. Do not wash or rinse the okra. Using a small paring knife, carefully shave off the tough okra stems and cut off the tops in a straight line, keeping the okra whole, and add the fresh or thawed okra to the stew.

Add the lemon juice; this will help the okra remain intact while cooking. If the stew appears overly thick and begins sticking to the bottom of the pot, add ½ to 1 cup of hot water as needed. Continue to simmer for another 10 minutes, just until the okra is fully cooked.

Once the okra has fully cooked, stir in the black pepper and allspice, and taste. Add additional seasoning if needed. Simmer for a few more minutes to allow the flavors to fully develop. Serve the stew hot, over rice.

VARIATION ❖ Substitute beef sirloin for lamb if you prefer.

VARIATION ❖ Substitute flat Italian green beans (romano beans) for the okra.

---

taboulie tip! The longer this stew slowly simmers, the more flavorful it will become and the more tender the meat will be.

بازيلا

Bazilla

green pea, lamb, and tomato stew

Bazilla, *which means "pea," is one of my go-to springtime ingredients, and I love it in this saucy one-bowl stew, a favorite of both my brothers, Freddy and Eddie Jr. Fresh, tender peas work so well with a fragrant tomato broth and hearty ground lamb. Bazilla is best served over* Rez b Shayriyeh *(page 165).*

❉ **MAKES 8 TO 10 SERVINGS**

2 tablespoons pure olive oil

2 tablespoons unsalted butter

1 pound finely ground lamb
  (from leg or shoulder)

2 small shallots, finely diced

1 large yellow onion, finely diced

6 to 8 medium tomatoes, cored and
  finely diced

1 teaspoon sea salt

½ teaspoon freshly ground
  black pepper

1 teaspoon ground allspice

2 pounds fresh sweet peas, or thawed
  frozen peas

Rez b Shayriyeh (page 165), for serving

In a heavy-bottomed pot, heat the olive oil and butter over medium-high heat until they start to sizzle and smoke slightly. Add the ground meat and cook, using the back of a spatula to break apart the meat, until it is thoroughly browned, 7 to 10 minutes.

Add the shallots and onion to the same pot and sauté until they are translucent and begin to caramelize, about 10 minutes.

Add the tomatoes to the pot, along with any juice that may have released and 2 cups of cold water. Season with the salt, pepper, and allspice and stir thoroughly. Bring to a boil uncovered. Reduce the heat to low and simmer for about 30 to 35 minutes, or until the meat is tender and the stew has thickened and is aromatic.

Add the fresh peas and simmer, uncovered, for another 5 to 10 minutes until the peas have cooked through. Taste a few peas to make sure they are tender but not overly squishy.

Once the peas are done, immediately turn off the heat and leave the pot on the stovetop, uncovered, until serving time so that the peas do not darken.

Serve hot, over rice.

VARIATION ❉ If you prefer, you can substitute 80 percent lean finely ground
beef or ground chicken for lamb.

كبة راهب

Kibbet Raheb

lemony lentil and swiss chard soup with bulgur wheat bites

In Arabic, Kibbet Raheb *translates as "Monk's Soup," as this dish, which dates back to biblical times, was often enjoyed during the fasting period of Lent, and on Good Friday among Lebanese Catholics. I love to make this hearty, lemony soup with soft bulgur bites as a warming springtime dinner or lunch, and I'll often make a big pot of it on a Sunday so I can heat it up throughout the week.* ✣ **MAKES 8 TO 10 SERVINGS**

SOUP

2 cups brown lentils

1 bunch Swiss chard

1 tablespoon sea salt

1 whole garlic head (about 10 cloves) peeled and finely mashed or pureed into a smooth paste

½ cup freshly squeezed lemon juice

⅓ cup olive oil

2 tablespoons fresh flat-leaf parsley leaves, coarsely chopped for serving

BULGUR WHEAT BITES

1 cup #1 fine bulgur wheat, soaked and softened

2 tablespoons shallots, finely minced

1 medium yellow onion, finely minced

⅓ cup fresh flat-leaf parsley leaves, finely chopped

½ cup unbleached all-purpose flour, plus more as needed

1 teaspoon sea salt

Spread the lentils out in a single layer on a clean kitchen towel, and run your fingers through to ensure that there are no small stones or impurities. Then, rinse lentils in a fine-mesh sieve under cold running water and drain over the sink.

Transfer the lentils to a very large pot and cover with 1 gallon (16 cups) of cold water. Place on the stovetop but *do not* turn on the heat.

Make the bulgur bites: Place the bulgur wheat in a large bowl, cover completely with 3 cups cold water, and set aside to soak and soften, about 20 minutes.

In a separate large bowl, combine all the remaining bulgur bite ingredients and mix together. After 20 minutes, test the bulgur wheat by squeezing some of the grains between your fingertips; it should be soft and squishy, with no firmness. If it is still firm, continue to soak it.

Once the bulgur has adequately softened, dip one of your hands into the bowl, and squeeze most of the water out of the grains over the bowl, leaving just a little bit of water so that the bulgur will bind together. Sprinkle the bulgur into the large bowl over the other ingredients, working in handfuls until all of the bulger has been added in. Using your hands, thoroughly mix all the ingredients together until they are well incorporated. Then, begin to knead the dough, plunging your fists in and then flipping the entire mixture over, until it comes together tightly. It should be sticky and moist, but not overly wet or dry. If the dough feels too wet, add additional flour by the teaspoon, and if it is too dry, add additional water by the teaspoon.

At this point, turn on the heat to medium under the large pot of lentils on the stovetop and cook, uncovered, watching for the pot to begin boiling.

Form the bulgur bites: Lightly flour a baking sheet or board and set aside.

Lightly flour a large counter or cutting board, and transfer the dough onto the surface. Using your hands, mold the mixture into a large ball, and flatten it down by pressing with the palms of your hands, beginning in the center of the dough and working your way out, until the dough is uniformly ½ inch thick.

Using a dough cutter or sharp knife, slice vertically through the dough, into 6 even strips, about 1 inch thick. Take each strip and roll it under your hands left to right, to form a breadsticklike shape that is long and thin. Then, using a sharp knife, cut across each strip horizontally, to create ½-inch cubes. Lightly roll them into balls, using the palms of your hands, and spread them out evenly on the floured baking sheet or board.

By now, the pot of lentils should be at a boil. Once the water is boiling, using a handheld strainer or large slotted spoon, carefully place the bulgur bites into the lentil liquid, adding them in small batches and tapping off any excess flour from the balls before placing them in the liquid. Gently stir to ensure that the balls do not stick to each other. Then, turn the heat to low and simmer, uncovered, for 10 to 12 minutes, just until the bites have cooked through.

While the bites simmer, thoroughly rinse the Swiss chard leaves under cold running water and shake off as much excess water as possible. Slice off the thick end and center stems and discard to save for another use. Layer the leaves on top of one another, roll them up, and slice across the leaves with a sharp knife, creating 1-inch-wide ribbons. Add to the pot, season with the salt, and simmer for 10 to 12 minutes until the greens are cooked through.

Once the greens have cooked, add the garlic paste, lemon juice, and olive oil and simmer for a few minutes more. Taste and add additional seasoning as needed. Sprinkle with the chopped parsley. Serve hot with warm Khebez Arabi (page 205).

VARIATION ❖ For a gluten-free version, replace the bulgur wheat with cooked and chilled quinoa, and use gluten-free flour instead of all-purpose flour.

Shish Barak

yogurt-mint soup with lamb dumplings

If there's one soup that signifies a special occasion in my family, it's Shish Barak, *and my siblings and I would never miss it! I can still see Mama stirring the steamy yogurt soup in the kitchen and carefully preparing the dumplings.*

It's a very special soup that requires a few hours of time, but it's truly worth it, and you would rarely find it in many Lebanese or Middle Eastern restaurants. ❖ **MAKES 8 TO 10 SERVINGS**

DUMPLING DOUGH

2 cups all-purpose, unbleached flour, plus additional for sprinkling

½ teaspoon sea salt

LAMB FILLING

½ pound freshly and finely ground lamb (from boneless leg or shoulder)

1 small yellow onion, finely minced

1 small bunch fresh mint leaves, finely minced

½ teaspoon sea salt

½ teaspoon fresh ground black pepper

SOUP

6 cups Laban (page 223), or store-bought laban, or plain full-fat yogurt, at room temperature (do not use Greek yogurt for this); I recommend Dannon.

1 egg white

1 teaspoon cornstarch

1 cup long-grain rice, uncooked

3 garlic cloves, finely mashed into a smooth paste

1 small bunch fresh mint leaves, finely minced

1 teaspoon sea salt

Make the dough: In a large mixing bowl combine the flour and salt, and thoroughly mix together using your hands to break up any small clumps. Using your hands, create a well in the center of the flour and pour ¾ cup lukewarm water. Using one hand to steady the bowl, start to slowly incorporate the flour with your other hand, sweeping along the sides of the bowl and then blending the flour into the water until all of the water has been completely incorporated into the flour. Mix the dough until it comes together, then create one large dough ball. Lift the ball of dough from the bottom and fold over the top a couple of times until you achieve a soft and pliable dough that is slightly moist to the touch and bounces back when touched. Make sure not to overmix the dough. If the dough is too dry, add a little more lukewarm water by the teaspoon, and if it is too moist, add a little more flour by the teaspoon. Cover with a clean kitchen towel and set aside momentarily.

Lightly flour a cutting board or clean counter top. Place the dough ball in the center and, using a dough cutter or sharp knife, slice the dough into two equal halves. Working with one half at a time, place the dough in the palms of your hands and tuck it under. Then, stretch the dough into a smooth, flat, round disk, place it on the board, and roll it out into a smooth and thin round shape, about ¼ inch thick.

Using a circular dough cutter or the rim of a small glass, cut out small rounds of the dough approximately 2 inches in diameter, and lay them flat on another lightly floured work surface or cutting board so that they are not touching or sticking to one another. Set the dough rounds aside.

Make the lamb filling: Lightly flour a baking sheet and set aside. In a large bowl, combine the lamb, onion, mint (reserving a bit for garnish), the salt, and pepper. Using your hands, mix all the ingredients together until they form a smooth mixture.

Scoop out ½ teaspoon of the meat filling and place in the center of each dough round, making sure not to overstuff. Place the dough round into the palm of your left hand, and using your right hand, fold one side over the meat in a small half-moon shape. With your fingertips, tightly pinch the edges along the seam, so they are securely closed. Now, bring both end points together and slightly overlap them to create a tortellini shape. Transfer the folded dumplings to the flavored baking sheet and set aside.

Make the soup: Bring 3 cups of water to a boil in a small pot over medium-high heat. Once the water is boiling, turn off the heat, and cover the pot. Pour the laban (yogurt) into a separate large, heavy-bottomed pot and whisk to dissolve any clumps. Thoroughly whisk the egg white and cornstarch into the yogurt. Turn the heat to medium-high and whisk, vigorously and continuously, until the yogurt reaches just below the boiling point, and is releasing hot steam. Immediately reduce the heat to a simmer.

Carefully add the hot water to the yogurt, whisking it in 1 cup at a time. Stir the rice into the yogurt-water mixture, then reduce the heat to a simmer and cook uncovered, for 10 to 15 minutes until the rice is tender, whisking periodically to keep the mixture smooth, and from sticking to the bottom of the pan.

Using a handheld strainer or large slotted spoon, carefully ladle in the lamb dumplings, working in small batches tapping off any excess flour from the dumplings before placing them in the liquid and making sure they do not stick together. Simmer, uncovered, for 10 minutes without stirring. The dumplings will float to the top of the pot when they are cooked.

Gently stir in the garlic paste and minced mint. Season with the salt, taste, and adjust the seasonings as needed. Cover the pot and turn off the heat. Serve the soup hot, warm, or at room temperature with additional minced mint and Crispy Pita Chips (page 206).

VARIATION ❖ If you prefer beef to lamb, feel free to substitute with 90 percent lean ground beef.

Makbouseh

summer squash stew

Makbouseh *translates literally as "to mix things up," which is exactly what this vibrant summertime stew does! We use the overflowing bounty of fresh vegetables from Mama's summer janah (garden) to flavor our* Makbouseh, *particularly including the kousa squash, which is a light green summer vegetable native to Lebanon. I've selected sweet, round Sicilian eggplant, because I love the tender texture and delicate taste. The colors and flavors that come out of this fresh and hearty vegetable stew are just like a plate full of summer!*

Makbouseh *can be served hot or cold, with or without* Rez b Heshwi *(see page 134) and pairs perfectly with my homemade Lebanese pasta,* Macaroune b Toum *(see page 163).* ✧ **MAKES 8 TO 10 SERVINGS**

⅓ cup extra-virgin olive oil

1 large Vidalia onion, finely diced

3 shallots, finely minced

6 garlic cloves, finely minced

2 medium Sicilian (see page 280) or Italian eggplants, half-peeled in vertical strips and cut into 1-inch cubes

2 medium kousa squash half-peeled in vertical strips and cut into 1-inch cubes

2 medium green zucchini, half-peeled in vertical strips and cut into 1-inch cubes

2 medium yellow squash, half-peeled in vertical strips and cut into 1-inch cubes

1½ teaspoons salt

6 large vine-ripened garden tomatoes

2 cups canned chickpeas, drained and rinsed

1 small long hot green or red pepper, seeded and finely diced

1½ teaspoons ground allspice

1 cup cherry or grape tomatoes

In a large, heavy-bottomed pot, heat the olive oil on medium-low heat. Add the onion and sauté, uncovered, until translucent, about 10 minutes. Add the shallots and garlic and sauté for 1 to 2 minutes until fragrant and lightly browned.

Add the eggplant, and cook for about 10 minutes, making sure that the pieces are coated in olive oil and well incorporated with the aromatics.

Add the kousa and cook for a couple of minutes then add the zucchini, yellow squash and season with 1 teaspoon of the salt, and sauté together for 10 to 15 minutes more, or until the squash pieces are softened and tender.

Slice each tomato in half horizontally, and squeeze the juice and seeds into the pot. Then, finely dice the juiced tomatoes and add these to the pot with the remaining ½ teaspoon salt. Stir to

continued

Stir in the chickpeas, peppers, and allspice and simmer the mixture, uncovered, for an additional 5 to 10 minutes, or until the chickpeas have heated through. Add the cherry tomatoes, and slowly simmer just until the tomato skin blisters slightly. The soup should be thick and juicy, and the squash, eggplant, and chickpeas tender but not mushy. Taste and adjust the seasonings as needed.

Serve hot, warm, or at room temperature.

———————

taboulie tip! Because of its smooth thin skin, small seeds, sweet taste, and tenderness, I think that this type of eggplant (Sicilian) makes all the difference in the taste and texture of my Makbouseh!

دجاج ورز

Djej wa Rez

lebanese-style chicken soup with long-grain rice

Every culture has their chicken soup, and I might be biased, but I think Djej wa Rez *is the absolute best! Fargee (chicken) and ruz (rice) come together in a "souper-soothing" recipe, which combines sweet Vidalia onions, heaps of fresh herbs, and an infusion of cinnamon. Toasted buttery vermicelli noodles add depth to this cold-weather comforting cure-all, which I find lighter and more flavorful than classic chicken noodle soup.* ❖ **MAKES 8 TO 10 SERVINGS**

One 3- to 4-pound whole chicken

1 small bunch fresh flat-leaf parsley

1 small bunch fresh thyme

1 small bunch fresh rosemary

1 teaspoon coarse sea salt, plus more if needed

1 cinnamon stick

2 cups long-grain rice, uncooked

4 tablespoons (½ stick) unsalted butter

1 small Vidalia onion, finely minced

2 small shallots, finely minced

2 angel hair noodle nests or 1 cup crushed vermicelli noodles (see page 279)

½ pound fresh sweet peas

3 carrots, peeled and cubed

½ teaspoon ground allspice

½ teaspoon ground *Sab'ah Baharat* (Seven-Spice, page 183)

Remove the chicken from its packaging and place on a baking sheet. Discard the neck, gizzards, and giblets or reserve for another use.

Place the whole chicken in a large, heavy-bottomed pot and cover with 16 cups of cold water. Place the pot on the stovetop, uncovered.

Wash all of the fresh herbs and add them to the pot. Add the coarse sea salt and cinnamon stick to the pot, and turn the heat to high. When the water comes to a rolling boil, about 15 minutes, foam will start to rise to the top of the pot. Using a slotted spoon or skimmer, skim off any foam and discard. As the soup continues to cook, continue to skim and discard the foam. Once the broth has stopped foaming, reduce the heat to low, add the rice, and simmer for about 30 minutes, or until the chicken and the rice are thoroughly cooked.

While the chicken is cooking, place a large sauté pan over medium-high heat and add the butter, onion, and shallots. Once the onion and shallots turn translucent, crush the angel hair or vermicelli noodles in your hands and into the pan and stir to combine with the onion and shallots. Toast the noodles thoroughly until they are a deep, dark brown color and give off a nutty aroma, then remove the pan from the heat and set aside.

Check the chicken at this point; it should be cooked through and tender—almost falling off the bone. Using tongs, remove it from the broth and place it on a cutting board. Allow it to cool just until it can be handled.

Add the peas, carrots, and noodles mixture to the broth and season with the allspice and seven-spice mix and stir thoroughly. Taste, and add additional salt if needed.

When the chicken is cool enough to handle, remove and discard the skin and bones. Using your hands or a fork and carving knife, shred the meat. Return the shredded chicken to the broth and simmer for 5 to 10 minutes to allow the chicken to absorb the flavor of the soup. Serve hot.

STREET-FOOD STARS

skewers & sandwiches

WALKING THE STREETS OF A LEBANESE CITY, ONE IS SURROUNDED BY the sights and scents of street food: the intoxicating aroma of sizzling meats and crispy falafel emanating from street vendors who skillfully stuff kabobs and other treats into fluffy warm pocket bread so fast it will make your head spin (and your stomach growl!) In this chapter, I'm showcasing our casual, and absolutely sensational street-food star sandwiches and skewers, from golden brown Falafel to Shawarma Lahem, saucy shaved lamb shawarma sandwiches. I couldn't resist including one of my personal favorites, Kafta Kababs, a mouthwatering meat kabob that I love snagging hot off the grill, especially in the summertime. With my sensational skewers and sandwiches, you can outshine even the most impressive street vendors and food trucks—all without a rotisserie, and right at home!

لحم مشوي

Lahem Mishwee
lamb meat and onion skewers

If I could choose my number-one summertime cookout dish, it would be Lahem Mishwee, *which simply means "grilled meat." Chunks of lamb, grilled with three types of onions on an open flame, makes for the most fork-tender, flavorful meat imaginable. Hot off the grill, the meat and caramelized onions are tucked into warm* Khebez Arabi *(page 205), and topped with* Toum *(page 175), a rich, creamy garlic sauce. Simple and oh-so-sensational, my* Lahem Mishwee *is a skewer star every time!* ❖ **MAKES 6 SERVINGS**

2 pounds boneless lamb shoulder or leg, cut into 2-inch cubes

⅓ cup plus 2 tablespoons extra-virgin olive oil

1 teaspoon sea salt

½ teaspoon ground black pepper

1 large yellow onion, cut into thick wedges

1 large red onion, cut into thick wedges

1 large Vidalia onion, cut into thick wedges

1 red bell pepper, cored, seeded, and cut into thick wedges

1 orange bell pepper, cored, seeded, and cut into thick wedges

1 yellow bell pepper, cored, seeded, and cut into thick wedges

12 to 14 wooden or metal skewers (if using wooden skewers, presoak in water for 30 to 60 minutes)

6 Khebez Arabi (page 205), or large pita breads, for serving

1 cup Toum (page 175), for serving

Preheat a grill to medium-high heat.

Place the lamb in a large mixing bowl and massage with ⅓ cup of the olive oil. Season evenly with sea salt and pepper and set aside.

Wash your hands before skewering your meat and set a large baking sheet near your work area.

Assemble your skewers by alternating pieces of lamb with onion and bell pepper wedges—each skewer should have 5 to 7 pieces of lamb. Set the skewers aside on the baking sheet as they are assembled.

Lightly brush the grill or a stovetop grill instead with the remaining 2 tablespoons olive oil to ensure that the skewers do not stick. Lay the skewers on the grill vertically, turning them periodically so that they grill evenly. This should take a total of 8 to 10 minutes; 4 to 5 minutes per side. Make sure not to overgrill your meat, or it will lose its natural juices.

Once cooked, immediately remove the skewers from the grill and serve hot with warm Khebez Arabi and Toum.

فلافل

Falafel
spiced chickpea fritters

If you're reading this, my guess is you've probably had a falafel before. These hearty, golden-brown chickpea fritters have gained popularity in the U.S. in recent years, and you can see them popping up in fast casual sandwich spots and Middle Eastern restaurants alike. But once you make falafel *(which means "pepper" in Arabic) from scratch, you'll never go back to store-bought. I like to serve these crunchy yet moist goodies with warm pita, tangy* Tahini Dressing *(page 49), herbs, and a sprinkling of* Kabis Lefet *(Pickled Turnips with Beet and Garlic, page 193). Good luck having time to wrap them up in pita, though, they usually get snapped up way before that!*

You will need to start this recipe a few days in advance, as the chickpeas must soak for 48 hours.

✧ **MAKES 6 SERVINGS (45 TO 50 FRITTERS)**

2 cups dried chickpeas	1½ teaspoons ground cumin
3 teaspoons baking soda	1½ teaspoons ground coriander
6 garlic cloves	1½ teaspoons sweet paprika
2 medium yellow onions	½ teaspoon cayenne pepper
1½ teaspoons sea salt	½ teaspoon crushed red pepper flakes
1 teaspoon freshly ground black pepper	4 cups vegetable oil, for frying

Two days before you plan to serve the falafel, place the dried chickpeas in a large mixing bowl and cover generously with cold water. Stir in 1 teaspoon of the baking soda, cover and set aside at room temperature to soak overnight. The baking soda will soften the chickpeas and balance the acid levels.

The following morning, drain the chickpeas, rinse, and return to the bowl. Cover completely with cold water, add 1 teaspoon of baking soda and soak overnight once again.

The next morning drain the chickpeas from the water, rinse, and lay out on paper towels or on a large, clean kitchen towel to thoroughly dry the chickpeas. You should have about 4½ to 5 cups. Make sure they are completely dry to make well-formed falafel.

While the chickpeas are drying, finely mince the garlic and onions in a food processor. Add the chickpeas in two batches and finely grind into a coarse meal, pausing periodically to scrape down the sides of the food processor bowl. Test the consistency by forming a small ball in the palm of your hand and squeezing it together. The ground chickpeas should be grainy and stick together with no lumps.

continued

Transfer the falafel mixture to a large mixing bowl, add all the salt, black pepper, cumin, coriander, paprika, cayenne, and red pepper flakes and mix well. If necessary, run a fork throughout the mixture to blend the spices evenly. Then, sprinkle in the remaining 1 teaspoon baking soda and fluff the mixture with a fork; this will help the falafel to rise. Set aside.

Line a baking sheet with parchment paper. Line a second baking sheet with paper towels. Set both baking sheets aside. Pour the vegetable oil into a large, deep frying pan, and place over medium heat until the oil registers between 350°F and 375°F on a deep-fry thermometer and begins to sizzle.

Meanwhile, using your hands, roll the falafel mixture into 1 tablespoon-size balls and gently press down to flatten slightly. Transfer the falafel to the parchment paper–lined baking sheet. Using a slotted spoon or skimmer, carefully lower and release the falafel balls into the hot oil and fry in batches of five to six at a time, submerging them completely in the hot oil. Let them settle into the oil, untouched, for 1 minute and then carefully turn them over and fry for 1 minute more, or until golden brown and crispy on the outside. Using a slotted spoon or handheld strainer, immediately remove the falafels and transfer to the paper towel–lined baking sheet to drain excess oil. Cover with aluminum foil to keep the falafel hot. Make sure the oil temperature remains constant throughout the frying, checking it periodically.

Serve hot with your choice of Lebanese accompaniments.

How to Make a Falafel Sandwich

Get ready to get your falafel fix on! My falafel fritters are feisty, flavor-filled, and will have you falling for more and more. Here's how to make my famous falafel street-food star wrap right at home!

Split one, warmed, large pita bread pocket into two halves. Take one half, place about 4 to 6 falafel fritters straight across and above the edge of the bread that is closest to you. Slightly open the falafel fritters by squeezing them with your fingertips. Spoon Tahini Dressing (see page 49) on top of the falafels, then layer finely diced tomatoes, scallions, Persian cucumbers, radishes, pickled turnips (see page 193), chopped fresh parsley and mint leaves, then finish with more tahini sauce. Roll the pita bread over once to completely enclose the toppings, bring in the sides of the bread, then tightly roll the rest of the pita to create a wrapped sandwich. You can wrap a thick napkin or paper towel around the bottom half of the falafel wrap to keep it together.

Korraysah

chickpea, potato, and bulgur patties

Korraysah *translates literally as "round," which is the shape that these hearty vegetarian patties take on. My grandmother, Sitto, often prepared* Korraysah *on Good Friday, and she and her children would distribute them to those in need throughout the village.*

These patties are a favorite of my sister Selma, a vegetarian, who says these beat any veggie burger she has ever tried. Light and crispy on the outside and moist on the inside, kharisah korraysah *make for a tasty snack or side dish, or as the star of a vegetarian main meal. I like to serve them with my garlic dipping sauce,* Toum *(page 175), and fresh lettuce for scooping, or on top of my* Hummus Salata *(page 46). You'll quickly find that these are a hit with meat lovers and vegetarians alike. Although I usually make* kharisah korraysah *with reconstituted dried chickpeas, I've included directions for canned chickpeas here for a quicker process but once again I prefer dried beans that are soaked overnight and uncooked for this recipe which makes for a tasty texture.* ❧ **MAKES 6 SERVINGS (12 PATTIES)**

3 medium potatoes

½ cup #1 fine bulgur wheat (see page 279), soaked and softened

One 15½-ounce can chickpeas (1½ cup)

1 small Vidalia onion, finely diced

1 small bunch fresh flat-leaf parsley leaves, finely minced

1 cup unbleached, all-purpose flour, plus more for cutting board

1 teaspoon sea salt

½ teaspoon ground white pepper

3 garlic cloves, minced (optional)

3 cups vegetable oil, for frying, plus 2 tablespoons

1 head Boston lettuce, for serving

Thoroughly wash the potatoes, put them in a large pot with cold water to cover, and place over medium-high heat. Bring to a rolling boil, then reduce the heat to medium-low and simmer, uncovered, for 20 to 25 minutes until the potatoes are cooked through and fork-tender. Drain the potatoes and immediately rinse under cold running water then submerge them in an ice-cold water bath. Transfer the cooled potatoes to a large bowl, cover with plastic wrap and refrigerate.

In the meantime, combine the bulgur wheat with 3 cups of cold water in a medium bowl to soak and soften about 20 minutes.

Drain the chickpeas and rinse thoroughly under cold running water. Pat dry on paper towels or a clean kitchen towel, spread out in an even layer onto a cutting board, and roughly chop. Pick out any skins that release from the chickpeas and discard. Put the chopped chickpeas in a large mixing bowl and set aside.

continued

Add the onion, parsley, flour, salt, white pepper, and garlic (if using) to the chickpeas in the bowl and thoroughly mix together with your hands.

By this time, the bulgur wheat should be softened. Test it by squeezing some of the wheat between your fingers, it should squish completely with no firmness. Working in handfuls, squeeze the excess water out of the soaked grains and sprinkle the grains into the onion-chickpea mixture.

Once the potatoes have cooled completely, remove them from the refrigerator, peel, and mash until smooth. Add the cold mashed potatoes to the chickpea-onion mixture and knead with your hands until all the ingredients are incorporated and the mixture has a doughlike consistency.

Form the patties: Lightly flour a cutting board or baking sheet. Lightly oil your hands with the vegetable oil, then take about ½ cup of the mixture and roll it into a ball. Gently press down on the ball between both palms to create a circular flat patty 1 to 1½ inches thick and 3 to 4 inches in diameter. Continue forming the rest of the patties with the remaining mixture, lightly oiling your hands with the vegetable oil periodically to prevent sticking, and placing the patties on the floured surface. You should have about 12 patties.

Fry the patties: Line a large baking sheet with paper towels and set aside. Pour the vegetable oil in a medium frying pan and place over medium-high heat. The oil level should come about ¾ inch up the side of the pan. Bring the oil to a temperature between 350°F and 375°F, or when you see the oil start to slightly smoke and sizzle. Once the oil is ready, lightly oil a large silicone spatula, slide the patty onto the spatula and carefully lower it into the hot oil while pushing it off with a spoon. Cook the patties, two to three at a time, depending on the size of your pan and your patties. When the edges of the patties turn golden brown, 2 to 3 minutes, carefully turn them over using 2 slotted spoons—a spatula will splatter hot oil over you! Fry on the opposite sides for an additional 2 to 3 minutes until golden brown.

Immediately remove the patties from the hot oil and transfer to the paper towel–lined baking sheet to soak up excess oil.

Serve the Korraysah hot on a lettuce leaf, topped with Toum (page 175), or Khyar b Laban (page 41), radish slivers, and fresh herbs.

VARIATION ❖ For a gluten-free version, substitute cooked cold quinoa for bulgur wheat, and replace the all-purpose flour with gluten-free flour.

————

taboulie tip! Make sure that the patties are not too thick otherwise they won't cook evenly inside!

كفتة كباب

Kafta Kababs
ground meat skewers

One of my favorite summertime memories as a little girl is the mouthwatering aroma of kabobs grilling outside. As I was playing in the backyard, I could never resist grabbing a kabob straight off the grill, almost burning myself because I was so eager and excited to taste one of these moist, meaty succulent skewers!

You can prepare my succulent kababs with lamb or beef, or both—laced with fresh parsley, onions, and a hit of allspice. Traditionally, the kabobs are formed into long sausagelike shapes on the skewer, but you can also make them into round patties for a very flavorful Lebanese take on a burger. I serve my "crave-a-licious" kafta kabobs with fresh and pickled vegetables, warm pita, and sauces like Tahini Dressing *(page 49) and* Khayer b Laban *(page 41).* ❖ **MAKES 6 SERVINGS (12 TO 14 SKEWERS)**

1 large yellow onion

3 sprigs fresh flat-leaf parsley leaves, finely minced

2 pounds finely ground lean lamb or beef

1 teaspoon sea salt

½ teaspoon freshly ground black pepper

½ teaspoon ground allspice

12 to 14 wooden or metal skewers (if using wooden skewers, presoak in water for 30 to 60 minutes)

Preheat a grill to high, or if using an oven, preheat to 450°F.

Quarter the onion and finely mince in a food processor. Transfer the minced onions in a fine-mesh sieve set over a bowl, and press down on the onions to remove any excess liquid. Discard the liquid and set the onions aside. Add the parsley to the food processor and pulse to finely chop. Return the drained onions to the food processor bowl. Add the ground meat and season with the salt, pepper, and allspice. Process to thoroughly blend all the ingredients, periodically pausing the processor to push the meat down and scrape it from the bottom and sides of the bowl. Transfer the meat mixture to a large mixing bowl.

Using your hands, mix the meat mixture together to make sure that all ingredients are evenly incorporated into a smooth mixture.

Make the kafta kabobs: Working in ⅓-cup portions, mold the meat mixture into a long sausage-like shape, about 6 inches in length. Then, roll the meat in between your palms to a thickness of about 1½ inches. Using the sharp end of the skewer, pierce through one end of the kabob and slide it through the other end; the meat should be about 1 inch away from the sharp tip of the skewer. Squeeze the meat one more time to ensure that it tightly adheres to the skewer. Continue making kabobs in the same manner with the remaining meat mixture. You should end up with 12 to 14 skewers.

continued

If using a grill, lightly brush it with oil. Place the kafta kabobs on the grill over a medium flame and cook, turning them periodically so that they cook evenly, 4 to 5 minutes per side, being careful not to overgrill them.

If roasting in the oven, place the kabobs on a lightly oiled baking sheet, spacing them evenly apart, and roast on the middle rack of the oven for 12 to 15 minutes, turning them over halfway through the roasting time.

Serve hot.

----

taboulie tip! Be sure not to overgrill these kabobs. They should be moist and juicy!

شاورما لحم

Shawarma Lahem
thinly sliced marinated meat sandwich

You've likely encountered shawarma at some point, perhaps at a food truck or roadside vendor: a large mass of meat rotating on a spit then thinly shaved into a pita with vegetable toppings and Tahini Dressing (page 49). Well, if you're a shawarma fan (and even if you're not yet, you will be), I've crafted an at-home recipe; no spit required! A bone-in leg of lamb is rubbed with my sensational shawarma spice mix, then marinated overnight with lemon juice, red wine vinegar, and olive oil. The next day, after 2 hours of roasting, the meat literally falls off the bone, and into warm pita bread! Finished with tahini sauce, parsley, and veggies, my shawarma is succulent, saucy, and a little bit spicy. ✣ **MAKES 6 SERVINGS**

MARINADE

1 tablespoon sea salt

1 tablespoon freshly ground black pepper

1 tablespoon ground allspice

1½ teaspoons ground cinnamon

½ teaspoon ground nutmeg

½ teaspoon ground cloves

½ teaspoon ground cardamom

1½ tablespoons sumac spice
 (see page 280)

1 cup extra-virgin olive oil

⅓ cup red wine vinegar

½ cup freshly squeezed lemon juice

MEAT

One 4- to 5-pound boneless or bone-in
 leg of lamb

5 garlic cloves, halved lengthwise

ROASTED VEGETABLES

1 large yellow onion, quartered

1 large red onion, quartered

1 large shallot, quartered

TOPPINGS

2 large red bell peppers

½ cup plus 1 tablespoon extra-virgin
 olive oil

1¼ teaspoons sea salt

2 large Vidalia onions, thinly sliced

3 vine-ripened garden tomatoes, thinly
 sliced

1 small bunch fresh flat-leat parsley
 leaves, coarsely chopped

1 small bunch fresh mint leaves, coarsely
 chopped

Tahini Dressing (page 49)

6 small Khebez Arabi (page 205), or
 large pita pockets, for serving

A day before you plan to serve the shawarma, combine all the seasonings and spices for the marinade in a large mixing bowl, making sure they are well blended. Whisk in the olive oil, vinegar, and lemon juice and set aside.

Place the lamb into a large mixing bowl or onto a nonreactive baking dish and, using a small, sharp knife, make 1-inch-deep slits all over and into the surface of the meat. Insert the garlic cloves into the slits, then pour the liquid marinade over the meat and thoroughly rub into the meat. Tightly cover the roast with plastic wrap and place in the refrigerator to marinate overnight.

continued

The next day, remove the lamb from the refrigerator and let the lamb come to room temperature before roasting. Preheat the oven to 425°F.

Bring 3 cups of water to a boil in a small pot, turn off the heat, and cover. Place the quartered onions on the bottom of a large roasting pan, and pour the hot water over them. Remove the lamb from the marinade, discard the liquid, and place lamb on top of a roasting rack set into the roasting pan. Roast the lamb in the center of the oven for 30 minutes. Then, lower the temperature to 350°F and roast for 1½ hours more, periodically basting the lamb with the juices it releases. You may need to add more hot water if the natural juices are evaporating.

While the lamb roasts, prepare the toppings. To roast the red bell peppers, you can use a broiler or a grill. If you are using a grill, fire it up. Drizzle 1 tablespoon olive oil over the red peppers, and sprinkle with ¼ teaspoon salt. Then, place the red peppers on the grill or under a broiler, and steadily rotate them using tongs so that they char evenly on all sides; this should take about 10 minutes. Once they are charred throughout, transfer them to a large mixing bowl, cover the bowl tightly with plastic wrap, and set aside to steam; this will facilitate peeling off the skins later.

Place 2 medium sauté pans over medium-low heat, and add 3 tablespoons of olive oil in each. Place the thinly sliced onions in one and the tomato slices in the other and season each with ½ teaspoon of the salt. Allow both the tomatoes and onions to caramelize for 5 to 7 minutes until softened, and the onions are golden brown. Remove from the heat and set aside.

By now, the bell peppers should have steamed sufficiently and cooled. Remove the plastic wrap from the bowl, and transfer the peppers to a cutting board. Using a sharp paring knife, scrape off the blackened skin and slice the peppers in half lengthwise. Remove and discard the stems and seeds, and thinly slice the peppers in long strips. Set aside.

At the end of the roasting time, check the lamb. The skin should be dark and the meat should be very fragrant. Remove the pan from the oven, and transfer the lamb to a large wooden carving board, cover it completely with aluminum foil, and allow it to rest for 10 minutes before carving. Turn off the oven. Strain the pan juices and reserve to pour over the shawarma if you like.

Arrange the Khebez Arabi breads or pita pockets on a large baking sheet, layering and overlapping them slightly. Place in the still warm (but turned off) oven for 2 to 3 minutes, flipping them over halfway so they are warmed through.

Once the lamb has finished resting, thinly slice the lamb against the grain and off the bone, using a very sharp carving knife and a carving fork. Pile the lamb in the warm pita pockets or bread, adding the roasted vegetables, spices, and Tahini Dressing.

NOTE You will need a large roasting pan with a rack.

شاورما دجاج

Shawarma Djej

thinly sliced marinated chicken sandwich

My Shawarma Djej *is a total crowd-pleaser that kids and adults alike can't get enough of. Super-succulent chicken, thanks to a spiced yogurt marinade, is very thinly sliced, tucked into warm pita, then topped with fresh and pickled vegetables, herbs, and* Toum *(page 175), my go-to tangy garlic sauce. If you prefer chicken breasts to thighs, feel free to use them, or do a combination of both.*

For an extra kid-friendly lunch or dinner, fry up some of my thick-cut Batata Maqlieh *(Twice-Fried French Fries, page 158) and serve with extra* Toum. *Taco night, who?* ✲ **MAKES 6 SERVINGS**

CHICKEN

- 2 cups Laban (page 223) or plain full-fat Greek yogurt
- ¾ cup extra-virgin olive oil
- ¼ cup white vinegar
- ⅓ cup freshly squeezed lemon juice
- 6 garlic cloves, finely minced
- 3 small shallots, finely minced
- 1 small yellow onion, finely minced
- 1 teaspoon sea salt
- ½ teaspoon ground white pepper
- ¼ teaspoon ground cardamom
- ¼ teapoon ground ginger
- 1 teaspoon cumin
- 1 teaspoon ground coriander
- 1 teaspoon garlic powder
- 2 pounds boneless, skinless chicken thighs, each sliced into three 1-inch strips

TOPPINGS

- 3 vine-ripened tomatoes, thinly sliced
- 1 large white onion, thinly sliced
- 3 Persian cucumbers, thinly sliced into matchsticks
- 6 red radishes, thinly sliced into matchsticks
- 6 pickled turnips (Kabis Lefet, page 193), thinly sliced into matchsticks
- 6 pickled cucumbers (Kabis Khayer, page 190), thinly sliced into matchsticks
- 3 scallions, ends trimmed, green and white parts thinly sliced
- 1 small bunch fresh flat-leaf parsley leaves, coarsely chopped

Toum Sauce (page 175)

6 small pita pockets warm, for serving

In a large mixing bowl, whisk the yogurt with ½ cup of the olive oil, the vinegar, and lemon juice. Add the minced garlic, shallots, onions, salt, white pepper, and spices and whisk again so that all the ingredients are well incorporated. Place the chicken strips into the marinade, submerging them entirely, and tossing to coat. Tightly cover the bowl with plastic wrap and refrigerate the chicken for at least 4 to 6 hours, or overnight.

When you are ready to cook the chicken, remove it from the refrigerator. Preheat the oven to 425°F.

Brush a large baking sheet with 2 tablespoons of the olive oil. Place the chicken strips on the baking sheet in an even layer, allowing any excess marinade to drip off. Discard the marinade. Place the baking sheet on the center rack of the preheated oven, and roast the chicken strips for 25 to 30 minutes, turning them over halfway through the roasting time, until they are completely cooked and golden brown.

Remove the chicken from the oven. Pour the remaining 2 tablespoons olive oil into a large sauté pan or cast-iron skillet and place over high heat. Once the oil begins to sizzle, add the roasted chicken strips, working in batches to avoid overcrowding the pan, and toss in the oil until they become crunchy and curl up slightly on the ends.

Immediately transfer the chicken strips to a large plate or serving platter, and cover with aluminum foil to keep hot.

Place the pita pockets in the still-warm (but turned off) oven to warm and soften for 2 to 3 minutes, then cover with foil to keep warm. Arrange all the fresh and pickled vegetables and herbs on the large serving platter, alongside a bowl of the Toum Sauce. Transfer the chicken strips to a serving dish, and serve making sandwiches as below.

How to Create a Chicken Shawarma Sandwich!

Place one warm, small pita pocket bread on a plate. Spread the Chicken Shawarma strips straight across the edge of the bread that is closest to you. Layer the freshly sliced vegetables, pickles, and herbs over the chicken strips and top with the Toum Sauce. Roll the pita bread over once to completely enclose the toppings, bring in the sides of the bread, then tightly roll the rest of the pita to create a wrapped sandwich. You can wrap a thick napkin or paper towel around the bottom half of the chicken wrap to keep it together.

NOTE You can also slice the warm pita pocket bread in half, and split it open using your fingertips. Simply stuff the chicken strips, tasty toppings, and sauce inside.

ASHA

main meals

STUFFED LEAVES & VEGETABLES
KHOUDRA
❀

sheikh el' mahshi . . . 92
STUFFED BABY EGGPLANT

kousa mahshi . . . 95
STUFFED KOUSA SQUASH

mahshi waraq enab . . . 99
STUFFED GRAPE LEAVES
WITH LAMB CHOPS

mahshi silik . . . 102
STUFFED SWISS CHARD LEAVES

mahshi malfouf . . . 105
STUFFED CABBAGE LEAVES

EGGS
BAYD
❀

bayd b halyoun . . . 109
ASPARAGUS-EGG SCRAMBLE

ejjeh . . . 110
FRESH HERB OMELET

bayd b lahem . . . 113
SPICED LAMB
AND EGG SCRAMBLE

bayd b batenjen . . . 114
BAKED EGGS
AND EGGPLANT

LAMB
XARUUF LAHEM

xaruuff mishwee . . . 117
ROASTED LEG OF LAMB WITH FREEKEH
AND SPRING VEGETABLES

kafta b sayniyeh . . . 120
LAMB, POTATO, AND TOMATO CASSEROLE

kibbeh kbekib . . . 123
MEAT AND BULGUR SPHERES STUFFED
WITH LAMB–PINE NUT FILLING

CHICKEN
DJEJ
❀

djej mishwee . . . 126
YOGURT-MARINATED CHICKEN
WITH QUINOA–PINE NUT PILAF

djej mahshi . . . 129
ROASTED CORNISH HENS STUFFED
WITH LONG-GRAIN RICE, MEAT, AND NUTS

djej b finden . . . 131
SHAWARMA-SPICED BAKED CHICKEN WITH
LEBANESE COUSCOUS "MOGHRABIEH"
AND WHITE WINE SAUCE

rez b heshwi . . . 134
ARABIC RICE, MEAT, AND NUT STUFFING

FISH
SAMAK
❀

sitto's samak mishwee . . .
GRILLED RED SNAPPER

siyediyeh . . . 138
SALMON AND SAFFRON RICE STEW

samak harrah . . . 143
BAKED BRANZINO
WITH SPICY TARATOUR SAUCE

WE'VE FINALLY ARRIVED AT THE CENTERPIECE OF THE MEAL: THE *ASHA*! If you're used to the anticipation of a dinner out, agonizing over whether you've ordered right, have no fear, you can't go wrong with even one recipe in this chapter. We Lebanese love stuffed vegetables, and I've included five varieties here, from lamb-filled eggplant and cabbage leaves to grape leaves and our go-to kousa squash. I've also included a variety of my favorite egg dishes, like Bayd b Halyoun (Asparagus-Egg Scramble), and Bayd b Batenjen (Baked Eggs and Eggplant), both of which make a satisfying breakfast or main meal! Lamb is the star meat in our cuisine, so of course I present you with a selection of my favorites, including my show-stopping Xaruuf Mishwee (Roasted Leg of Lamb with Freekeh and Spring Vegetables), and a home-style Lamb, Potato, and Tomato Casserole known as Kafta b Sayniyeh. And, of course, I love to cook with organic, free-range chickens—who can resist a yogurt-marinated chicken (Djej Mishwee, or my famous Lebanese long grain and wild rice, meat, and nut-stuffed Cornish Hen (Djej Mahshi). . . . Can you say fabulous? Last, I've included another of my go-to ingredients: fabulous, flaky, fresh fish. Try two of my favorites: my grandmother's grilled fresh red snapper (Sitto's Samak Mishwee), and Siyediyeh, a fresh salmon and saffron rice stew—they'll surely become part of your repertoire. I hope you enjoy serving these mouthwatering main meals at your table, which is always the best table in the house!

بشيخ المحشي

Sheikh El Mahshi
stuffed baby eggplant

Sheikh *means an "Arabic leader" or "patriarch," and although this recipe uses small, adorable eggplants, the flavor is as mighty as any sheikh! I get very excited whenever I come across these mini eggplants, and love to stuff them with this mouthwatering lamb–pine nut filling. Although my* Sheikh El Mahshi *is a more involved recipe, it's completely worth the extra TLLC (tender loving Lebanese care). Whether you dress it up for a formal dinner, or serve it home-style as a comforting casserole,* Sheikh El Mahshi *will become a favorite for sure.* ❖ **MAKES 24 EGGPLANTS (6 TO 8 MAIN-COURSE SERVINGS)**

24 baby Indian eggplants, at room temperature, washed and peeled (see page 280)

11 tablespoons (1 stick plus 3 tablespoons) unsalted butter

2 teapoons plus ¼ teaspoon sea salt

1 large Vidalia onion, finely minced

1 pound ground lamb

½ teaspoon freshly ground black pepper

1 teaspoon ground allspice

1 teaspoon Sab'ah Baharat (Seven-Spice, page 183)

⅓ cup pine nuts

1 small bunch fresh flat-leaf parsley leaves, finely chopped

5 vine-ripened tomatoes, finely diced

¼ cup extra-virgin olive oil

Preheat the oven to 350°F.

Gently remove the crown stem of each eggplant while retaining the small spiral stem. Then, using a small-sharp knife, create a thin but deep (without going all the way through) vertical slit down the center of each eggplant leaving ½ inch from the top and bottom. Set the eggplants aside.

Heat 3 tablespoons of the butter in a large sauté pan over high heat until the butter sizzles. Place 12 of the eggplants in the pan, season with ½ teaspoon of the salt and brown evenly until all sides are golden brown. Transfer onto a baking sheet. Repeat the process with the remaining 12 eggplants, using 3 more tablespoons of butter and ½ teaspoon of the salt. Transfer the eggplants to the baking sheet, turn off heat, but keep the pan on the stovetop for later use. Allow the eggplants to rest while you prepare the stuffing.

In the same sauté pan, melt 3 tablespoons of the butter over medium heat until shimmering. Add the onion and sauté until slightly translucent. Add the ground lamb, increase the heat to high, and cook, stirring continuously, until the meat is cooked through; continuously stirring the meat will decrease the amount of liquid it releases. Season with 1 teaspoon of the salt, the pepper, ½ teaspoon of the allspice, and ½ teaspoon of the seven spice. Stir until the seasonings are entirely incorporated.

Meanwhile, melt the remaining 2 tablespoons butter in a small sauté pan over medium-low heat. Add the pine nuts and the remaining ¼ teaspoon salt. Toss the pine nuts until they are nicely toasted and turn golden brown. Transfer the pine nuts to the meat mixture and turn the heat off under both pans. Add 2 tablespoons of the parsley to the meat mixture and set it aside.

Drizzle the bottom of a medium 9 x 13-inch casserole with the olive oil. Spread half of the diced tomatoes on the bottom of the casserole. Using your fingers, split apart each eggplant to create an opening large enough to receive the filling. Stuff 1 tablespoon of the filling into each eggplant and, using the back of your thumb, gently press the filling into the bottom. Take another tablespoon of the filling and stuff this over the first tablespoon of filling so that it sits on top of each eggplant. You will have about 2 cups left of stuffing. Place the stuffed eggplants into the prepared casserole, packing them closely in horizontal rows, then cover with the remaining diced tomatoes. Top the tomatoes with the remaining meat mixture and season with the remaining ½ teaspoon allspice and ½ teaspoon of seven spice. Sprinkle with the remaining chopped parsley.

Place the casserole on the center rack of the preheated oven and bake for approximately 30 minutes, or until golden brown and bubbly. Turn off heat, remove the casserole from the oven, and set aside to cool for a couple minutes before serving.

Serve hot over rice-vermicelli pilaf Rez b Shayriyeh (page 165).

Kousa Mahshi

stuffed kousa squash

Originating in the Middle East, kousa is a small, thin-skinned light green variety of summer squash. Previously unknown in the West, kousa is now popping up all over the States, from local farmers' markets and stands to regional and chain grocery stores. I'm pretty lucky, though, I don't have to go far for my squash—just to Mama's garden!

Other than the tender, savory lamb-rice stuffing, my favorite thing about this comforting hearty dish is that it's a two-for-one. Not only do you end up with mouthwatering stuffed squash, it also makes a very tasty tomato soup, which can be served with or without the squash. I like to pair Kousa Mahshi *with my refreshing* Khyar wa Banadoura; *the crisp Persian cucumbers and fresh tomatoes in the salad work really well with the stewed meat and squash. If you prefer beef to lamb, feel free to use freshly ground sirloin or 80/20 percent lean meat.* ❖ **MAKES 6 SERVINGS (12 KOUSA SQUASH)**

12 kousa squash, at room temperature	1 cup tomato paste
4 tablespoons (½ stick) unsalted butter, melted	4 tablespoons finely chopped fresh mint leaves
2 tablespoons pure olive oil	2½ teaspoons sea salt
½ pound finely ground lamb or beef	½ teaspoon freshly ground black pepper
1 cup long-grain rice, rinsed in cold water, and uncooked	2 to 3 tablespoons freshly squeezed lemon juice

Core and clean the kousa: Using a small, sharp paring knife, cut off the top stems evenly. Next, using the sharp tip of a zucchini corer (see page 281) trace a small circle in the center of the kousa top, and use this as your guide as you carefully continue to core the squash, scooping the flesh into a separate bowl. Remove as much of the inside flesh as possible, then clean the side walls of the squash, carefully scraping the insides, being careful not to pierce or puncture the skin. Place the cored squash in a colander and rinse with cold water so that no scraps remain inside. Drain the squashes upside down in the colander.

Make the stuffing: Heat 2 tablespoons of the melted butter and the olive oil in a medium sauté pan over medium-high heat. Once the oil and butter are shimmering, add the ground meat and cook until browned, stirring constantly with a wooden spoon to break up the meat. Once the meat has browned, remove it from the heat and transfer it to a large mixing bowl to cool.

continued

Once the meat has cooled, add the long-grain rice to the bowl along with half of the tomato paste, 2 tablespoons of the chopped mint, 1 teaspoon of the salt, the black pepper, and the remaining 2 tablespoons melted butter. Mix with your hands until all the ingredients are fully incorporated.

Stuff the kousa: Using your hands, gently stuff each squash with the rice-meat mixture using your index finger, pressing the stuffing downward until it reaches the bottom of the squash. Make sure to stuff the squash all the way to the top without overstuffing, as this will cause the kousa to crack when it is cooked.

Cook the kousa: Fill a large pot with a gallon (16 cups) of cold water. Stir in the remaining tomato paste, 1 teaspoon salt, and lemon juice. Place each squash into the liquid, then cover the pot and place over medium-high heat. Bring the liquid to a boil, then immediately reduce the heat to low and simmer the kousa for about 30 minutes.

After 30 minutes, check the kousa for doneness by removing one squash and lightly pressing the skin with your fingertips—it should be tender to the touch without being too firm or overly soft. When sufficiently cooked, remove the remaining squash from the pot, place on a serving platter, and cover with aluminum foil to keep them warm.

Stir the remaining 2 tablespoons mint and salt into the pot of broth and simmer for just a few minutes so that the flavors can infuse into the soup. Serve hot, first ladling the broth into shallow, rimmed soup bowls and then placing the squash in the broth.

VARIATION ❖ For a vegetarian version, simply omit the meat.

———

taboulie tip! Since you will be coring the squash, make sure to select kousa that are small, slender, short, and straight, not large or crooked.

taboulie tip! Make sure that your kousa squash are at room temperature, and not cold, before coring, which will minimize the chance of the kousa squash from cracking.

taboulie tip! Once the kousa squash are completely cooked, immediately remove from the pot otherwise the squash will likely overcook and crack open

محشي ورق عنب

Mahshi Waraq Enab

stuffed grape leaves with lamb chops

When you think of grape leaves, appetizers and mezza platters immediately come to mind. While we do often serve our Mahshi Waraq Enab *(Stuffed Grape Leaves) as part of our mezza at the start of a meal, I also love to serve them layered with succulent lamb chops as a main course. Filled with ground lamb, long-grain rice, and herbs, my grape leaves are simmered in a lemon-garlic broth alongside lamb chops, and served all together, generally with my* Khyar b Laban *(Cucumber, Yogurt, and Mint Salad, page 169).*

✢ **MAKES 60 STUFFED GRAPE LEAVES (6 TO 8 SERVINGS)**

60 fresh grape leaves, medium-sized (see page 99), or one 16-ounce jar grape leaves

2½ to 3 tablespoons freshly squeezed lemon juice, if using jarred grape leaves

FILLING

1 pound finely ground lamb

1 cup long-grain rice, rinsed in cold water and uncooked

2 tablespoons fresh mint leaves, finely chopped

1 teaspoon sea salt

½ teaspoon freshly ground black pepper

LAMB CHOPS

4 small or 2 large lamb chops

1 teaspoon sea salt

1 teaspoon freshly ground black pepper

2 tablespoons unsalted butter

2 tablespoons pure olive oil

6 garlic cloves

LEMON COOKING WATER

6 cups cold water

2½ to 3 tablespoons freshly squeezed lemon juice

6 garlic cloves, mashed into a smooth paste

½ teaspoon sea salt

Prepare the grape leaves: If using fresh grape leaves, cut off the small stem, being careful not to cut the leaves, then rinse under cold water and drain. Set aside 5 whole grape leaves for later use, then fill a medium pot with 4 cups of cold water and bring to a boil, reduce heat to medium-low and maintain a steady simmer. Add the leaves and blanch for just 2 to 3 seconds so that both sides wilt slightly. Immediately transfer to a colander to drain excess water. When all the leaves are blanched, place them onto a clean kitchen towel or paper towels and set aside to drain completely.

If using jarred grape leaves: Drain the liquid from the jar, remove the leaves and set aside 5 grape leaves for later use. Rinse the remaining leaves in a colander then place in a bowl of cold water with the lemon juice. Soak for 20 to 30 minutes then drain, and remove excess water by laying the leaves flat onto a clean kitchen towel or paper towels. Transfer the leaves to a cutting board, and cut off the small stems from the top of the leaves, being careful not to tear the leaves.

Make the filling: In a large mixing bowl, combine the ground meat, uncooked rice, mint, 1 teaspoon of the sea salt, and ½ teaspoon of the pepper. Thoroughly mix all the ingredients by hand, and set aside.

Fill and roll the grape leaves: On a clean surface or cutting board, carefully lay out some of the grape leaves in horizontal rows. Smooth out the edges of the leaves with your fingertips, smooth side down, veins side up, with the top of the leaves facing you. Next, take approximately 1 teaspoon of the meat mixture and spread it out lengthwise in a straight line just below the top stems of the leaf. Tightly roll the leaf over just once to completely enclose the filling. Then, turn in the outer wings (sides) of the leaf on each side, tucking them in and under tightly and then rolling to the end of the leaf. Continue with all the remaining filling, making sure not to overstuff the leaves.

Cook the lamb chops: Season the lamb chops on both sides with the sea salt and pepper. Heat the butter and olive oil in a large cast-iron skillet or sauté pan over high heat until it is lightly smoking. Place the lamb chops on the hot pan and sear for 2 to 3 minutes on each side until golden brown and slightly crisp. Remove from the pan and set aside on a separate plate.

Lay the reserved 5 leaves on the bottom of a large pot, covering the entire surface area. Then, begin to tightly layer the rolled grape leaves in horizontal and vertical rows, alternating the direction after each completed layer, and adding 2 garlic cloves with each layer; you will have 3 layers. Then, on the top and final layer, lay the small seared lamb chops.

Prepare the lemon water: Place a large dinner plate, or any plate that can fit inside the pot over the grape leaves, bottom facing up, covering as many of the grape leaves as possible. Pour the cold lemon water over the plate until the liquid level reaches just slightly above the plate. Cover the pot with a lid and bring to a boil. Reduce the heat to medium-low and simmer slowly for 40 to 45 minutes until almost all of the liquid has been absorbed or evaporated.

Remove the lid and, using tongs, remove the plate and set aside one grape leaf to cool for tasting. The meat should be completely cooked, and the rice cooked to al dente, not firm nor mushy. If the rice and/or meat are not fully cooked, simply add a little more plain hot water to the pot and continue to simmer the grape leaves slowly with the plate on top. Once the grape leaves have fully cooked, remove from the heat and leave them in the pot to stay hot and set aside until ready to serve.

To serve, arrange the grape leaves on a large platter along with the lamb chops. Finish with fresh sprigs of mint and sliced lemon rounds, and serve with Khyar b Laban (cucumber-mint yogurt sauce, page 169) and warm pita pocket or Khebez Arabi (page 205).

Mahshi Silik

stuffed swiss chard leaves

I never understand why Swiss chard doesn't get the love and recognition that kale does. These calcium-packed leaves are one of my absolute favorite vegetables, and I am always smitten with the many-colored stalks I see at the farmers' market and in Mama's glorious garden.

My **Mahshi Silik** *features tender Swiss chard leaves stuffed with a super-succulent chopped chickpea-rice filling then simmered in a lemon-garlic broth. I often serve my stuffed chard leaves cold as part of a mezza platter, or warm as a vegetarian main dish with my Kibbet Raheb Soup (page 60). Either way, you just can't go wrong—especially enjoyed alongside my Hummus Salata (page 46) for a double dose of chickpeas.* ✣ **MAKES 36 TO 42 LEAVES (6 SERVINGS)**

2½ teaspoons sea salt

2 bunches Swiss chard

½ cup canned chickpeas

½ cup long-grain rice, rinsed in cold water and uncooked

1 small white onion, finely minced

8 garlic cloves, 4 finely minced, 4 left whole

3 scallions, ends trimmed, green and white parts thinly sliced

1 small bunch fresh parsley leaves, finely minced

1 small bunch fresh mint leaves, finely minced, plus extra left whole for garnish

½ cup freshly squeezed lemon juice plus 1 lemon, sliced, for garnish

⅓ cup extra-virgin olive oil

In a large pot, bring 8 cups of cold water and 1 teaspoon of the sea salt to a rolling boil. Fill a large mixing bowl with cold water and ice cubes and set aside.

Place the chard leaves in a colander and thoroughly wash and drain, shaking off any excess water. Trim off the thick stems and devein the leaves, carefully carving out the stems by trimming all around them with a small sharp knife so that only the large, tender leaves remain. Now, lightly slice vertically down the center of each leaf so that you have 2 equal halves. Then, slice both halves horizontally into 2 to 3 segments, so that there are 3 to 4 large pieces per leaf half. You should have 35 to 40 leaf segments total. Reserve 4 to 5 leaf segments and set aside (do not blanch them).

Place the remaining 30 to 35 Swiss chard segments into the boiling water for approximately 10 to 15 seconds at the most, just enough to quickly blanch the leaves. Immediately remove them using a slotted spoon and place in the ice-water bath to stop the cooking process so the leaves retain their bright green color. Make sure not to overcook the leaves, they should just wilt slightly. Then, drain the blanched leaves and lay over clean paper towels to absorb any excess water and set aside.

Make the stuffing: Drain the chickpeas from the canning liquid and thoroughly rinse under cold water. Then, evenly spread out the chickpeas on a cutting board and roughly chop them. Place the chickpeas in a large mixing bowl with the rice, minced onion, and minced garlic. Add the scallions, parsley, and mint and pour in 2½ to 3 tablespoons of the lemon juice and all of the olive oil. Season with 1 teaspoon of the salt and thoroughly mix all the ingredients with your hands, until they are all well incorporated.

Stuff the chard leaves: Lay 6 to 8 leaves out on a large, clean surface, vein side up and shiny smooth side down. Smooth the edges out with your fingertips, and then take 1 teaspoon (depending on the size of the leaf) of the stuffing and spread it out evenly in a straight line just above the edge of the leaf that is closer to you. Be sure not to overstuff the leaves. Then, roll the leaf over once to completely enclose the filling, then bring in the sides of the leaf and tuck under. Roll the rest of the leaf to the end, set aside, and continue to roll the rest of the leaves (see photos on page 101 for techniques).

Lay the reserved unblanched leaf segments on the bottom of a large pot. Lay the stuffed Swiss chard leaves in the pot in two layers, alternating horizontal and vertical rows and placing 4 whole garlic cloves in between the layers. If your pot is too small for just two layers, make more layers, and just divide the 4 garlic cloves evenly among them.

Place a large dinner plate, or any plate that can fit inside the pot over the stuffed leaves, bottom facing up. In a separate bowl, combine 6 cups of cold water with the remaining lemon juice, the remaining ½ teaspoon sea salt, and the remaining 4 minced garlic cloves. Thoroughly stir this mixture together and pour over the plate in the pot until the water level reaches slightly above the top of the plate.

Cover the pot and place on the stovetop over medium-high heat. Bring to a rolling boil then immediately reduce the heat to low and simmer slowly for 25 to 30 minutes until almost all of the water has evaporated and the stuffing is tender and al dente but not undercooked or mushy. Immediately remove the pot from the heat, turn off the heat, and remove the cover. Allow the stuffed Swiss chard leaves to settle for 5 to 10 minutes, then transfer them to a serving platter.

Arrange in rows and garnish with fresh lemon slices and fresh mint leaves.

Serve warm, at room temperature, or cool.

NOTE You can also use dried and reconstituted chickpeas (see method on page 11).

Mahshi Malfouf
stuffed cabbage leaves

Many people associate stuffed cabbage leaves with Eastern European cuisine, but my Mahshi Malfouf, *which translates literally as "stuffed cabbage," is a classic Lebanese dish that will entice even the strictest cabbage cynic out there. I use Savoy cabbage—usually plucked from Mama's garden—in this harvest-time dish, as I find it sweeter and tenderer than many other cabbage varieties. Stuffed with a savory blend of lean lamb, long-grain rice, and chopped tomatoes, these tasty parcels are then slowly simmered in a broth spiked with tangy pomegranate molasses. If you can't find ground lamb (or prefer beef), feel free to substitute with 80/20 percent ground beef.* ✣ **MAKES 60 STUFFED CABBAGE LEAVES (6 SERVINGS)**

2 teaspoons sea salt

1 head Savoy cabbage
(about 1½ pounds)

2 pounds finely ground lamb

2 cups long-grain rice, rinsed in cold
water and uncooked

3 vine-ripened tomatoes, finely diced

10 garlic cloves, 5 finely minced,
5 left whole

½ teaspoon freshly ground black pepper

½ teaspoon ground allspice

Ripe tomato slices, for serving

Fresh mint sprigs, for serving

Khebez Arabi (page 205), for serving

CABBAGE COOKING LIQUID

2½ to 3 tablespoons freshly squeezed
lemon juice

3 tablespoons tomato paste

3 tablespoons pomegranate molasses
(see page 280)

1 teaspoon sea salt

Fill a large pot with 8 cups of cold water and 1 teaspoon of the sea salt and bring to a boil. Meanwhile, fill a large mixing bowl with cold water and ice cubes and set aside.

Place the cabbage on a thick cutting board and remove the central core with a small, sharp paring knife, by making deep cuts around the core, then pulling the core out with your fingers. Place the cored cabbage under cold running water and wash thoroughly, but do not separate the leaves.

Once the water is boiling, place the entire head of cabbage, core side down, into the water and submerge for several minutes. As the leaves separate from the head, remove them from the hot water and transfer them to the ice-water bath immediately to stop cooking, and retain their shape and light green color. Once you have removed all of the leaves, reserve the heart of the cabbage and set aside.

Strain the blanched leaves from the ice water and place on a paper towel–lined baking sheet to absorb any excess water. Set aside.

continued

In a large mixing bowl, combine the ground meat, rice, tomatoes, and garlic. Season with the remaining salt, the pepper, and allspice and mix all the ingredients together using your hands, so they are completely incorporated into a smooth, moist mixture. Set aside.

Prepare the cabbage leaves for stuffing: Lay the leaves flat on a cutting board, smoothing the edges with your fingers. Set aside 3 large cabbage leaves and reserve for later use. With a small sharp knife, slice each remaining large leaf in half lengthwise and then again widthwise to create 4 equal segments. Shave off any thick stems going through the leaves. For medium-size leaves, you can just cut them in half; smaller leaves can be left whole.

Now, lay 6 to 8 leaves on the cutting board, shiny leaf side down and vein side up. Scoop ½ to 1 teaspoon (depending on the size of the leaf) of the filling, and spread the mixture out in an even line just above the bottom edge of the leaf. Begin to tightly roll the leaf over once to completely enclose the mixture, and then bring the sides in while tucking under and continuing to tightly roll the leaf to the end. Place the rolled leaf into the palm of your hand and gently squeeze out as much excess water as possible. Set aside and continue to roll the remaining leaves, making sure not to understuff or overstuff.

Place the 3 reserved whole leaves on the bottom of a large pot so that the entire surface is covered. Place the reserved cabbage heart into the center of the pot and begin to layer the stuffed leaves around it, starting at the bottom of the pot and interchanging vertical and horizontal rows. You should have 3 rows. Pack the leaves closely together and add a few whole garlic cloves with each complete row.

In a large mixing bowl, combine the ingredients for the cabbage cooking liquid by whisking together the lemon juice, tomato paste, pomegranate molasses, and salt with 6 cups of cold water.

Take a large dinner plate that will fit inside the pot, and place it, bottom side up, tightly covering the leaves. Then, pour the cooking liquid over the top of the plate until it reaches just slightly above the plate's rim. Gently press down on the bottom of the plate as you pour the cooking liquid so that the plate does not float up to the surface of the pot.

Cover the pot with a lid and place on the stovetop over medium-high heat. Bring to a rolling boil, then immediately reduce the heat to medium-low and simmer for 30 to 35 minutes, or until all of the cooking liquid has been absorbed. After 30 minutes, taste a stuffed leaf. The meat and rice should be cooked through and the leaves should remain intact. If the rice is still firm, add some hot water to the pot over the plate and simmer, covered, for several minutes more until the rice is cooked through. Once the filling is cooked, turn the heat off, remove the lid and the plate, and allow the leaves to settle in the pot for a few minutes before transferring to a large serving platter and serving.

Serve hot or warm with the fresh sliced tomatoes, mint sprigs, and Khebez Arabi (page 205).

Bayd b Halyoun

asparagus-egg scramble

Bayd b Halyoun, *which translates literally as "Eggs with Asparagus," is a wonderful springtime breakfast and a family favorite. Growing up in Lebanon, my mother would collect fresh wild asparagus for this scrumptious scramble that my Sitto (grandmother) would make during the Lenten season.* Bayd b Halyoun *is satisfying, filling, and brings back wonderful memories for my mother. Make sure to select long, thin asparagus spears, which will be more tender and sweeter than the thicker ones.* ✢ **MAKES 6 SERVINGS**

⅓ cup extra-virgin olive oil

1 large shallot, finely minced

3 garlic cloves, finely minced

10 thin asparagus spears, finely diced

1 teaspoon sea salt

6 large eggs

¼ cup heavy cream, half-and-half, or whole milk

2 generous pinches freshly ground black pepper

Heat the olive oil in a large sauté pan (preferably copper) or cast-iron skillet over medium-low heat. Add the shallots and garlic and sauté, stirring occasionally, until the shallots are translucent and have softened slightly. Add the asparagus and season with ½ teaspoon of the salt. Toss thoroughly with the shallots and garlic, and coat completely with the olive oil. Sauté until the asparagus has softened slightly, but is still bright green and slightly crunchy, 4 to 5 minutes.

Meanwhile, crack the eggs into a large mixing bowl. Pierce the yolks with a sharp knife or fork, then pour in the cream, season with the pepper and remaining ½ teaspoon salt, and whisk vigorously until creamy.

Slowly pour the beaten eggs over the asparagus mixture and reduce the heat to low. Gradually scramble the eggs into the vegetables by stirring slowly until the eggs are completely cooked through, but still golden yellow, moist, and soft.

Serve hot.

Ejjeh

fresh herb omelet

Ejjeh *simply means "omelet," and this open-faced herb-filled version is very simple and very satisfying. Ideal for breakfast, or a light lunch,* Ejjeh *especially entices me in the spring, when I can use Mama's fresh herbs and the brown, white, and green organic eggs from our free-range chicken coop.*

❖ **MAKES 6 INDIVIDUAL OMELETS**

12 large eggs

⅓ cup heavy cream, half-and-half, or whole milk

3 scallions, ends trimmed, finely minced

1 small bunch fresh flat-leaf parsley leaves, finely minced

1 small bunch fresh chives, finely minced

1 small bunch fresh mint leaves, finely minced

1 teaspoon sea salt

1 teaspoon ground white pepper

3 tablespoons unbleached, all-purpose flour

3 tablespoons clarified or unsalted butter

3 tablespoons extra-virgin olive oil

Crack the eggs into a large mixing bowl, and poke each yolk with a small knife or fork to break open. Vigorously whisk the eggs until the whites and yolks are completely blended together, then add the cream or milk and whisk until soft and smooth.

Fold in the scallions and all of the herbs, and season with the salt. Then add the flour and whisk until it has completely dissolved. The mixture should be slightly substantial with small bubbles on the surface.

Meanwhile, melt 1 tablespoon of the butter and 1 tablespoon of olive oil over medium-low heat in a small sauté pan (preferably copper) or a cast-iron skillet. Once the butter and oil start to foam slightly, ladle about ½ cup of the egg mixture into the center of the pan. Lift the pan handle and gently swirl the pan in a circular motion so that the egg mixture coats the bottom of the pan. Allow the mixture to set for about 10 seconds, then gently run a silicone spatula around the side walls of the pan, slightly lifting the omelet's edges so they do not stick. When the omelet turns light golden brown, 2 to 3 minutes, flip over by sliding the spatula under the center and swiftly turning it. Cook for an additional 2 to 3 minutes, then transfer to a baking sheet and cover with aluminum foil. Continue to make omelets with the remaining egg mixture. After about 3 omelets you will need to add more butter and oil in the pan. You should end up with about 12 small omelets.

Serve the omelets warm or at room temperature with my Batata b Zeit home fries (page 157), or Khebez Arabi (page 205).

بيض برليون

Bayd b Lahem
spiced lamb and egg scramble

If you haven't noticed, we Lebanese just love our lamb—we put it everywhere, even in scrambled eggs! My Bayd b Lahem, *which translates literally to "Eggs with Lamb," is a hearty, savory dish that can be served any time of day. Aromatic onions and garlic are combined with succulent spiced lamb and fluffy eggs, and finished off with refreshing chopped mint and butter-toasted pine nuts. The mix of textures, not to mention flavors, is unbeatable in this dish, which makes a wonderful main course for a brunch party.*

✴ **MAKES 6 SERVINGS**

⅓ cup extra-virgin olive oil

1 medium yellow onion, finely minced

3 garlic cloves, finely minced

1 teaspoon sea salt

½ pound finely ground lamb

½ teaspoon freshly ground black pepper

6 large eggs

2 tablespoons unsalted butter

⅓ cup pine nuts

½ teaspoon allspice

½ teaspoon Sab'ah Baharat (Seven-Spice, page 183)

1 small bunch fresh mint leaves, finely minced

Heat the olive oil in a large copper sauté pan or cast-iron skillet over medium-low heat. Once the oil is hot, add the onion and garlic, and season with ½ teaspoon of the salt. Sauté until the onion is translucent and somewhat softened.

Increase the heat to high, and add the ground lamb. Using the back of a wooden spoon, break up the meat and mix in with the onion and garlic. Sauté until the meat is browned and completely cooked through, about 5 to 10 minutes. Reduce the heat to low, season with the black pepper and the remaining ½ teaspoon salt, and stir thoroughly.

While the lamb is cooking, crack the eggs into a large mixing bowl, and pierce the yolks with a sharp knife or fork. Vigorously whisk the eggs until creamy, then slowly pour over the cooked lamb mixture. Cook, stirring continuously with a spatula to scramble the eggs into the meat mixture, and until they are completely cooked but still soft and moist. Turn off the heat.

Melt the butter in a small sauté pan over medium-low heat. Once it starts to sizzle, stir in the pine nuts, completely coating them in butter. Cook, stirring continuously, until the pine nuts are a light golden brown. Turn off the heat, transfer the pine nuts to the lamb mixture, and fold them in gently. Season the scrambled eggs and lamb with the allspice and sab'ah baharat spice and sprinkle with the minced mint. Serve hot.

بيض بالباذنجان

Bayd b Batenjen
baked eggs and eggplant

Eggplants are one of my absolute favorite vegetables—so much so that Mama plants a wide array of different varieties just for me each year. In my Bayd b Batenjen, *I like to use white Italian eggplants because of their very delicate flavor. If you can't find them, purple Italian eggplants will work just fine.*

Flavored with garlic, shallots, and Vidalia onions, this standout dish looks impressive, but is super simple to make. I love the combination of the eggplant and luscious egg yolks, sprinkled with allspice and served hot as a filling breakfast, lunch, or one-skillet dinner. ❖ **MAKES 6 SERVINGS**

⅓ cup extra-virgin olive oil

1 large Vidalia onion, finely minced

1 large or 2 small shallots, finely minced

6 garlic cloves, finely minced

1 teaspoon plus ¼ teaspoon sea salt

2 medium white or purple Italian eggplants, peeled and diced into 1-inch cubes

5 large eggs

¼ teaspoon ground white pepper

¼ teaspoon ground allspice

Preheat the oven to 350°F.

Heat the olive oil over medium heat in a large oven-safe sauté pan or cast-iron skillet until shimmering. Add the onion, shallots, and garlic, season with ½ teaspoon of the salt, and sauté until the onion and shallots are translucent and softened.

Toss the eggplant cubes into the sauté pan and season with 1½ teaspoons of the salt. Stir thoroughly to combine with onion and shallots, then reduce the heat to low. Slowly sauté the eggplant cubes until they have cooked down to about half of their original size, and the flesh appears translucent and light golden brown, about 5 to 7 minutes. Turn off the heat.

Crack the eggs on top of the eggplant mixture in a circular pattern evenly distributed throughout (if you imagine the pan as a clock, crack the eggs at 12, 3, 6, and 9 o'clock and then the last one in the center of the pan). Sprinkle the eggs with the remaining ¼ teaspoon salt, the white pepper, and allspice.

Transfer the pan to the center of the preheated oven and bake for 12 to 15 minutes until the egg whites are cooked but the yolks are still slightly runny. Remove from the pan (use an oven mitt!) and cool slightly before serving.

VARIATION ❖ Feel free to add finely diced tomatoes if you wish.
I prefer plum or campari tomatoes for this dish.

Xaruuf Mishwee
roasted leg of lamb with freekeh and spring vegetables

In my family, Xaruuf Mishwee *is always served at our Easter celebration as a return to meat after the Lenten season. My springtime roast begins with a leg of lamb stuffed with garlic cloves and marinated overnight in fresh herbs. A slow roast makes for melt-in-your-mouth tenderness, perfectly complemented by freekeh (fire-roasted baby wheat), and steamed spring vegetables with a garlic-herb butter sauce.*

There's no need to limit yourself to just once a year for this dish; it makes a showstopping centerpiece for Christmas, New Years' Eve, or any large holiday or celebration. I love to make it on my favorite holiday— Valentine's Day—and share the love with my whole family. ✢ **MAKES 10 TO 12 SERVINGS**

LAMB

One 8- to 10-pound bone-in leg of lamb

10 garlic cloves, 5 left whole and 5 finely minced

⅓ cup extra-virgin olive oil

1 tablespoon sea salt

½ tablespoon ground white pepper

1 small bunch fresh mint leaves, half finely minced and half left whole

1 small bunch fresh flat-leaf parsley leaves, half finely minced and half left whole

1 small bunch fresh chives, half finely minced and half left whole

1 small bunch fresh thyme sprigs, leaves picked, half finely minced and half left whole

1 small bunch fresh rosemary, leaves picked, half finely minced and half left whole

1 large Vidalia onion, quartered

1 large red onion, quartered

3 large shallots, quartered

1 cup clover or alfalfa sprouts, for garnish

FREEKEH

2 cups freekeh (see page 279)

⅓ cup extra-virgin olive oil

1 Vidalia onion, finely minced

2 shallots, finely minced

1 teaspoon sea salt

4½ cups water, vegetable, beef, or chicken broth

SPRING VEGETABLES

12 spring onion bulbs

2 cups sugar snap peas

12 baby carrots, peeled with stems left on

12 asparagus spears, thick ends removed

8 tablespoons (1 stick) unsalted butter, softened

3 garlic cloves, finely minced

3 tablespoons fresh mint, minced

3 tablespoons fresh flat-leaf parsley leaves, minced

3 tablespoons fresh chives, minced

1 teaspoon sea salt

Place the leg of lamb on a large baking sheet. Using a small, sharp knife, make small 1-inch-deep slits throughout the lamb leg, piercing through the skin into the meat. Slice the whole garlic cloves in half and stuff them into the slits.

In a large mixing bowl, whisk together the olive oil, salt, pepper, and minced herbs. Generously rub the herbed oil all over the lamb leg, and cover the baking sheet with plastic wrap. Transfer the lamb to the refrigerator and marinate for at least 6 hours and up to 12.

After marinating, remove the lamb from the refrigerator and discard the plastic wrap.

Preheat the oven to 450°F. In a small pot, bring 3 cups of cold water to a boil.

Place the quartered onions, shallots, and whole herbs on the bottom of a large roasting pan and cover with the boiling water. Place a rack on top and lift the lamb leg onto the rack. Transfer the roasting pan to a lower rack in the preheated oven and roast the lamb for 30 minutes. Reduce the oven temperature to 350°F, and continue to roast for 2½ to 3 hours, basting the lamb periodically with the juices it releases. If the pan juices are evaporating too quickly, simply add additional hot water to the bottom of the pan.

When the meat is fully cooked, it should be pinkish in the center, dark brown on the outside, and register an internal temperature of 160°F. Remove the lamb from the oven and turn off the heat. Cover the lamb with aluminum foil and allow to rest for 10 to 15 minutes.

While the lamb is cooking, begin cooking the freekeh: place freekeh in a large mixing bowl, and run your fingers through the wheat and discard any particles if necessary. Rinse under cold running water three times, skimming off any skins that may rise to the top of the bowl. Set aside.

In a large pot, combine the olive oil, onion, and shallots and sauté over medium-low heat until the onion and shallots are translucent and lightly browned. Stir in the freekeh, completely coating the grains in the oil and mixing well with the onion and shallots. Season with the sea salt and stir steadily for a few minutes to toast the grains. Pour the water or broth into the pot, cover, and bring to a boil. Reduce the heat to low and allow the freekeh to slowly simmer, covered, for 45 minutes to 1 hour while absorbing liquid. If the liquid is absorbed too quickly, add more hot water or broth and cook until the freekeh is tender.

Once the freekeh is tender, remove the pot from the heat and let the freekeh stand, covered, for 5 to 10 minutes. Remove the lid, and fluff the grains with a fork. Re-cover to keep hot until ready to serve.

While the freekeh is simmering, prepare the spring vegetables. Using a large double boiler or steamer pot, bring 6 cups of cold water to a rolling boil in the bottom pot. Cut an X in the bottom of each spring onion bulb. Place all the vegetables in the steamer basket and steam, covered, for 10 to 15 minutes so that the vegetables are cooked through, but still slightly crunchy. While the vegetables are cooking, fill a large bowl with cold water and ice cubes. When the vegetables are cooked, transfer them to the ice bath.

In a large sauté pan, melt the butter over medium-low heat. Stir in the garlic and herbs. Once the butter and herbs start to slightly sizzle, add the steamed vegetables to the pan and season with salt. Briefly toss to coat the vegetables completely with the butter sauce, then turn off the heat, and cover to keep warm.

To plate the meal, cover a large serving platter with the sprouts. Place the lamb leg in the center of the platter, either left whole or carved. Spread the freekeh all around the lamb, and arrange the vegetables on top of the grains. Pour the herb-butter sauce from the sauté pan into a small bowl and serve alongside the platter. Strain the pan juices from the roasting pan and spoon over the lamb meat just before serving.

NOTE You will need a long, large roasting pan with a rack.

Kafta b Sayniyeh
lamb, potato, and tomato casserole

Kafta, which means "to beat" or "to grind," refers to the thoroughly ground and mixed lamb in this soul-warming casserole. Sayniyeh *means "pan," and in this case, the casserole dish pan in which the luscious meat and spiced tomato broth are cooked. Growing up, my siblings and I referred to this dish as "Skiboo," as my grandmother would cook it for us often and wave us to the table saying "Skiboo, Skiboo," pointing to the dish. We soon discovered that Skiboo, Skiboo actually means "Eat, Eat!"*

In the winter months, I often serve Kafta b Sayniyeh *spooned over* Rez b Shayriyeh, *a rice pilaf (page 165) with some toasted pine nuts—it will warm you from bottom to top.* ❖ **MAKES 6 SERVINGS**

1 pound finely ground lamb or beef sirloin

1 medium yellow onion, finely minced

2 small bunches fresh parsley leaves, 1 bunch finely minced, 1 bunch coarsely chopped

2 teaspoons sea salt

1 teaspoon freshly ground pepper

½ teaspoon ground allspice

½ teaspoon Sab'ah Baharat (Seven-Spice, page 183)

8 tablespoons (1 stick) unsalted butter, cut into tablespoon-size pieces

3 large Yukon gold potatoes, peeled and sliced into ½-inch-thick rounds

6 tomatoes, sliced into ½-inch-thick rounds

3 tablespoons extra-virgin olive oil

Preheat the oven to 350°F.

In a large mixing bowl, combine the lamb, onion, and minced parsley. Add 1 teaspoon salt, ½ teaspoon pepper, and spices and mix together, using your hands, until all the ingredients are completely incorporated. Using your fists, gently punch into the meat mixture to help it bind together.

Form into patties, rolling about 2 tablespoons of the mixture into a ball between your palms, and then pushing down into the center to form a 3-inch-round patty. Repeat with the remaining meat mixture. Set the patties aside on a plate. You should have about 12.

In a large sauté pan, melt 3 tablespoons of the butter over medium heat. Once the butter begins to sizzle, add the meat patties in small batches, and sear for 2 to 3 minutes per side until cooked through and golden brown. Set the cooked patties aside on a clean plate and turn off the heat, but reserve the natural juices in pan on the stovetop.

Melt 3 more tablespoons of the butter in the same sauté pan with the juices until the butter sizzles. Place the potato slices in the pan in small batches, season with ½ teaspoon of the salt and

pepper, and sauté for 2 to 3 minutes on both sides until the potatoes are slightly cooked through and lightly browned. Set the cooked potatoes aside, then add the remaining 2 tablespoons butter to the same sauté pan. Add the tomatoes and cook in the same method, seasoning with the remaining ½ teaspoon of the salt. Set aside.

Generously drizzle the olive oil into a medium 9 x 13-inch casserole dish and rub the oil onto the bottom and sides of the dish. Spread one-third of the tomatoes evenly on the bottom of the dish. Then, spread half of the meat patties on top of the tomatoes, then half of the potatoes on top of the meat. Repeat with another layer of tomatoes, the remaining meat patties, and the remaining potatoes, and finish with one final layer of tomatoes on top. Sprinkle the coarsely chopped parsley over the tomatoes, and bake the casserole on the center rack of the preheated oven for about 30 minutes, or until golden brown and bubbly.

Remove from the oven, turn off the heat, and set the casserole aside to set and cool slightly. Serve with Rez b Shayriyeh (page 165).

كبة كبكيب

Kibbeh Kbekib

meat and bulgur spheres stuffed with lamb–pine nut filling

In Lebanese cuisine, any dish that combines cracked bulgur wheat and ground lamb is known as kibbeh. Kibbeh also has a number of different spellings, including kibbe *and* kibbee. *This one is my absolute favorite; I can't get enough of the out-of-this-world taste and texture of these little, addictive nuggets.*

Bulgur wheat is blended with ground lamb and onion, and stuffed with Heshwi, *the traditional kibbeh stuffing of ground lamb, chopped herbs, spices, and buttery toasted pine nuts. Baked with butter, the end result is crispy on the outside shell, with a succulent meaty filling inside. Paired with warm* Khebez Arabi *(page 205) and a drizzle of* Labneh *(page 225), there's really nothing more traditional or delicious.*

❉ MAKES 10 TO 12 KIBBEH, DEPENDING ON SIZE

KIBBEH BASE

½ cup #1 fine bulgur wheat
  (see page 279)

1 small yellow onion, finely grated

1 pound finely ground lean lamb

1 teaspoon sea salt

½ teaspoon freshly ground black pepper

2 tablespoons extra-virgin olive oil

HESHWI (KIBBEH STUFFING)

12 tablespoons unsalted butter
  (6 tablespoons cold and cut
  in halves)

2 tablespoons olive oil

1 medium yellow onion, finely diced
  (about ⅓ cup)

½ pound finely ground lamb

1 teaspoon sea salt

½ teaspoon freshly ground pepper

½ teaspoon ground allspice

⅓ cup fresh mint leaves, finely chopped

⅓ cup pine nuts

Preheat the oven to 425°F.

Make the heshwi: In a medium skillet over medium-high heat, melt 2 tablespoons of butter with 2 tablespoons of olive oil. Add the diced onions and cook until translucent. Add the ground lamb and sauté until it is completely browned and cooked through. Once the meat is cooked, season it with salt, pepper, and allspice. Remove from the heat, add the chopped mint and set aside to cool.

In a small sauté pan, melt 2 tablespoons of butter over medium-low heat. Add the pine nuts and toss to coat completely. Toast until they are a light golden brown. Remove from the heat and mix into the meat heshwi.

continued

Make the kibbeh base: Place the bulgur wheat in a large bowl and lightly rinse with cold water to slightly moisten. Do not soak the bulgur wheat in the water. Add the grated onion and thoroughly mix to combine, then begin to knead the bulgur wheat mixture by pounding it with your fists.

In the bowl of a food processor, combine the lamb, salt, and pepper with a couple of ice cubes and pulse to thoroughly blend together. Once finely blended, transfer the mixture to a large freezer bag, smooth out the mixture, release any air pockets, and tightly seal and secure. Place in the freezer for about 10–15 minutes until ice cold but not frozen.

Remove the mixture from the freezer and add to the bulgur wheat mixture and mix together so that all the ingredients are fully incorporated. Knead the mixture by pounding it together with your fists until it is soft and pliable but not mushy. If the mixture feels too stiff, gradually add small amounts of ice water to loosen.

Now it's time to make the kibbeh spheres: Fill a small bowl with ice cubes and ice-cold water and set on the countertop. Then, place the heshwi next to the bowl with the kibbeh base. Coat a baking sheet with the 2 tablespoons softened butter and place it next to your work area.

Lightly dip your hands in the cold water and take about 2 tablespoons of the kibbeh base and roll it into a small oval ball in the palms of your hands. Then, place the oval ball in one hand, and, with your other hand, use your index finger to poke a small hole in one end of the oval, pointing inwards to the middle. Now, gently begin to rotate your finger into the hole in a circular motion until you have created a deeper and wider hole within the kibbeh shell. Make sure not to break through the kibbeh walls or tear the outside. If you do, simply start over or seam it back together and smooth with your fingertips (see photos opposite).

Now, take about ½ tablespoon of the heshwi and fill the hole by slightly pressing it down into the bottom of the kibbeh ball and working your way up to about ¼ inch from the top. Be careful not to overstuff. Then, close the hole by lightly dipping your fingers in the ice-cold water and tightly squeezing the opening ends together. Seam and smooth out the top tip and place on the buttered baking sheet. Repeat this technique with the remaining base and filling; you should have between 10 and 14 kibbeh (see photos opposite).

Next, place one of the halves of cold butter onto the top of each kibbeh sphere and bake for approximately 30 minutes, turning the spheres over halfway through. They should be golden brown and crispy on the outside. Remove from the oven and lightly shake the pan back and forth to roll the kibbeh balls around with baking juices and butter.

Serve straight out of the oven with Labneh (page 225), drizzled with olive oil, sea salt, and chopped mint leaves and with warm Khebez Arabi (page 205).

NOTE You will need a food processor.

دجاج مشوي

Djej Mishwee
yogurt-marinated chicken with quinoa-pine nut pilaf

My Djej Mishwee *always produces the moistest grilled chicken—a far cry from the rubbery versions that are all too widespread. Why? This life-changing marinade of rich laban yogurt, fresh herbs, garlic, and lemon juice tenderizes the meat while adding a tart, tangy flavor. I serve this juicy chicken in the summertime over pine nut–laced quinoa and zesty olives for a beautiful rustic meal. Feel free to use a combination of legs, wings, and thighs in addition to the breasts if you prefer.* ❖ **MAKES 6 SERVINGS**

2 cups Laban (page 223) or plain
   Greek yogurt

⅓ cup extra-virgin olive oil, plus
   2 tablespoons for brushing the
   grill and finishing

2½ to 3 tablespoons freshly squeezed
   lemon juice

6 garlic cloves, mashed into a smooth
   paste

2 tablespoons fresh flat-leaf parsley
   leaves, finely minced, plus
   1 tablespoon for garnish

2 tablespoons fresh mint leaves, finely
   minced, plus 1 tablespoon for garnish

1 teaspoon sea salt

6 skinless, bone-in chicken breasts

1 cup Zaytoun olives (see page 184),
   pitted and chopped, for garnish

1 lemon sliced, for garnish

QUINOA–PINE NUT PILAF

2 cups white quinoa, rinsed

4 cups water or chicken broth
   (or a combination of the two)

1 teaspoon sea salt

2 tablespoons unsalted butter

⅓ cup pine nuts, toasted

In a large mixing bowl, whisk together the yogurt, the ⅓ cup of olive oil, lemon juice, garlic, herbs, and salt until smooth. Transfer half of the mixture to a separate bowl, cover with plastic wrap, and place in the refrigerator for later use.

Add the chicken breasts to the mixing bowl and toss to coat completely in the yogurt mixture. Cover with plastic wrap and refrigerate for at least 2 to 3 hours or up to overnight. Remove from the refrigerator.

Preheat an outdoor grill or indoor grill pan to medium-high heat. When the grill is hot, brush it with 1 tablespoon of the olive oil. Let any excess marinade drip off the chicken, place it on the grill, and cook 30 to 35 minutes, turning periodically until the breasts are evenly grilled on all sides and golden brown, and their internal temperature registers 160° to 165°F; do not allow the breasts to blacken or burn.

Remove the chicken from the grill, place it on a baking sheet, cover with aluminum foil, and set aside to rest for 5 to 7 minutes.

While the chicken is grilling, prepare the quinoa. Place the quinoa in a fine mesh sieve and thoroughly rinse under cold water then transfer into a medium pot, cover the quinoa with 4 cups of cold water or broth, season with salt, and cover. Bring to a gentle boil over medium-high heat, then immediately reduce the heat to low and simmer, covered, for 15 to 20 minutes or until almost all of the liquid has been absorbed and the quinoa is tender. Turn off the heat and allow the quinoa to settle for 5 to 7 minutes.

Meanwhile, toast the pine nuts. Heat the butter in a small sauté pan over medium heat, add the pine nuts and toss continuously until they are light golden brown and coated with the butter.

Fluff the quinoa with a fork, spread out on a serving platter, and sprinkle with the toasted pine nuts. Arrange the chicken breasts on top, either whole or sliced. Drizzle the remaining 1 tablespoon olive oil over the chicken, and top with the reserved minced herbs and chopped olives. Place the lemon slices around the platter and serve with the reserved yogurt-garlic sauce.

دجاج محشي

Djej Mahshi

roasted cornish hens stuffed with long-grain rice and meat

Growing up, whenever the weather turned cool and the leaves began to fall from the trees, my mother would make Djej Mahshi—*one of my family's all-time favorite meals. Beautifully browned and slightly crisp on the outside, the Cornish hens are filled with a fragrant rice, meat and nut* Heshwi, *or filling. Whether you make this for a special weeknight or weekend meal, or during the holiday season,* Djej Mahshi *is always a magnificent and memorable dish!* ❖ **MAKES 6 INDIVIDUAL-PORTION HENS (WHICH CAN BE SPLIT FOR 12 SERVINGS)**

1 large yellow onion, quartered

1 large red onion, quartered

3 shallots, quartered

½ small bunch fresh rosemary, washed and left whole

½ small bunch fresh sage, washed and left whole

½ small bunch fresh flat-leaf parsley leaves, washed and left whole

½ small bunch fresh thyme, washed, half left whole, half stemmed and leaves picked

2 teaspoons sea salt

1 teaspoon freshly ground black pepper

6 Cornish hens, necks and giblets removed

⅓ cup extra-virgin olive oil

1 recipe Rez b Heshwi Stuffing, cooked and divided (see page 134, half should be completely cool, half should be warm/hot)

6 small wooden skewers, soaked in cold water for 30 to 60 minutes

Preheat the oven to 450°F.

In a small pot, bring 3 cups of cold water to a boil. Turn off heat and set aside.

In the bottom of a large roasting pan, combine the onion and shallots and lay the rosemary, sage, parsley, and the whole thyme on top. Season with 1 teaspoon of the salt, ½ teaspoon of the black pepper, and cover with the 3 cups of hot water. Place a roasting rack on top and set aside.

Drizzle the hens evenly with olive oil and season with the remaining 1 teaspoon of sea salt, ½ teaspoon of black pepper, and the reserved thyme leaves. Thoroughly rub the hens so they are coated with oil and seasonings.

Put half of the cooled Rez b Heshwi stuffing into a bowl for filling the hens, and keep the rest of the stuffing warm in a pot for serving. Spoon the stuffing into each hen, making sure to push it down to the bottom of the cavity until the stuffing reaches about ¼ inch from the top. Then, enclose the stuffing by weaving a wooden skewer in and out of the top cavity skin until it is completely sewn up and the stuffing is enclosed.

continued

Lay the hens, breast side up, on the roasting rack, cover with aluminum foil, and roast on the center rack of the preheated oven for 30 minutes.

Reduce the heat to 350°F, remove the foil, and roast for about 1 hour, or until the hens are golden brown and cooked completely through (to an internal temperature around 160°F), basting the hens with the pan juices every 30 minutes. Let the hens rest at room temperature for 5 to 10 minutes before carving and serving. During this time, you may need to very gently reheat the reserved rice before putting it on a large serving dish.

Serve the hens over the hot rice, and ladle some of the pan juices over, so the meat remains moist. Remove the roasting rack and strain the onions and remaining pan juices into a fine-mesh sieve. Serve the remaining pan juices alongside the hens and rice.

NOTE You will need a large roasting pan and rack.

شاورما دجاج

Djej b Finden

shawarma-spiced baked chicken with lebanese couscous "moghrabieh"
and white wine sauce

Shawarma spices flavor chicken breasts and thighs in my one-pot, low-and-slow Djej b Finden. *The moist, tender chicken shares the stage with pearl onions and cremini mushrooms—all finished with fresh herbs, butter, and white wine sauce over Lebanese couscous,* Moghrabieh.

I like to sear the chicken first to seal in all the natural juices before braising it with aromatics and herbs. I created this recipe several years ago for an artistic foundation's benefit dinner, and it was a hit with everyone, including me! This spiced chicken can be presented as a formal, special-occasion meal, or as a rustic comfort food served straight from the pot. ✣ **MAKES 6 SERVINGS**

3 bone-in chicken breasts (skinless)

3 bone-in chicken thighs (skinless)

2½ teaspoons Chicken Shawarma Spice (page 179)

12 tablespoons (1½ sticks) unsalted butter

3 tablespoons extra-virgin olive oil

1 pound pearl onions

1½ teaspoons sea salt

1 pound cremini mushrooms, quartered

1½ cups white wine

½ teaspoon ground white pepper

1 cup chicken broth

¼ cup fresh thyme leaves

2 tablespoons fresh rosemary leaves, minced

2 tablespoons fresh sage leaves, minced

2 tablespoons shallots, minced

2 tablespoons unbleached, all-purpose flour or cornstarch

MOGHRABIEH

2 cups Moghrabieh (see page 279) or couscous

1 teaspoon sea salt

4 tablespoons unsalted butter

1 teaspoon Chicken Shawarma Spice (page 179)

1 cup chicken broth

Preheat the oven to 325°F.

Pat the chicken breasts and thighs dry with paper towels and place on a large baking sheet. Generously season both sides of the chicken pieces with 2 teaspoons of the shawarma spice.

Melt 3 tablespoons of the butter with the olive oil in a large, heavy-bottomed oven-safe pot or Dutch oven over medium-high heat. Once it starts shimmering, add the chicken and sear in small batches for 4 to 5 minutes on each side, until crisp and golden brown. Transfer the chicken to a plate.

In the same pot, melt 3 tablespoons of the butter over medium-high heat. Once the butter is shimmering, add the pearl onions, season with ½ teaspoon of the salt and cook, tossing occasionally, until golden brown. Transfer the onions to a plate.

continued

Melt 3 tablespoons of the butter in the same pot until shimmering. Add the mushrooms, season with ½ teaspoon of the salt and cook, tossing occasionally, until they are slightly softened but still maintain their shape. Return the onions and chicken to the pan.

With the heat still on medium-high, pour the white wine into the pan and deglaze, scraping up any browned bits on the bottom of the pan with a wooden spoon. Season with the remaining ½ teaspoon salt and the white pepper and allow the wine to cook off for just a few minutes.

Add half of the thyme, half of the rosemary, half of the sage, and all of the shallots and stir thoroughly. Stir in the chicken broth and bring to a boil. Turn off the heat, cover the pot, and transfer to the center rack of the preheated oven. Braise for 30 to 35 minutes.

Meanwhile, prepare the Moghrabieh. In a large pot, bring 8 cups of water to a rolling boil over medium-high heat and season with the ½ teaspoon sea salt. Once the water is boiling, stir in the Moghrabieh with a wooden spoon and cook, uncovered, for 10 to 12 minutes until the grains have swelled, doubled in size, and cooked through. Drain and strain.

Melt the butter in a large pan over medium heat until shimmering. Add the Moghrabieh to the pan with the butter and toss for a few minutes to coat completely. Season with the remaining ½ teaspoon sea salt and 1 teaspoon of the shawarma spice and thoroughly stir. Pour in the chicken broth and simmer, uncovered, for 5 to 7 minutes so that the Moghrabieh absorbs the majority of the chicken broth. Remove from the heat and allow to rest for a few minutes.

Once the chicken has cooked through—the thickest part of the breast should register 160°F, and the juices should run clear—remove it from the oven. Transfer the chicken, onions, and mushrooms to a serving platter and cover with aluminum foil to keep warm.

Strain the pan juices through a fine-mesh sieve and pour back into the pot. Whisk ½ cup cold water with the flour or cornstarch until smooth, then stir into the strained pan juices. Heat the mixture over high heat, stirring continuously, until it begins to thicken. Finish by stirring in the remaining 3 tablespoons butter and the remaining ½ teaspoon shawarma spice. Cook for another few minutes until the sauce is smooth and shiny. Turn off the heat.

Spoon the Moghrabieh onto a large serving platter, layer the chicken on top, and surround with the mushrooms and onions. Spoon the sauce on top, and sprinkle with the remaining thyme, rosemary, and sage. Serve immediately.

NOTE If you cannot find Moghrabieh, substitute Israeli couscous or regular couscous. When using regular couscous, the cooking method will be different, and should be prepared according to the package directions using the ingredients above.

Rez b Heshwi

arabic rice, meat, and nut stuffing

Succulent ground meat, fresh herbs, and traditional spices come together in my moist and meaty Rez b Heshwi, *which makes a mouthwatering stuffing for turkey, chicken, Cornish hen, and lamb. In my family, we always serve it for Thanksgiving, for a Lebanese twist on tradition. Simply heated up and served plain, it makes for a spectacular side dish, too.* ✦ **MAKES 6 TO 12 SERVINGS**

8 tablespoons (1 stick) unsalted butter

1 pound ground meat (lamb or 80/20 percent beef)

3 cups long-grain rice

1 cup wild rice

8 cups cold water or 4 cups cold water and 4 cups chicken, turkey, or vegetable broth

1 ½ teaspoons sea salt

½ teaspoon freshly ground black pepper

½ teaspoon ground allspice

½ teaspoon Sab'ah Baharat (Seven-Spice, page 183) (optional)

2 tablespoons fresh rosemary leaves, finely minced

2 tablespoons fresh sage leaves, finely minced

2 tablespoons fresh chives, finely minced

2 tablespoons fresh flat-leaf parsley leaves, finely minced

2 tablespoons fresh mint leaves, finely minced

¼ cup pine nuts

¼ cup raw whole walnuts

¼ cup raw whole almonds

¼ cup raw slivered almonds

¼ cup marcona almonds (optional)

In a large, heavy-bottomed pot, melt 4 tablespoons of the butter over medium-high heat. Once the butter starts to sizzle, add the meat and cook until browned, breaking it up with a wooden spoon and stirring continuously.

Add the long-grain and wild rice and toast the grains for 2 to 3 minutes, blending them in with the meat. Pour the water or broth into the pot and season with 1 teaspoon of salt, the pepper, allspice, sab'ah baharat, and fresh herbs. Stir to completely incorporate all the ingredients. Taste the broth and add additional salt or seasonings as needed.

Cover the pot and bring to a rolling boil over medium-high heat. Once boiling, reduce the heat to low and simmer, covered, for 25 to 30 minutes until all the water has been absorbed. Test this by dipping the handle of a wooden spoon in the pot; if the handle comes out clean the rice is ready, if the handle is wet, then simmer for a few more minutes and test again. The rice should be tender but not mushy. Once cooked, remove the pot from the heat.

While the rice is cooking, toast the nuts. In a large sauté pan, melt the remaining 4 tablespoons butter over medium heat. Add the nuts, sprinkle with the remaining ½ teaspoon salt and toss to coat completely. Once the nuts are light golden brown and fragrant remove from the heat and transfer to a bowl.

Lightly fluff the rice with a fork and transfer to a large serving bowl. Top with the toasted nuts and serve, or completely cool and use for stuffing.

NOTE For a vegetarian version, substitute diced portobello or baby bella mushrooms for the meat, and use vegetable broth or water as a cooking liquid.

Sitto's Samak Mishwee

grilled red snapper

Growing up, my mother vividly remembers local fish merchants coming from Tripoli to her family's small village, offering the fresh catch of the day. My Sitto (grandmother) was a great lover of seafood, and would enthusiastically snap up these glorious, still-wet-from-the-sea fish. She would prepare the fish simply, with olive oil, lemon, garlic, and fresh herbs—all grilled over smoky charcoal. I, too, love fish, and I love preparing it as simply as my grandmother, and I'm sure you will, too. ❖ **MAKES 6 SERVINGS**

3 whole red snapper (about 2 pounds each), cleaned

⅓ cup plus 3 tablespoons extra-virgin olive oil

1½ teaspoons sea salt

1 teaspoon ground white pepper

3 sprigs fresh flat-leaf parsley, stemmed, leaves left whole, plus 1 tablespoon minced leaves for garnish

3 sprigs fresh mint, leaves picked and left whole, plus 1 tablespoon minced leaves for garnish

3 sprigs fresh thyme, plus 1 tablespoon leaves picked and left whole for garnish

12 garlic cloves, 6 left whole and 6 smashed into a smooth paste

2 lemons, sliced into rounds

⅓ cup freshly squeezed lemon juice

1 lemon, sliced, for serving

Preheat a charcoal or gas grill to medium-high heat, about 400°F.

Rinse the fish under cold running water and pat dry. Line a baking sheet with aluminum foil, then drizzle with 1 tablespoon of the olive oil. Lay the fish vertically on the oiled foil, and make three even slits on one side of each fish, using a small, sharp knife to score all the way to the bone. Lightly season the inside and outside of the fish with 1 teaspoon of sea salt and white pepper, then stuff each fish with a sprig of parsley, mint, and thyme, 2 garlic cloves, and 2 lemon rounds. Combine 1 tablespoon of the olive oil and 3 tablespoons of the lemon juice in a small bowl, then drizzle over the fish.

In a small bowl, combine the garlic paste and the remaining ½ teaspoon of sea salt. Whisk in the ⅓ cup of olive oil and the remaining lemon juice to form a creamy basting sauce.

Brush the grill or grill pan with the remaining 1 tablespoon olive oil, then place each fish onto the preheated grill on an angle. Grill for 4 to 5 minutes on each side, basting the fish frequently with oil, lemon, and garlic sauce. Once the skin is crisp and the inside is flaky and white, remove from the grill and transfer to a clean baking sheet.

Debone the fish, sprinkle with herbs and grated lemon peel, surround with lemon slices, and serve.

صيادية

Siyediyeh

salmon and saffron rice stew

Siyediyeh *literally means "fish and rice" in Arabic, which are the main components of this Lebanese fisherman's stew that combines very fresh fish, homemade fish stock, and long-grain rice. I have refined the traditional version a bit, and have included saffron and turmeric to flavor the rice and turn it a gorgeous golden color, and have added a crunchy nut topping and butter sauce. My Auntie Layla inspired this dish, after making a similar version for a family party. I instantly loved* Siyediyeh *and now make it frequently, often serving it with my peppery watercress* Jarjir Salata *(page 44).* ❖ **MAKES 6 TO 12 SERVINGS**

FISH STOCK

2 pounds fish heads and bones from a non-oily white fish (snapper, sole, or bass)

2 tablespoons extra-virgin olive oil

2 tablespoons unsalted butter

1 large Vidalia onion, finely diced

3 shallots, finely diced

1 large leek, washed thoroughly, white and light green parts sliced

2 celery stalks, sliced

1 teaspoon sea salt

1 cup dry white wine

3 sprigs fresh flat-leaf parsley

3 sprigs fresh thyme

1 dried bay leaf

1 tablespoon whole black peppercorns

RICE

¼ cup olive oil

1 teaspoon saffron threads

1 large onion, finely diced

2 cups long-grain rice

1 teaspoon sea salt

1 teaspoon ground turmeric

TOASTED NUTS

4 tablespoons unsalted butter

⅓ cup pine nuts

¼ cup blanched whole almonds

¼ cup slivered almonds

¼ cup marcona almonds

¼ cup cashews

½ teaspoon sea salt

SALMON

3 pounds salmon fillets

1 tablespoon olive oil

1 teaspoon sea salt

1 teaspoon ground white pepper

SAUCE

Remaining fish stock

1 tablespoon unsalted butter

1 tablespoon freshly squeezed lemon juice

½ teaspoon sea salt

1 tablespoon fresh flat-leaf parsley leaves, minced

In a large mixing bowl, soak the saffron threads in 2 cups of hot water. Set aside to steep for approximately 2 hours. Reserve for the rice.

Make the stock: Remove the gills and any blood from the fish heads, and thoroughly wash the bones and heads under cold running water. Cut the fish bones into 4- to 5-inch pieces and set aside in a bowl. Heat the olive oil and butter in an 8-quart pot over medium heat until shimmering. Add the onion, shallots, leek, and celery to the pot and season with the salt. Stir to completely coat the aromatics with the butter and oil and cook until softened and translucent, 5 to 7 minutes. Increase the heat to high, add the fish heads, and cook for 5 to 7 minutes. Pour the white wine and 6 cups of cold water into the pot to completely cover the bones. Add the parsley, thyme, bay leaf, and whole peppercorns and bring to a rolling boil, skimming any foam that rises to the surface. Reduce the heat to low and simmer, continuously skim off any foam as it cooks uncovered, for about 30 minutes.

After 30 minutes, turn off the heat, and allow the stock to settle for about 5 minutes. Carefully strain the stock through a large fine-mesh sieve into a 4-quart stockpot. Reserve 2 cups of stock for cooking the rice.

Prepare the rice: Heat the olive oil into a large, heavy-bottomed 8-quart stockpot over medium heat. Once the oil is shimmering, add the onion and stir to coat in the oil. Cook, stirring occasionally, until softened and light golden, about 5 to 7 minutes.

Add the rice, season with salt and turmeric, stir to coat in the oil and onion, and toast for a few minutes to release a nutty aroma. Strain the reserved saffron soaking liquid through a fine-mesh sieve over the rice, then pound the threads in a stone mortar and pestle into a smooth paste, and add the paste to the rice. Pour in 2 cups of fish stock and stir to combine. Cover the pot with a lid and bring to a rolling boil over high heat. Reduce the heat and simmer, covered, for 15 to 20 minutes until all of the liquid has been absorbed. Remove from the heat and fluff the rice with a fork. Set aside.

While the rice is cooking, prepare the salmon and toast the nuts. Heat a grill or grill pan to 400°F. Lay a large sheet of aluminum foil in front of you and place the fish on top. Lightly drizzle with the olive oil and season with the salt and white pepper. Then, place another sheet of foil over the fish to create a pouch. Fold the edges in to tightly seal the fish. Place the pouch on the hot grill, cover, and cook for 15 minutes until the fish is opaque and flaky. Remove from the heat and let the fish rest in the foil for a few minutes, then carefully open the foil packet and let the fish rest for 3 to 5 minutes.

Toast the nuts: Heat the butter over medium-low heat. Add all the nuts and season with the salt. Stir to coat with the butter, then toast, tossing, until golden brown. Transfer to a plate.

Make the sauce: Reduce the remaining fish stock by half over high heat. Reduce the heat to low and stir in the butter and lemon juice to make the sauce. Season with the sea salt and parsley. Remove from the heat and pour the sauce into a small bowl for serving.

Just before serving, fluff the rice with a fork and spoon it onto a large serving platter. Flake the fish on top of the rice, and then scatter the toasted nuts on top. Serve hot or warm with the sauce.

NOTE You can swap in red snapper, halibut, or cod for the salmon, and use white, brown, basmati, or jasmine rice instead of long-grain rice.

ة حرة سمك

Samak Harrah

baked branzino with spicy taratour sauce

"Samak" meaning fish and "Harrah" meaning hot, together translates to spicy fish! It is also a famous dish in our family and my brother Eddie Jr.'s favorite fish dish of all time. I am a fan of the delicate and mild flavor of Branzino, a Mediterranean Sea Bass; here it is simply baked before it is finished off with my spicy tahini sauce, Taratour, *then topped with toasted pine nuts and parsley.* ❈ **MAKES 6 SERVINGS**

1 recipe Taratour Sauce (page 172)

2 tablespoons extra-virgin olive oil

3 medium to large branzino (Mediterranean sea bass, about 1½ pounds each), cleaned

1 teaspoon plus ¼ teaspoon sea salt

1 teaspoon ground white pepper

2½ to 3 tablespoons freshly squeezed lemon juice

2 lemons, sliced into rounds

2 tablespoons unsalted butter

⅓ cup pine nuts

3 sprigs fresh flat-leaf parsley leaves, minced

Preheat the oven to 350°F. Drizzle 1 tablespoon of the olive oil on the bottom of a 9 x 13-inch casserole.

Rinse the fish under cold running water, pat dry with clean paper towels and place on a board. Using a small, sharp knife, make three, evenly spaced shallow slits on an angle on the top side of each fish. Season both sides of each fish with salt and white pepper, and drizzle with the remaining 1 tablespoon olive oil and the lemon juice. Lay the fish on the casserole and surround with the lemon rounds.

Bake on the center rack of the preheated oven for 25 to 30 minutes until the flesh of the fish is opaque and flaky with a crisp, caramelized outer skin. When there is 10 minutes of cooking time left, remove the fish from the oven and generously pour the taratour sauce on top until the fish is completely covered, reserving 1 cup of sauce for serving. Return the fish to the oven and bake for 5 to 7 minutes more, or until the sauce is hot and bubbly. Remove from the oven and set aside briefly.

Melt the butter in a small saucepan over medium heat. Add the pine nuts and season with ¼ teaspoon of the salt and toss to coat. Cook, stirring continuously, until light golden brown. Remove from the heat and set aside.

Debone and fillet the fish, transfer to a serving platter, and surround with the baked lemon slices. Spoon the reserved taratour sauce over the fish and finish with the pine nuts and minced parsley. Serve hot or warm with any remaining taratour sauce on the side.

NOTE You can use already filleted branzino, whole or filleted cod, red snapper, or any flaky fish in this recipe.

TASHQUILA

side dishes

VEGETABLES
KHOUDRA
·

sabenegh . . . 147
SAUTÉED SPINACH AND ARUGULA GREENS
WITH BULGUR WHEAT

loubieh b zeit . . . 148
STEWED GREEN BEANS

foul . . . 151
FAVA BEANS WITH GARLIC AND LEMON

hindbeh . . . 152
SAUTÉED DANDELION GREENS
WITH CARAMELIZED ONIONS

makmoura . . . 155
CARAMELIZED CABBAGE WITH
BULGUR WHEAT

khoudra mishwiyeh . . . 156
CARAMELIZED VEGETABLES WITH HERBS

STARCHES
·

batata b zeit . . . 157
LEBANESE-STYLE HOME FRIES

batata maglieh . . . 158
TWICE-FRIED LEBANESE FRENCH FRIES

macaroune b toum . . . 163
HOMEMADE PASTA IN GARLIC SAUCE

rez b shayriyeh . . . 165
LONG-GRAIN RICE AND
VERMICELLI PILAF

A TRUE LEBANESE MEAL IS NEVER COMPLETE WITHOUT AT LEAST ONE or two side dishes (usually more). I find that my glorious greens, beans, and grains enhance whatever main dish I'm serving, and occasionally even outshine the star! In this chapter, I've included a large variety of sides that pair perfectly with my Asha (Main Meals) and Shawraba (Soups and Stews), like traditional Rez b Shayriyeh (Long-Grain Rice and Vermicelli Pilaf), and not one but two types of fries! Stewed Green Beans in oil, or Loubieh b Zeit, and caramelized cabbage Makmoura make wonderful, easy-to-prepare side dishes and complements to Salatas and Mezza. For anyone who is vegetarian (like my sister Selma), gluten-free, vegan, or just a veggie lover, like yours truly, this chapter is created just for you!

Sabenegh

sautéed spinach and arugula greens with bulgur wheat

For us Lebanese, there are never enough greens! We love to grow many different varieties in our jinah (gardens), and serve them in simple but sensational dishes. Sabenegh, which translates to "spinach," is a more substantial side, thanks to the addition of bulgur wheat. I like to serve it around the holiday season—often at Thanksgiving or Christmas, as it makes an excellent counterpoint to roasted and braised meats.

✤ **MAKES 6 SERVINGS**

⅓ cup #2 medium bulgur wheat (see page 279)

⅓ cup extra-virgin olive oil plus 2 tablespoons

3 small shallots, thinly sliced into half-moons

1 large yellow onion, thinly sliced into half-moons

1 teaspoon sea salt

One 8-ounce bag fresh baby spinach greens, washed thoroughly

One 8-ounce bag fresh baby arugula, washed thoroughly

½ teaspoon ground allspice

In a medium mixing bowl, cover the bulgur wheat in 3 cups of lukewarm water and set aside to soak and soften, about 20 minutes.

Combine the olive oil, shallots, and onion in a large sauté pan over medium heat, and season with ½ teaspoon of the sea salt. Cook, stirring occasionally, until they caramelize to a light brown color, 5 to 7 minutes; do not burn.

Reduce the heat to low, add the spinach and arugula greens to the pan in small batches, and season with the remaining ½ teaspoon salt and 2 tablespoons of olive oil. Once the spinach and arugula have cooked down, 2 to 3 minutes, reduce the heat to low and test the bulgur grains. They should be soft when squeezed between your fingers; if they are still hard, let soak for a bit longer. When the bulgur is ready, squeeze out the excess water in handfuls over the soaking bowl, and then sprinkle the grains over the greens in the pan, stir and cook for just a couple minutes to warm through and immediately remove the pan from the heat. Finish by sprinkling the allspice all over the greens and grains.

Serve hot, at room temperature, or warm.

VARIATION ✤ For a gluten-free version, substitute cooked quinoa for the bulgur wheat.

لوبيا بزيت

Loubieh b Zeit

stewed green beans

Loubieh b Zeit *is one of my simplest yet most versatile side dishes, and I often make it for a big meal with friends and family. Whether you're serving meat, fish, poultry, or an assortment of other vegetables, these green beans are a tasty complement. Slowly stewed with very few ingredients, the* loubieh *(flat Italian green beans, sometimes called romano beans) turn juicy and succulent, with a sweet earthiness from the caramelized onions and aromatic allspice.* ❖ **MAKES 6 SERVINGS**

⅓ cup extra-virgin olive oil

1 large yellow onion, finely diced

1 pound fresh flat Italian green beans
    (romano beans), rinsed, trimmed,
    and snapped in half

1 teaspoon sea salt

½ teaspoon ground allspice

Heat the olive oil in a large, heavy-bottomed pot over medium heat until shimmering. Add the onion and stir to completely coat in the oil. Sauté until the onion begins to soften and turn translucent, then continue to cook, stirring, until caramelized and light brown, 5 to 7 minutes.

Add the green beans and ½ cup of cold water. Season the beans with the salt and toss all the ingredients together. Cover the pot, increase the heat to medium-high, and bring to a boil. Reduce the heat to low and simmer for 30 to 45 minutes until the beans are fully cooked, tender and juicy, and most of the cooking liquid has been absorbed.

Remove the beans from the heat and sprinkle with the allspice. Serve hot, warm, or at room temperature.

VARIATION ❖ For Loubieh b Banadoura, add whole and minced garlic cloves, finely diced tomatoes, and 1 cinnamon stick to the simmering mixture.

———

taboulie tip! Look for long, fresh, and slender beans that are vibrant green in color which will be more tender in taste.

فول

Foul

fava beans with garlic and lemon

Pronounced "fool," this sensational veggie side is one of my favorites in the spring, when the fava beans are in season and especially fresh. Tossed simply with mashed garlic, olive oil, and lemon juice, Foul is a super-flavorful dish that just happens to be vegan, low-fat, gluten-free, and heart healthy! ❋ **MAKES 6 SERVINGS**

1 teaspoon sea salt

1 pound fresh fava beans, shelled, washed, and drained

3 garlic cloves

¼ cup extra-virgin olive oil

2 to 3 tablespoons freshly squeezed lemon juice

Fresh flat-leaf parsley leaves, chopped for garnish (optional)

Boston lettuce leaves, for scooping (optional)

Bring 8 cups of cold water to a rolling boil in a large pot over high heat and season with ½ teaspoon of the salt. Reduce the heat to medium and maintain a steady simmer. Submerge the beans in the hot water and cook, uncovered, for about 10 minutes until tender but still bright green. While the beans are cooking, fill a large mixing bowl with cold water and ice cubes.

Once the beans are cooked, drain them and transfer to the ice-water bath to stop the cooking process. While the beans are cooling, finely mash the garlic cloves into a smooth paste using a garlic press, or mortar and pestle. Stream the olive oil and lemon juice into the garlic paste mixing continually until a creamy consistency is achieved.

Drain the favas from the ice-water bath and remove the outer skins by gently squeezing each bean with your fingertips; the skin should pop right off. Put the beans into a large bowl, season with remaining ½ teaspoon salt, and pour in the garlic-lemon-olive oil mixture. Gently toss so that all of the beans are evenly coated.

Serve at room temperature with chopped parsley or lettuce leaves for scooping if you wish.

————

taboulie tip! Fresh fava beans are in season in the spring and early summer months, and typically can be found at fresh farmers' markets. Select slender, smooth, and bright green bean pods that are approximately 5 to 7 inches long, firm, and filled out along the entire length, but not over-bulging.

هندبة

Hindbeh

sautéed dandelion greens with caramelized onions

While dandelion greens have only recently become popular in the United States, they have long been an essential ingredient in Lebanese cuisine. Each spring in Mama's garden I can hardly wait to see these gorgeous greens arrive. The minute they sprout in her garden, Mama knows to tell me, and we pick and prepare them that very day. Although Hindbeh *is a side dish, my family and I often enjoy it as a main course simply scooped up with some warm Arabic bread, such as* Khebez Arabi *(page 205). Sautéed with sweet Vidalia onions, olive oil, and salt,* Hindbeh *is a must-make, quick side that is especially good with soups like* Kibbet Raheb *(page 60), egg dishes like my herb omelet* Ejjeh *(page 110), and* Bayd b Halyoun, *an asparagus and egg scramble.* ❖ MAKES 6 SERVINGS

½ tablespoon plus ½ teaspoon sea salt

2 bunches fresh dandelion greens, thoroughly washed, stemmed, and coarsely chopped into 2-inch pieces

⅓ cup plus 2 tablespoons extra-virgin olive oil

1 large Vidalia onion, thinly sliced into half-moons

In a large pot, bring 8 cups of water and the ½ tablespoon of the salt to a boil. Add the chopped greens to the boiling water, pushing them down so they are fully submerged. Boil the greens, uncovered, for 15 to 20 minutes, making sure to periodically push them down so they blanch evenly. While they are cooking, fill a large mixing bowl with ice cubes and cold water. After about 15 to 20 minutes, test the tenderness of the greens by rubbing a stem or two between your fingers. If they are slightly squishy, then they are cooked.

Immediately remove the greens from the heat, drain, and transfer to the ice-water bath to stop the cooking process and set the color.

While the greens are cooling, combine the ⅓ cup of the olive oil and onion slices in a large sauté pan over medium-high heat and sauté, stirring occasionally, until caramelized to a golden brown color, 10 to 12 minutes; do not burn.

When the onions have caramelized, reduce the heat to low. Drain the cooled greens in a colander, and squeeze as much excess water as possible with your hands. Add the blanched greens to the sauté pan, pulling apart the small clumps with your hands. Stir into the caramelized onions to combine, season with the remaining ½ teaspoon salt and sauté until the greens are heated through. Taste, and add additional seasonings as needed.

Drizzle with the remaining 2 tablespoons olive oil and serve warm, at room temperature or cold.

———————

taboulie tip! Boiling the dandelions removes the bitterness and tenderizes the greens.

Makmoura
caramelized cabbage with bulgur wheat

Makmoura *is a dish I often serve in the fall when cabbage is in season and even sweeter and tenderer than usual. For an extra treat for the eye* and *the taste buds, I like to prepare my* Makmoura, *which means "cabbage with wheat," with both red and green cabbage leaves. Although it tastes like you've been slaving over the stove all day, this side is an easy one to put together, and pairs particularly well with my* Basal wa Banadoura Salata *(page 45).* ❖ **MAKES 6 SERVINGS**

⅓ cup #2 medium bulgur wheat
 (see page 279)

½ head savoy cabbage, thinly sliced

½ head red cabbage, thinly sliced

⅓ cup extra-virgin olive oil, plus
 2 tablespoons

1 large yellow onion, thinly sliced into
 half-moons

1 large red onion, thinly sliced into half-
 moons

1 teaspoon sea salt

¼ teaspoon crushed red pepper flakes

In a medium mixing bowl, cover the bulgur wheat in 3 cups of lukewarm water. Set aside to soak and soften, about 20 minutes.

Remove the thick outer leaves from the cabbages and discard or compost. Slice the cabbages in half and, using a sharp, serrated knife, slice through the leaves to make thin shreds. Set aside.

Heat the olive oil in a large sauté pan over medium heat, add the onion slices, and season with ½ teaspoon of the salt. Cook until translucent and light golden brown, 10 to 12 minutes.

Reduce the heat to low, add the shredded cabbage to the sauté pan in small batches pulling the shreds apart as you add them in. Season the cabbage-onion mixture with the remaining ½ teaspoon salt, and 2 tablespoons olive oil and toss to combine. Sauté the cabbage-onion mixture for 7 to 10 minutes continuously tossing, until the cabbage softens and turns light golden brown.

By this time, the bulgur should be softened. Test some grains between your fingers; they should be soft. Working in handfuls, squeeze the excess water out of the bulgur into the soaking bowl, and sprinkle the softened grains into the cabbage-onion mixture. Cook briefly, tossing with the other ingredients, until the bulgur is warmed through.

Season with the crushed red pepper flakes and serve hot or warm.

VARIATION ❖ For a gluten-free version, substitute cooked quinoa for the bulgur wheat.

Khoudra Mishwiyeh
caramelized vegetables with herbs

Khoudra Mishwiyeh *is a dish that came about spontaneously. On one balmy summer day I had just placed my luscious* Kafta Kababs *(page 80) on the hot grill when I realized that there was nothing for my vegetarian sister, Selma, to eat. I rushed out to Mama's garden and gathered a basket of different veggies including peppers, three types of onions, and herbs. I caramelized the vegetables over the grill, and then topped them with fresh herbs and a lemony vinaigrette. It was an instant hit, and has become a favorite among my family, served at each and every summer cookout.* ❖ **MAKES 6 SERVINGS**

1 large yellow onion, finely sliced into half-moons

1 large red onion, finely sliced into half-moons

1 large Vidalia onion, finely sliced into half-moons

3 shallots, finely sliced

1 whole head garlic, peeled, half the cloves left whole and half sliced

1 pound sweet mini peppers or bell peppers, cored, seeded, and sliced

1 pound baby bella mushrooms, stemmed and quartered

3 scallions, ends trimmed, green and white parts finely diced

1 small bunch fresh chives, finely diced

1 small bunch fresh flat-leaf parsley leaves, coarsely chopped

1 small bunch fresh mint leaves, coarsely chopped

1 teaspoon sea salt

1½ teaspoons freshly ground black pepper

⅓ cup extra-virgin olive oil

2 to 3 tablespoons freshly squeezed lemon juice

Heat the grill to medium-high heat or preheat the oven to 425°F.

Spread the onions and shallots out in an aluminum foil–lined grilling basket. If roasting in the oven, spread out on a large lightly oiled baking sheet. Layer the whole and sliced garlic cloves on top of the onions and shallots then cover the garlic with the peppers. Place the mushrooms on top of the sliced peppers and then top with scallions, chives, parsley, and mint. Season the mixture with salt and pepper and drizzle with olive oil and lemon juice. Lightly toss the mixture with your hands to ensure that all of the vegetables are coated with the lemon juice and olive oil. Cover with plastic wrap and marinate at room temperature for about 30 minutes.

If using the grilling basket, enclose the vegetables with the foil to form a pouch and roast over the grill for about 20 minutes. Remove the pouch from the grill and let sit for 5 to 7 minutes, then carefully open the pouch, making sure not to burn yourself on the steam that will be released.

If using the oven, roast the vegetables on the baking sheet for about 30 minutes. Remove from the oven and serve immediately. Serve hot or warm.

بطاطا بزيت

Batata b Zeit

lebanese-style home fries

My Batata b Zeit *are an extra-flavorful spin on home fries. I often make these tasty potatoes in the spring when the green garlic and fresh herbs have begun to sprout. Sprinkled with sumac spice, these crisp potatoes make a perfect side for egg dishes such as* Bayd b Lahem *(page 113) and* Bayd b Batenjen *(page 114).*

✴ MAKES 6 SERVINGS

⅓ cup extra-virgin olive oil

1 large Vidalia onion, thinly sliced into half-moons

3 shallots, thinly sliced

1½ pounds new potatoes, peeled and thinly sliced into half moons

3 green garlic shoots or 3 spring garlic cloves, minced

½ teaspoon sea salt

2 scallions, ends trimmed, finely diced

1 small bunch fresh flat-leaf parsley leaves, finely chopped

1 small bunch chives, finely diced

½ teaspoon sumac spice (see page 280)

Pour the olive oil in a large sauté pan or skillet over medium heat. Add the onion and shallots and sauté until softened and translucent, about 5 minutes.

Stir in the potatoes and garlic and season with the salt. Cook, stirring frequently so they do not stick to the bottom of the pan, until they are light golden brown and crispy on the outside, about 15 minutes.

Reduce the heat to low, add the scallions, parsley and chives and toss to combine. Finish with the sumac spice. Serve immediately.

VARIATION ✴ Add sliced baby bella mushrooms and hot peppers with the potatoes or finish with crushed red pepper flakes, for a spicy version that my sister, Selma, loves!

―――――――

tabouli tip! For the crispiest home fries, cook the potatoes in a cast-iron skillet.

بطاطا مقلية

Batata Maqlieh
twice-fried lebanese french fries

Everyone loves French fries, and we Lebanese are no exception! You'll find Batata Maqlieh, *which translates to "fried potatoes," on any traditional Lebanese table. We put them in pita sandwiches, serve them with meat, and, of course, eat them plain. When I visited my Sitto in Lebanon, there was never a meal without her special fries, which always brought a smile to everyone's face. When it comes to* Batata Maqlieh, *don't even think about reaching for the ketchup; my creamy garlic* Toum *(page 175) is the perfect accompaniment to these crispy-crunchy delights!* ❖ **MAKES 6 SERVINGS**

3 large Yukon gold potatoes, peeled

4 cups vegetable oil

½ teaspoon sea salt

1 recipe Toum (page 175)

1 small bunch fresh flat-leaf parsley leaves, finely minced

Thoroughly wash the peeled potatoes under cold running water and pat dry. Cut the potatoes lengthwise down the center and then cut them into ½-inch-thick strips. Place the potato strips into a large mixing bowl and cover with cold water, so that they release some of their starch and do not brown. Drain the strips and spread out onto paper towels to thoroughly dry.

Line a baking sheet with paper towels and set aside. Pour the vegetable oil into a large, heavy-bottomed pot so that it comes only 3 to 4 inches up the sides of the pot. Heat on medium-high until the temperature registers 325°F.

Using a handheld strainer or slotted spoon, carefully submerge about a quarter of the potatoes into the hot oil. Allow them to fry, undisturbed, for 2 to 4 minutes on each side, gently turning them halfway through the cooking time, until they are light golden brown. Immediately remove the first batch, straining the excess oil over the pot, and transfer the fries directly to the paper towel–lined baking sheet to drain. Repeat with the remaining potato strips, frying them in small batches and maintaining a steady oil temperature of 325°F.

While the fries are draining and cooling, bring the oil temperature up to 375°F. Working in small batches, submerge the fries into the hot oil for a second time and fry until they are deeper golden in color and crispy.

Drain the fries on paper towels and sprinkle with sea salt.

Spoon the Toum sauce over the fries, sprinkle with parsley, and serve hot.

مكرون بثوم

Macaroune b Toum
homemade pasta in garlic sauce

Macaroune b Toum *is a very special family dish filled with memories. When my grandmother prepared this traditional garlicky pasta dish, she would instruct my mother and her siblings to gather small branches from the Zaytoun olive trees outside. The children would then sharpen the branches and use them instead of forks to eat the pasta pieces. My mother continued this wonderful tradition with my siblings and me growing up in Syracuse, New York. These memories, traditions, and dishes that have passed through the generations always make me so proud of my Lebanese heritage.* ❖ **MAKES 6 SERVINGS**

4 cups all-purpose unbleached flour, plus additional for sprinkling

1 teaspoon sea salt

⅓ cup extra-virgin olive oil

1 small bunch fresh mint leaves, finely minced

Toum Sauce (page 175, made without the lemon)

Put the flour into a large mixing bowl and run your fingers through it to break up any clumps. Add ½ teaspoon of the sea salt and mix in thoroughly. Using your hands, create a well in the center of the flour and pour 1½ cups of lukewarm water into the well. Using one hand to steady the bowl, begin to incorporate the flour with your other hand, sweeping along the sides of the well and then blending the flour into the water. Be sure to gather the loose flour that sits at the bottom of the bowl and blend it with the water as well. Once the water has been entirely incorporated into the flour, and the mixture has come together, lift the dough from the bottom of the bowl and fold it over on itself. Do this a few times, then roll the dough together with your fists until it is smooth, slightly moist, and bounces back when touched. Make sure not to overwork the dough. If the dough is too dry, add a little lukewarm water by the ½ teaspoon, and if it is too moist, add a little more flour by the teaspoon. Shape the dough into a ball and set aside.

Lightly flour a cutting board or clean countertop. Place the dough ball in the center and, using a dough cutter or sharp knife, slice the dough into quarters. Working with a quarter at a time, place the dough in the palms of your hands and tuck it under. Then, stretch the dough into a smooth, flat, round disk, place it on the board, and roll it out into a rectangle about ¼ inch thick.

Slice the dough into long, 1-inch vertical strips, and then slice horizontally into 2-inch pieces. Lightly flour the small pieces and continue in the same manner with the remaining dough.

Flip a colander upside down. Take each piece of dough and roll over the holes of the colander, rolling the dough back and forth to create tiny circles in the pasta. Repeat with the remaining strips. Set pieces aside on the floured board.

continued

Bring 8 cups of water and the ½ teaspoon salt to a rolling boil in a large pot. Using a slotted spoon or handheld strainer, submerge the pasta pieces into the boiling water adding in small batches, shaking out any excess flour beforehand. Stir gently with a wooden spoon so that the pasta doesn't stick to the bottom of the pot. Reduce the heat to medium and cook for about 5 to 7 minutes, or until the pasta is tender and has risen to the top.

While the pasta is cooking, prepare the Toum according to the recipe directions on page 175 but omit the freshly squeezed lemon juice. The sauce should have a creamy consistency.

As soon as the pasta has cooked, transfer it to a large mixing bowl, and toss with the sauce to coat. Sprinkle with minced mint leaves and serve hot.

رز بشعيرية

Rez b Shayriyeh

long-grain rice and vermicelli pilaf

In Arabic, Rez b Shayriyeh, *simply means "rice with thin noodles." It's an absolute staple in Lebanese cuisine, and the foundation on which many other rice dishes are built. Crisp vermicelli noodles are blended with light, fluffy long-grain rice for a hearty base for any sauce, soup, or stew.* ✦ **MAKES 6 SERVINGS**

3 tablespoons unsalted butter

½ cup crushed vermicelli noodles,
  or 1 angel-hair noodle nest
  (see page 279)

2 cups long-grain rice, unrinsed

1 teaspoon sea salt

In a medium pot, melt the butter over medium-high heat. Crush the vermicelli noodles over the melted butter and stir to make sure that all of the pieces are coated in the butter. Continue to fry, stirring constantly until the noodles are crisp and a deep, dark golden brown, 2 to 4 minutes. Reduce the heat to low and stir in the rice and sea salt. Then, increase the heat to medium and toast the rice with the noodles for a couple of minutes, stirring continuously.

Pour in 4¼ cups cold water and stir a few times so that all the ingredients are incorporated. Taste the cooking liquid; it should be slightly salty. If not, add more salt by the pinch, making sure not to oversalt.

Cover the pot, increase the heat to high, and bring to a rolling boil, 5 to 7 minutes. Once the water boils, immediately reduce the heat to low and simmer, covered, for 15 to 20 minutes until all of the water has been absorbed. Test the rice by placing the handle of a wooden spoon into the center of the pot and quickly removing it. If the tip is moist then continue to simmer, if it comes out dry, the rice is cooked. Make sure not to stir or uncover the rice during the simmering process.

Once the rice is cooked, immediately remove it from the heat. It will be moist and buttery. Fluff with a fork just before serving. Serve hot or warm.

VARIATION ✦ Instead of white rice, you can substitute brown rice, just be aware of the additional cooking time needed. Also orzo can be used instead of vermicelli noodles.

———————

tabouilie tip! Do not stir the rice while it is cooking. Simply follow my fool-proof recipe and you will have perfect rice every time, I promise, and no rice-cooker needed!

SALSAT, BHARAT & KABIS

sauces, spices & pickles

SAUCES
SALSAT
⁕

hyar b laban . . . 169
CUCUMBER-MINT-YOGURT
SAUCE

tahini dressing . . . 172
SESAME SEED SAUCE

taratour . . . 172
SPICY TAHINI SAUCE

toum . . . 175
GARLIC, OLIVE OIL,
AND LEMON SAUCE

SPICES
BHARAT
⁕

bhar falafel . . . 176
FALAFEL SPICE

*bhar shawarma
lahmeh* . . . 179
MEAT SHAWARMA SPICE

*bhar shawarma
djej* . . . 179
CHICKEN SHAWARMA SPICE

zaatar . . . 180
THYME SPICE

sab'ah baharat . . . 183
SEVEN-SPICE

PICKLES
KABIS

kabis zaytoun . . . 184
PICKLED CRACKED
GREEN OLIVES

kabis batenjen . . . 187
PICKLED STUFFED
BABY EGGPLANT

kabis khyar . . . 190
PICKLED
PERSIAN CUCUMBERS

kabis lefet . . . 193
PICKLED TURNIPS
WITH BEET AND GARLIC

WHENEVER PEOPLE TRY MY FOOD, I ALWAYS FIND THEY ARE MOST fascinated by the lingering tastes of the sauces and spices, often asking, "What's in that?" We have a few master sauces that are absolutely essential to cooking the Lebanese way: garlicky Toum, Tahini Sauce, and yogurt sauce, Khyar b Laban. Unlike European sauces, which are often made from cream and butter, Lebanese sauces are mostly based around nuts and seeds, garlic, fresh herbs, lemon juice, and olive oil. Spices are used subtly, with a light and delicate hand. Warm, earthy, and exotic, our spice blends are used to build flavor in dishes, not overpower them. Although we do use some hot spices like cayenne and Aleppo pepper, these are used for finishing dishes and adding a little kick at the end. Here are some of our most famous spices and seasoning staples that you should have on hand. Pickles are an important part of the seasonal way of life in Lebanon. In the summer months, we preserve and pickle fresh foods harvested at their peak to enjoy throughout the colder, less fertile months. Once you try the crunchy, slightly acidic homemade version, you'll never go back. Kabis Lefet (Pickled Turnips with Beet and Garlic) are always served with Falafel, and you absolutely must try Kabis Batenjen (Pickled Stuffed Baby Eggplant)—you'll see eggplant in a whole new way!

خيار بلبن

Khyar b Laban
cucumber-mint-yogurt sauce

Made with homemade thick strained yogurt and refreshing Persian cucumbers, Khyar b Laban *is cooling and creamy, with a garlicky tang—and finds its way into pretty much every meal I make! I love to slather this sauce onto* Lahem Mishwee *(Lamb Meat and Onion Skewers, page 73) and* Mahshi Waraq Enab *(Stuffed Grape Leaves, page 99). Even served over a warm bowl of long-grain rice, such as* Rez b Shayriyeh *(page 165), this yogurt sauce brightens everything up, and it takes almost no time to make.*

✣ **MAKES 4 CUPS**

4 cups Labneh (page 225) or plain, full-fat Greek yogurt, chilled

3 garlic cloves

1 Persian cucumber, finely minced

1 small bunch fresh mint leaves, finely minced

1 teaspoon sea salt

Put the labneh into a large mixing bowl and whisk to dissolve any lumps, and until it is silky smooth.

Using a mortar and pestle or a garlic press, create a smooth paste from the garlic cloves. Add the garlic and cucumber to the yogurt.

Remove the mint leaves from the stems. Layer the leaves on top of each other and roll them up. Then, thinly slice horizontally through the mint leaves to create thin ribbons. Sprinkle the ribbons all over the yogurt. Season the yogurt mixture with the salt and mix together thoroughly. Taste and add additional seasoning if needed.

Cover the sauce with plastic wrap and refrigerate for at least 30 minutes to 1 hour before serving.

NOTE Khyar b Laban can be made up to two days in advance, and tastes better the longer it sits in the refrigerator.

Tahini Dressing
sesame seed sauce

Tahini is a staple sauce in so many Middle Eastern cuisines, and the food of Lebanon is no exception. This recipe, which combines tahini with garlic and lemon, is served with many of my savory dishes and used in salad dressings. I often just eat it plain with fresh-cut vegetables or Crispy Pita Chips *(page 206).*

When making this garlic-laced tahini dressing or dipping sauce, it's very important to select the best-quality tahini you can find. ❖ **MAKES 2½ CUPS**

3 garlic cloves	1 cup freshly squeezed lemon juice
1 cup tahini (see page 280)	1 teaspoon sea salt

In the bowl of a food processor, finely mince the garlic cloves. Vigorously shake the container of tahini and then allow it to settle. Stir the oil and tahini paste together so they are completely incorporated and blended together.

Pour 1 cup of the tahini into the food processor over the garlic, and add ⅓ cup of cold water. Blend all the ingredients together, then add the lemon juice and salt. Run the processor for a few minutes, pausing to scrape down the sides and bottom of the bowl. The dressing should be creamy and not too thick. Serve at room temperature or cold.

Taratour
spicy tahini sauce

Taratour, also spelled Tarator *and* Taratoor *refers to a class of sauces made with tahini.* Taratour *is most frequently served with fresh fish dishes, like my* Samak Harrah *(page 143), but it seems to go with everything from chicken and fish to steak and shrimp.* ❖ **MAKES 2½ CUPS**

3 garlic cloves	1 cup freshly squeezed lemon juice
⅓ cup pine nuts, toasted	1 teaspoon sea salt
2 sprigs fresh flat-leaf parsley leaves, minced	1 teaspoon cayenne pepper
1 cup tahini (see page 280), thoroughly stirred	2 tablespoons extra-virgin olive oil

In the bowl of a large food processor, finely mince the garlic, toasted pine nuts, and parsley. Pour in the tahini and ⅓ cup of cold water and puree until fully blended, scraping down the bottom and sides of the bowl. Add the lemon juice, season with the salt and cayenne and process until smooth and creamy. With the food processor running, stream in the olive oil until the sauce thickens and will coat a wooden spoon. To test the texture, run your finger along the back of the spoon. It should make a clear line through the sauce. Serve the sauce at room temperature.

Toum

garlic, olive oil, and lemon sauce

Toum, *which means "garlic," is an essential sauce in Lebanese cuisine, full-bodied, flavorful, and slightly zesty. With just four ingredients, this garlicky sauce is a perfect complement to many dishes, especially grilled meats and kabobs, Lebanese French fries,* Batata Maqlieh *(page 158), and many of the greens found in my* Tashquila *(Side Dishes) section.*

Since this staple sauce, which is found on every Lebanese table, is made almost entirely of mashed garlic, it's very important to select very fresh garlic. Look for pure white heads where the cloves are tightly nestled together and the skins are somewhat moist. I've found that Italian and German varieties offer a lovely flavor without being too pungent or spicy—perfect for preparing Toum.

To make Toum, *I always use a* jidan, *a mortar and pestle. However, you can also use a food processor to puree the ingredients.* ❖ **MAKES 1 CUP**

8 to 10 garlic cloves (about 1 head)

½ tablespoon sea salt

1 cup extra-virgin olive oil

2½ to 3 tablespoons freshly squeezed
lemon juice

Peel the garlic cloves and cut off any tiny green shoots that you may see. If using a mortar and pestle, place all of the cloves into the mortar with the salt and firmly pound the cloves down to flatten, then smash them into a smooth paste by vigorously moving the pestle in a circular motion. The consistency should be very creamy. If using a food processor, make sure to scrape down the sides of the bowl to ensure that all of the garlic is fully processed and smooth.

Slowly stream ½ cup of the olive oil into the garlic paste, mixing the two together so that the oil entirely emulsifies into the garlic, and the mixture thickens substantially. Once the first half of the olive oil is incorporated, slowly stream in half of the lemon juice, mixing vigorously so that the lemon juice blends in completely and the mixture does not separate. Repeat with the remaining half of the olive oil and the remaining lemon juice.

Serve at room temperature.

بـرهـا - فلافل

Bhar Falafel

falafel spice

Spicy and savory with a hit of brightness from ground coriander, my Falafel Spice gives the Falafel
Chickpea Patties *(page 75) the perfect flavor profile. I kick up the heat with a touch of cayenne pepper and
crushed red pepper flakes, and then mellow it all out with sweet, sultry paprika. This spice mix looks just as
beautiful as it tastes, and if you're in need of more than ½ cup, this recipe is easily doubled (and tripled!)*
✧ **MAKES ½ CUP**

1 ½ tablespoons sea salt

1 tablespoon freshly ground black pepper

1 ½ tablespoons ground cumin

1 ½ tablespoons ground coriander

1 ½ tablespoons sweet paprika

1 teaspoon cayenne pepper

1 teaspoon crushed red pepper flakes

In a small mixing bowl, combine all the ingredients and stir thoroughly, using a fork to break
up the small spice particles. Store the spice mix in a glass jar and tightly secure with a lid. For
optimal freshness, always store spices in a cool, dry, dark area.

Bhar Shawarma Lahmeh

meat shawarma spice

Used for marinating red meat, my shawarma spice mix is an earthy blend of allspice, cinnamon, cloves, and nutmeg, with tangy notes of ginger and sumac. You can use it as a dry rub or mix with olive oil, red wine vinegar, and lemon juice for a wet marinade. ❖ **MAKES ½ CUP**

1 tablespoon sea salt

1 tablespoon freshly ground black pepper

1 tablespoon ground allspice

1½ teaspoons ground cinnamon

½ teaspoon ground cloves

½ teaspoon ground cardamom

½ teaspoon ground nutmeg

1½ teaspoons ground dried ginger

1½ tablespoons sumac spice
(see page 280)

For this meat blend and my chicken blend that follows: In small mixing bowls, combine all the ingredients for each blend and stir thoroughly, using a fork to break up the small spice particles. Store the spice mixes in glass jars and tightly secure with a lid. For optimal freshness, always store spices in a cool, dry, dark area.

بهار شاورما دجاج

bhar shawarma djej

chicken shawarma spice

Slightly more mellow than the meat shawarma spice mix, my chicken shawarma spice mix is still very robust and flavorful, with delicate white pepper playing off fragrant cumin, coriander, and cardamom. Ginger and garlic powder add a hint of intensity, which brightens up chicken. This mixture makes for an excellent dry rub, but is especially delicious as a marinade with olive oil, lemon juice, red wine vinegar, garlic paste, and thick labneh yogurt. The addition of labneh in the marinade will ensure very moist and juicy chicken. ❖ **MAKES ½ CUP**

1 tablespoon sea salt

1 tablespoon ground white pepper

1 tablespoon ground cumin

1 tablespoon ground coriander

1½ teaspoons ground cardamom

1½ teaspoons ground ginger

1½ teaspoons garlic powder

زعتر

Zaatar

thyme spice

Zaatar, *which translates as "thyme," is a signature Lebanese spice that has been used for centuries. During my trip to Lebanon, I vividly remember my Aunt Antoinette toasting the sesame seeds in my grandmother's outdoor oven for a fresh batch of zaatar. Every time I make zaatar, I'm reminded of that amazing, aromatic memory, and my mother's stories of harvesting wild thyme as a child in Lebanon. This super simple spice mix is used in so many of my recipes, from topping* Manoush b Zaatar *pies (page 209) to sprinkling over* Labneh *(page 225), and on my* Shanklish *yogurt cheese balls (page 236).*

Zaatar can vary widely from region to region, and mine is a traditional old-world Lebanese version that you'll be putting in everything from salad dressing to meat marinades. ❖ **MAKES 1⅓ CUPS**

1 cup dried wild thyme or Greek oregano

¼ cup sumac spice (see page 280)

½ cup sesame seeds, lightly toasted until golden brown

1½ teaspoons sea salt

In a mortar and pestle (in Lebanese we call it a jidan), a spice grinder, or a food processor combine the dried wild thyme or Greek oregano with the sumac spice and finely grind. Transfer to a medium mixing bowl and stir in the lightly toasted sesame seeds and sea salt and mix thoroughly so that all of the herbs and spices come together and are intermingled with one another. For optimal freshness, always store spices in a cool, dry, dark area.

———

taboulie tip! For best results, be sure to add in the toasted sesame seeds while they are still hot so that the oil coats the herbs to bring out the fullest flavor, and also helps this mixture to blend beautifully together!

سبع بهارات

Sab'ah Baharat

seven-spice

Sab'ah Baharat *is the ultimate signature spice in Lebanese cuisine. Slightly sweet and very aromatic, this combination, which includes cardamom, allspice, and cinnamon is something I use absolutely all the time; I call it my fairy dust! Whether I'm sprinkling it onto lamb or beef before roasting or into rice pilaf or stews, it's a spice that brings out bold, robust flavors. During the holidays, I love to make batches of* Sab'ah Baharat *and give it to friends as a gift, in a glass bottle with a ribbon attached.* ⟡ **MAKES ½ CUP**

1½ teaspoons sea salt	1½ teaspoons ground cardamom
1 tablespoon freshly ground black pepper	1½ teaspoons ground cumin
1 tablespoon ground allspice	½ teaspoon ground cloves
1½ teaspoons ground cinnamon	½ teaspoon ground nutmeg

In a small mixing bowl, combine all the ingredients and stir thoroughly, using a fork to break up the small spice particles. Store in a glass jar and tightly secure with a lid. For optimal freshness, always store spices in a cool, dry, dark area.

VARIATION ⟡ For a roasted variation, gently roast the spices in a dry pan,
then finely grind and blend together.

Kabis Zaytoun

pickled cracked green olives

Ever since I can remember, my mother has told me stories about picking olives from the trees in her family's bustan *(farm and olive orchards). During the picking season, from late August to October, Mama would lay a carpet underneath the olive tree and shake the branches. After the carpet was covered with olives, she'd gather them in a basket, then return home to carefully crack each olive with a small spoon, to decrease bitterness. After the olives were cracked, my mother and grandmother would pickle them in large terra-cotta pots to enjoy year-round.*

Zaytoun are my favorite of all the pickles, and I could (and sometimes do!) eat them morning, noon, and night. After one zesty, slightly spicy Zaytoun, you won't be able to stop! I love to serve my Zaytoun with fresh sliced vegetables or with Labneh *(page 225) and* Khebez Arabi *(page 205). Zaytoun are absolutely always a part of the mezza platter, whether at home or in restaurants. Though the recipe takes four days, it's mostly inactive, and definitely worth it!* ✦ MAKES TWO 16-OUNCE JARS

2 pounds fresh, raw, uncured small green
    olives (see page 281)

1 cup all-natural canning and pickling salt
    (see page 279)

2 lemons, thinly sliced into rounds

6 small, hot green thai chili peppers,
    whole

1 small bunch fresh dill sprigs, thick
    stems discarded

4 tablespoons extra-virgin olive oil

1 fresh egg

Rinse the olives in a large colander under cold running water. Lay a clean kitchen towel or paper towels on a large cutting board and place the rinsed olives on the clean towel, working in batches.

Using a wooden pestle or a wooden spoon and rolling pin, lightly hit each olive until it cracks just slightly on one side, resulting in a small slit through the olive skin revealing the center pit. Do not remove the pit. Put the cracked olives in a large mixing bowl.

Completely cover the olives with cold water and 3 tablespoons of the canning pickling salt. Set aside on the countertop to soak for 24 hours. Drain, rinse with cold water, and return to the bowl. Submerge in fresh cold water, add 3 more tablespoons of salt and let rest for 24 hours again. Repeat the soaking/draining process until you have done it three times for three days in a row.

On the fourth day, equally divide the olives, lemon slices, thai chile peppers, and dill sprigs between the two jars. Pour 2 tablespoons of olive oil over the olives in each jar along with 3 tablespoons of salt per jar; you should have about 1 inch of headspace at the top of the jar.

continued

Then, pour 2 cups of cold water in a large mixing bowl. Dissolve 4 tablespoons of salt in the water, then place the fresh egg in the bottom of the bowl. Wait for it to float to the top, indicating that there is enough salt in the water. If the egg does not float to the top, add another tablespoon of salt—you should use between 4 and 5 tablespoons of salt.

Once the egg has floated to the top, ladle in the salt water until the liquid level reaches about ½ inch from the top of each jar. Wipe off any excess pickling liquid from the outside of the jars and tightly seal with the canning lids.

Leave in a cool, dry place for about 4 weeks to pickle, then refrigerate and enjoy.

NOTE You will need two sterilized 16-ounce jars, seals, and lids.

كبيس لفت

Kabis Batenjen
pickled stuffed baby eggplant

Every fall, Mama and I wait patiently (or not so patiently) for our eggplants to spring from the ground. After two seasons of lovingly watering and weeding our plants, we excitedly pluck these adorable little veggies from the ground and get ready to pickle them! We also source additional eggplants from the wonderful farmers' markets near our house, showing off our spoils like small, shiny, edible trophies.

You can use baby Indian or baby Italian eggplants for this, just make sure they are between 2 and 2½ inches long. Italian eggplants are deep purple, and Indian are a light purple, and the color of the skin and the bright green tops should be vibrant, with the skin smooth, shiny, and unbruised.

While eggplants aren't usually a pickle one finds in the U.S., they are absolutely delicious with a little acidic tang, and can be found in many different varieties throughout the Middle East, and in India as well.

✳ **MAKES TWO 16-OUNCE JARS**

1½ tablespoons coarse sea salt

24 baby Indian or Italian eggplants
(2 to 2½ inches long, see page 280)

2 garlic heads (18 to 20 cloves)

1 red jalapeño pepper, finely minced

1 green jalapeño pepper, finely minced

1 each red, green, yellow, and orange
Hungarian hot wax pepper

Seeds from 1 pomegranate

1 cup red wine vinegar

1 tablespoon plus 2 teaspoons
all-natural canning and pickling salt
(see page 279)

Fill a large pot with 8 cups of cold water and season with ½ teaspoon of the coarse sea salt. Cover the pot and bring to a boil over high heat. Remove the lid and continue to boil.

While you wait for the water to boil, thoroughly wash the eggplants in cold running water, without bruising or scraping the skin.

Shave down the thick top stems of each eggplant and pluck them off. Then, using a small, sharp knife, make a small central slit to create a lengthwise pocket for the stuffing, stopping within ½ inch of the top and bottom, but do not cut through completely. Then, carefully submerge the eggplants into the boiling water, gently pressing down with a wooden spoon when they pop up to the surface. Boil uncovered for 10 to 12 minutes until they are slightly soft to the touch. Remove them from the water and drain, bottom side up, in a large colander to remove any excess water. Allow the eggplants to cool until they can be handled.

While you are waiting for the eggplants to cool, prepare the stuffing: Using a food processor, finely mince the garlic cloves. Slice vertically through each hot pepper, and remove the seeds and devein. Add all the peppers to the food processor and finely mince with the garlic. Transfer

the garlic-pepper mixture to a small mixing bowl. Stir in the pomegranate seeds and any natural juices released from the pomegranate. Season with the remaining 1 teaspoon coarse sea salt, and stir to completely mix the ingredients.

By now, the eggplants should have cooled. Place each eggplant in the palm of your hand and squeeze gently to open the center slit. If it doesn't immediately open, gently pry the opening with your fingers, and push the eggplant flesh down to make space for the stuffing. Fill each eggplant with about 1 teaspoon of the stuffing mixture, pushing it down with your fingers. Press the sides of the eggplants together after filling to seal in the stuffing.

In a large mixing bowl, combine the red wine vinegar, 1 cup of cold water, and 1 tablespoon of the pickling salt. To make pickling solution, stir together and set aside.

Carefully layer the stuffed eggplants into two 16-ounce sterilized jars, compactly placing them in from bottom to top until you have about ½ inch of headspace at the top. Place 1 teaspoon of the canning and pickling salt in each jar, then gently pour the pickling solution over the eggplants, leaving about ½ inch of headspace from the top.

Wipe any excess pickling solution from the jars and tightly seal. Set in a cool, dry place for 2 to 3 weeks to pickle, then refrigerate after opening.

NOTE You will need 2 sterilized 16-ounce jars, seals, and lids.

———————

tabouie tip! Select baby Indian or baby Italian eggplants that are picked at their peak!
The eggplants should be fresh, firm, and flavorful for optimal taste and texture.
Be sure not to select eggplants that are soft, shriveled, or discolored.

کبیـــی باذنجـان

Kabis Khyar

pickled persian cucumbers

Growing up, my siblings and I didn't really snack on junk food. When we came home from school in the afternoons, it wasn't chips, cookies, or candy that we went for, but crunchy, briny pickles. My mother would slice her homemade Kabis Khyar *(better than any store-bought fluorescent green pickle) into long, thin strips and sprinkle a little sea salt on top. These pickles were, and still remain, one of my absolute favorite snacks.*

I like to use Persian cucumbers to pickle, as they are most similar to the slim Mitte *variety we pickle in Lebanon. The most important part of* Kabis Khyar *is, of course, the cucumbers, so pay attention to which ones you're using; they should be firm, slender fresh ones that are vibrant green, with no discolorations or bruises.* ❖ **MAKES TWO 16-OUNCE JARS**

2 bay leaves

8 to 10 garlic cloves (about 1 head), peeled

1 small bunch fresh dill, thick stems discarded

1 small bunch fresh celery stalk leaves

2 teaspoons dill seeds

2 teaspoons coriander seeds

1 tablespoon plus 2 teaspoons all-natural canning and pickling salt (see page 279)

16 Persian cucumbers, thoroughly rinsed

2 green jalapeño peppers, whole or sliced (depending on spiciness level)

1 cup white wine vinegar

In the bottom of each of two 16-ounce sterilized jars, layer 1 bay leaf, 2 to 3 garlic cloves, half the fresh dill, half the celery leaves, 1 teaspoon of the dill seeds, 1 teaspoon of the coriander seeds, and 1 teaspoon of the canning and pickling salt.

Place 8 whole cucumbers into each jar, tightly packing them in a circular pattern starting from the outside in. Nestle either the whole jalapeños right in the center of the cucumbers (if you prefer less spiciness), or slice the jalapeño peppers in half lengthwise and add the two segments into the center of the jar. Top with 2 to 3 more whole garlic cloves, leaving about ½ inch of headspace at the top of the jars.

In a large mixing bowl, combine the white wine vinegar and 1 cup of cold water, then stir in the remaining 1 tablespoon of pickling salt. Pour the mixture over the cucumbers to completely cover them, so that the liquid level is about ½ inch from the top of the jar. Wipe off any excess pickling solution from the jars, and tightly seal them.

Store in a cool, dry place for 1 to 2 weeks to pickle, then refrigerate and enjoy!

NOTE You will need two sterilized 16-ounce jars, seals, and lids.

Kabis Lefet

pickled turnips with beet and garlic

Crunchy and tangy, my pickled turnips get their neon pink color from pieces of fresh beet, which add a sweetness in addition to a gorgeous hue. With a hint of garlicky flavor, Kabis Lefet are a classic accompaniment to Falafel (page 75) and other skewers and sandwiches. I also love to add Lefet, literally translating to "turnip" to my many fresh salads for their tangy taste and crunchy texture. We even serve these perfectly pink pickles with Mjadrah (Lentil Soup, page 53) and other stews. Sometimes, I just love to munch on these tasty turnips straight from the jar! ❖ MAKES TWO 16-OUNCE JARS

3 large turnips, scrubbed but not peeled

3 tablespoons coarse sea salt

1 large beet

8 garlic cloves, peeled and left whole

1 cup red wine vinegar

1 tablespoon all-natural canning and pickling salt (see page 279)

Cut the turnips in half, and then slice each half into ½-inch-thick half-moons. Place the turnip slices in a colander over a large mixing bowl and rub with the coarse sea salt. Cover with plastic wrap and set aside at room temperature overnight.

The next day, drain and discard the liquid from the turnips and thoroughly wash the turnips under cold running water.

Cut off the top and bottom roots of the beet, peel, and slice in half. Then, slice each half into ½-inch-thick half-moons, to resemble the turnip slices.

Line up the two sterilized 16-ounce jars and fill them with even layers of turnips, then beets, then garlic cloves, in that order—until you reach about ½ inch from the top of the jars.

In a large bowl or pitcher, combine the red wine vinegar, 1 cup of cold water, and the canning and pickling salt. Pour this pickling solution over the turnips and beets until the liquid reaches ½ inch from the top of the jars. Wipe any excess pickling solution from the jars and tightly seal. Set in a cool, dry, undisturbed area for at least 2 weeks to pickle.

Refrigerate after opening.

NOTE You will need two sterilized 16-ounce jars, or four sterilized 8-ounce jars, seals, and lids.

————

tabouli tip! Do not peel the turnips! We are leaving on the skin, which adds tons of texture to its crunchy taste.

KHEBEZ, ALBAN & AJBAN

— ✳ —

breads, yogurt & cheese

BREADS
KHEBEZ

⟡

ajin . . . 198
ALL-PURPOSE YEASTED BREAD DOUGH

kourban . . . 202
LEBANESE HOLY BREAD

khebez arabi . . . 205
THIN POCKET BREAD

khebez mahamas . . . 206
CRISPY PITA CHIPS

manoush b zaatar . . . 209
THYME-TOPPED BREAKFAST
FLATBREAD

fatayer . . . 210
MEAT- AND SPINACH-STUFFED TRIANGULAR
TURNOVER PIES

sambousek . . . 214
BAKED LEBANESE DUMPLINGS

sfiha baalbakiyeh . . . 217
MEAT PASTRIES FROM BA'ALBEK

lahmeh b ajin . . . 221
INDIVIDUAL LAMB PIES

YOGURT
ALBAN

⟡

laban . . . 223
UNSTRAINED LEBANESE YOGURT

labneh . . . 225
STRAINED LEBANESE YOGURT

labneh b zeit . . . 226
LABNEH WITH OIL AND SPICES

CHEESE
AJBAN

⟡

jebneh mchallale . . . 229
SYRIAN STRING CHEESE

labneh b zeit kabis . . . 232
CREAMY CHEESE BALLS PRESERVED
IN OLIVE OIL

jeben . . . 233
ARABIC BASKET CHEESE

shanklish . . . 236
SPREADABLE CHEESE BALLS WITH

OLIVE OIL AND SPICES

BREAD, YOGURT, AND CHEESE ARE THREE EXTREMELY IMPORTANT aspects of Lebanese cuisine; some might say the basic tenets. To make your own loaves and dairy is to live and breathe Lebanese culture, and I've included a number of personal and family favorites alongside traditional classics. Our all-purpose yeasted Ajin dough is used throughout my recipes and books, and is the basis for so many of my other dishes, including Lahmeh b Ajin (lamb pies) and Khebez Arabi (the Lebanese version of pita.) While we traditionally bake our bread in a *saj,* a dome-shaped metal oven, all of our recipes—from Mama's savory dumplings called Sambousek to thyme and Zaatar coated flatbreads—adapt well to conventional ovens. Even though baking bread may seem intimidating, it's a truly enjoyable and rewarding process, and when you taste the results you surely won't regret it! And, with my special thin Arabic rolling pin, the results will be better than you can imagine (see page 281).

If you're like most people, you've got at least one container of yogurt in your refrigerator. And perhaps more than one. In recent years, dairy aisles have exploded with yogurt varieties, providing a wealth of options in flavor, brand, and fat content. So, why make your own? Well, *laban*, Lebanese yogurt made from *haleeb* (milk) and *rawbi* (starter yogurt) is an indispensable ingredient that is very easy and very economical. With no preservatives or additives found in other yogurts, laban is luscious, pure, and used in everything from sauces to soups to salads and spreads, and even sweets and drinks. Another essential ingredient in Lebanese cuisine is *labneh*, strained yogurt made from laban that is reminiscent of very spreadable, mild cream cheese. After trying my Laban and Labneh recipes, you'll become a convert immediately!

Typically enjoyed at breakfast time or as a part of the mezza, *Ajban* (cheese) is a staple in Lebanese cooking. While it is less common to prepare homemade cheese in the States, in the old country, it is a rewarding part of daily life. While I've only included a few Ajban varieties here, they will be enough to whet your appetite for cheese making! From my basic Jeben (Arabic Basket Cheese) recipe, a super-creamy variety that can be made sweet or savory, to salty Syrian string cheese Jeben Mchallale adorned with nigella seeds to my two spreadable stars—Labneh b Zeit Kabis and spicy Shanklish—you'll be able to create a wealth of homemade Ajban varieties to serve and eat daily. I always use the freshest milk possible when making cheese, as it will ensure the freshest results at the end.

عجين

Ajin
all-purpose yeasted bread dough

When I think of ajin, *which means dough in Arabic, I immediately think of my mother. Every Sunday for as long as I can remember, I've seen my Mama making this dough in the biggest stainless steel mixing bowl you can imagine. In one sitting, she'll make up to fifteen pounds of ajin for use in all of our family's favorite bread dishes like* Manoush *(breakfast pies, page 209),* Fatayer *(triangular spinach and meat pies, (page 210),* Lahmeh b Ajin *(open-faced meat pies, page 221), and, of course,* Khebez Arabi *(Arabic pocket bread, page 205). There are just so many things you can make with ajin, and lucky for you, I've got a lot of ideas!*

Once baked, the dough is delicate and satisfying, soft on the inside and just a bit crispy outside.

✧ **MAKES 2 POUNDS DOUGH**

1 teaspoon yeast, dry powder or solid

1 teaspoon sugar

4 cups plus 1 teaspoon unbleached, all-purpose flour

1 teaspoon sea salt

2 tablespoons plus 1 teaspoon extra-virgin olive oil

In a small bowl, combine the yeast, sugar, 1 teaspoon of the flour, and ¼ cup of lukewarm water. Thoroughly mix the ingredients with a fork to dissolve any clumps and set aside at room temperature to rise. Once the yeast begins to foam and form small bubbles at the surface, 3 to 5 minutes, it is ready.

While you are waiting for the yeast to foam, place the remaining 4 cups of flour into a large mixing bowl and add the salt. Working in a circular motion, thoroughly mix in the salt with your fingers and break up any lumps of flour. Now, create a deep hole in the center of the flour and pour the 2 tablespoons of olive oil, 1½ cups of room-temperature water, and the yeast mixture into the well. First, mix all the ingredients loosely together with your hands starting from the outside of the bowl and working your way into the center so that the ingredients are evenly incorporated. Then begin to knead the dough by punching and rolling into it with your fists, then flipping the dough over and repeating the process. The dough should be moist but not too sticky. If it is too dry add more lukewarm water by the teaspoon, and if it is too wet, add a bit more flour by the teaspoon. Once it is soft and bounces back when you press into the dough, it is ready. Pour the remaining 1 teaspoon of olive oil in the bottom of the bowl and roll the dough in the oil until it is completely coated.

If you are using the dough that day, securely seal it in plastic wrap and cover with a large clean kitchen towel. Set aside at room temperature for 2 to 2½ hours to rest and rise. Once the dough has doubled in volume, it is ready to use.

If you plan on using the dough more than 2½ hours later, cut the dough into halves (1 lb each), seal in a plastic bag, and refrigerate. Once you are ready to use your dough, remove it from the refrigerator and allow it to rest at room temperature for 1 hour before using.

NOTE The temperature of your kitchen is an important factor in this recipe, as is the time of year. If it is colder, it will take longer for the dough to rise, and if warmer, it will take less time. The time can vary between 1 hour and 2½ hours.

NOTE This recipe can be doubled, but allow for additional preparation and resting time.

———————

taboulie tip! Use bottled springwater for best results.

Kourban

lebanese holy bread

Meaning "sacrifice" in Arabic, Kourban *is the blessed bread of the Maronite Catholics and Orthodox Christians in Lebanon and Syria. Traditionally prepared for Holy Communion and other church celebrations,* Kourban *is also sold in bakeries and prepared at home. Mahlab and mastic spices make this circular holy bread, which is scented with either orange blossom or rose water, simply magical. I particularly love it toasted with plenty of soft, sweet butter on top. When Mama and I prepare this bread, we always bless the loaf by drawing a cross into the dough before it rises, and using an Aramaic holy seal in the dough before baking.* ✴ **MAKES 2 POUNDS DOUGH, 12 LOAVES**

1 teaspoon yeast, dry powder or solid

1 teaspoon sugar

4 cups plus 3 tablespoons unbleached all-purpose flour

1 teaspoon sea salt

1 teaspoon finely ground mahlab spice (see page 280)

1 teaspoon finely ground mastic (see page 280)

1½ cups whole milk

3 tablespoons rose water (see page 280)

In a small bowl, combine the yeast, sugar, 1 teaspoon of the flour, and ⅓ cup of lukewarm water. Stir thoroughly with a fork to dissolve any clumps and let proof for 3 to 5 minutes at room temperature.

While the yeast proofs, combine 4 cups of the flour, the salt, mahlab, and mastic in a large mixing bowl. Stir the ingredients together thoroughly, then create a well in the center, and pour in ½ cup of water, milk, and the yeast mixture. Using your hands, sweep the flour into the liquid well, working your way around the bowl until all of the flour and liquid are combined. Then, begin to knead the mixture just until it comes together; do not overknead. Form the dough into one large ball in the center; the dough should be smooth and bounce back when you press it gently.

Cover the dough with a large kitchen towel and place the dough in a warm, undisturbed area to rest and rise for about 2 to 3 hours, or until the dough has doubled in volume.

Remove the towel, and transfer the dough to a clean, lightly floured surface. Divide the dough into 12 equal portions and form into smooth, round dough balls by taking each portion in your hands, one at a time, and rolling and tucking the dough under itself. Cover the balls with a large, clean kitchen towel and allow to rest for 30 minutes at room temperature.

Uncover the dough balls, lightly flour, and roll each into ¼-inch-thick rounds. Place the dough balls onto parchment paper–lined baking sheets, spacing them 2 to 3 inches apart. Cover the baking sheets with large, clean kitchen towels and let the dough rest for 30 to 60 minutes until doubled in volume.

Uncover the dough balls, and if you have a holy bread seal, lightly flour it, and press it firmly into the center of the dough. Then, using a toothpick, prick five tiny holes around the design, or just into the dough, to keep it from puffing up too much in the oven.

Preheat the oven to 375°F.

Bake the breads on the center rack of the preheated oven for 20 to 25 minutes until golden brown. While the breads are still warm, dip a clean towel into the rose water and lightly wipe both sides of the loaves. Enjoy warm with softened butter. Store leftover breads in an airtight container for up to 2 weeks.

خبز عربي

Khebez Arabi
thin pocket bread

Khebez, *which means "bread" in Arabic, is an irreplaceable part of Lebanese cuisine. Omitting khebez from a meal would be unthinkable, and don't even* think *about entertaining without it! So important to us is khebez, that if you accidently drop some on the floor, you must immediately pick it up and kiss it to let God know how highly you regard it.*

The Lebanese version of pita bread, khebez often replaces utensils—who needs a fork, knife, or spoon when you can scoop up mezza, stews, and meat dishes with warm, fluffy pocket bread? Whether served from a street stall or in the house, our sandwiches are always wrapped in fresh khebez, and we even have a class of dishes called fatteh, *that uses the day-old bread as its base, and includes our famous* Fattoush *salad (page 34).*

To enjoy Lebanese food is to enjoy khebez, and I hope you enjoy making and eating it as much as my family does! ✳ **MAKES EIGHT 9-INCH POCKET BREADS**

2 pounds Ajin (All-Purpose Yeasted
   Bread Dough, page 198), at room
   temperature

⅓ cup flour, for the work surface and
   dough

Preheat the oven to 500°F. Before you begin to roll out the dough, place 2 or 4 baking sheets into the preheated oven.

Lightly flour a work surface and place the dough in the center, sprinkling a little flour on top. Using a sharp knife or dough cutter, cut the dough into two equal halves then cut each half into quarters for a total of 8 pieces.

Working one by one, take each dough piece into the palms of your hands and tuck it underneath itself. Then roll between the palms of your hands to shape a small ball. Place the balls on a lightly floured surface and allow to rest for 10 to 15 minutes, which will make it easier to roll. Then, stretch it out into a smooth, circular flat shape making sure not to pull so hard as to create holes. Place the flat dough on the floured work surface and roll it out to a thickness of about ¼ inch, and approximately 9 inches in diameter. Repeat with the 7 remaining pieces of dough.

Carefully place the rolled-out dough rounds onto the hot baking sheet, two to a sheet, and place on the center rack of the oven. Bake for 5 to 7 minutes until the dough puffs up and turns light golden brown. Remove from the oven immediately and cover the breads with a clean kitchen towel or wrap in a plastic bag to retain the heat.

Serve the khebez immediately, hot out of the oven or warm.

NOTE You will need a thin Arabic rolling pin (see page 281).

خبز محمص

Khebez Mahamas

crispy pita chips

Pita chips are one of those things that are absolutely always better when homemade. Not only are they not loaded with additives and preservatives, they aren't heavily salted or deep-fried, and are totally fresh! They are so incredibly easy to make, but keep one thing in mind: you'll never have enough! I always double or triple my recipe, and use a number of different seasonings and spices on top. Serve with dips or spreads in the Mezza section (see pages 10–28), with Salatas (Salads, see pages 32–49), and Shawraba (Soups and Stews, see pages 52–69). ❖ **MAKES 80 PITA PIECES**

6 loaves pocket pita bread (about 6-inch loaves), at room temperature

½ cup plus 2 tablespoons extra-virgin olive oil

4 teaspoons sea salt

Preheat the oven to 450°F.

Split each loaf of bread into equal halves, using a small paring knife to make the initial slit and then tearing gently with your hands. Layer the two halves on top of one another and slice in half. Slice into 8 wedgelike pieces similar to a pizza or pie; you should have 16 pita pieces per loaf (8 per half).

Brush 2 tablespoons of the olive oil onto the bottom of a large baking sheet and arrange 20 pita pieces in one even layer on the pan. Drizzle 2 tablespoons of olive oil over the pieces, distributing it evenly, and season with 1 teaspoon of the salt. Bake for 12 to 15 minutes in the preheated oven until the pieces are visibly crispy, crunchy, and light golden brown. Remove from the oven and transfer to a cooling rack.

Repeat with the remaining pita pieces, working in batches of 20, using 2 tablespoons of olive oil and 1 teaspoon of sea salt each time. Once the pieces have baked and cooled, store them in a large sealable bag or container.

VARIATIONS ❖ PITA CHIP SEASONINGS
Sprinkle spices evenly on the pita pieces prior to baking.

SUMAC & SESAME SEEDS: 2 tablespoons of each

ZESTY ZAATAR: 2 tablespoons zaatar (page 180)

SMOKY: 2 tablespoons Aleppo pepper and 1 tablespoon smoked paprika

SWEET & SPICY: 2 tablespoons crushed red pepper flakes, 1 tablespoon cayenne pepper, and 1 tablespoon sweet paprika

GARLIC & FRESH HERB: 2 tablespoons each of minced garlic, parsley, mint, and chives.

Manoush b Zaatar

thyme-topped breakfast flatbread

Manoush b Zaatar, *a classic breakfast dish throughout Lebanon is a filling, slightly spiced, and totally delicious way to start the day. As a child, my mother was told that this tasty bread was good for the memory and would help her perform well in school! Manoush really wakes you up, with its soft fluffy bready center and zesty zaatar topping. Serve it any time of day, though, it makes a great complement to salads, soups, and meat dishes. I love to have my manoush spread with* Labneh *(page 225), a drizzle of olive oil, and topped with salt, pepper, and crushed red pepper flakes. Sliced cucumbers, tomatoes, and fresh herbs also make a tasty accompaniment.* ❖ **MAKES EIGHT 9-INCH FLATBREADS**

½ cup extra-virgin olive oil

½ cup zaatar (page 180)

Unbleached, all-purpose flour, for the work surface

2 pounds Ajin (page 198), at room temperature

In a medium mixing bowl, blend the oil and zaatar together into a creamy paste that is fluid but not runny. Taste it, it should be zesty and earthy. Make any adjustments as needed.

Preheat the oven to 500°F. Before you begin to roll out the dough, place two baking sheets into the preheated oven. If you have four baking sheets and can fit them in your oven, feel free to bake all the pieces at the same time (2 pieces per sheet).

Lightly flour a clean work surface. Place the dough on the floured work surface. Using a dough cutter or sharp knife, cut the dough into 2 equal halves and then cut each half into quarters for a total of 8 pieces.

Flatten the dough pieces out onto the flour, lightly pressing down with your fingertips. Using a rolling pin, roll out each dough piece into a circular shape, approximately 9 inches in diameter and ¼ inch thick. Try to make them as uniform in size and shape as possible, then create an edge by pinching the outer edges along around the dough so that the zaatar filling will not leak out.

Next, spread 2 tablespoons of the zaatar mixture onto each dough round, using the back of the spoon to smear the paste evenly onto the dough, starting in the center and working your way around to the edges until the whole pie is coated. Carefully place the dough rounds on the baking sheets (two to a sheet).

Transfer the baking sheets to the top and center racks of the preheated oven and bake for 5 to 7 minutes until the pies are golden brown and you start to see small bubbles appearing. The edges should be crispy, and the pies will be very aromatic. Repeat with the remaining pies, keeping the first batch warm for serving. Serve hot.

مطاير

Fatayer

meat- and spinach-stuffed triangular turnover pies

Fatayer are simple to make, and even simpler to eat! I love making these stuffed pies as a party snack; everyone loves them and you can make them as large or as small as you like. This recipe is for medium-size Fatayer, which make a great dinner appetizer or lunch main course. Thanks to Mama's trick of brushing them with olive oil as soon as they come out of the oven, mine are shiny, moist, and crisp on the outside.

I often make both the spinach and lamb varieties, so that everyone has a taste of both and carnivores and vegetarians alike are satisfied! But feel free to make one or the other! Even though I'm a veggie lover, I do have to admit that the lamb Fatayer are my favorite. ❖ **MAKES SIXTEEN 5-INCH TURNOVERS**

⅓ cup unbleached, all-purpose flour, for the work surface

2 pounds Ajin (page 198), at room temperature (cut into 1 pound dough balls)

¼ cup extra-virgin olive oil, for brushing

LAMB FILLING

4 tablespoons (½ stick) unsalted butter

2 tablespoons olive oil

1 medium yellow onion, finely diced

½ pound finely ground lamb

1 teaspoon sea salt

½ teaspoon freshly ground black pepper

½ teaspoon ground allspice

1 small bunch fresh flat-leaf parsley leaves, finely minced

¼ cup pine nuts

SPINACH FILLING

½ pound spinach leaves, shredded

1 small yellow onion, finely diced

2½ to 3 tablespoons freshly squeezed lemon juice

¼ cup extra-virgin olive oil

1 teaspoon sea salt

½ teaspoon crushed red pepper flakes

Preheat the oven to 450°F.

Lightly flour a clean work surface or cutting board.

If you are making the lamb filling, prepare it before you roll out the dough, so that it has time to cool before stuffing. In a large sauté pan on medium-high heat, melt 2 tablespoons of the butter and the 2 tablespoons of the olive oil until shimmering. Add the onion and cook, tossing continuously, until slightly softened and translucent, about 10 minutes. Add the lamb and cook, stirring occasionally, until completely browned, breaking up the meat with a wooden spatula. Season with the salt, pepper, and allspice. Sprinkle with the fresh parsley and turn off the heat.

continued

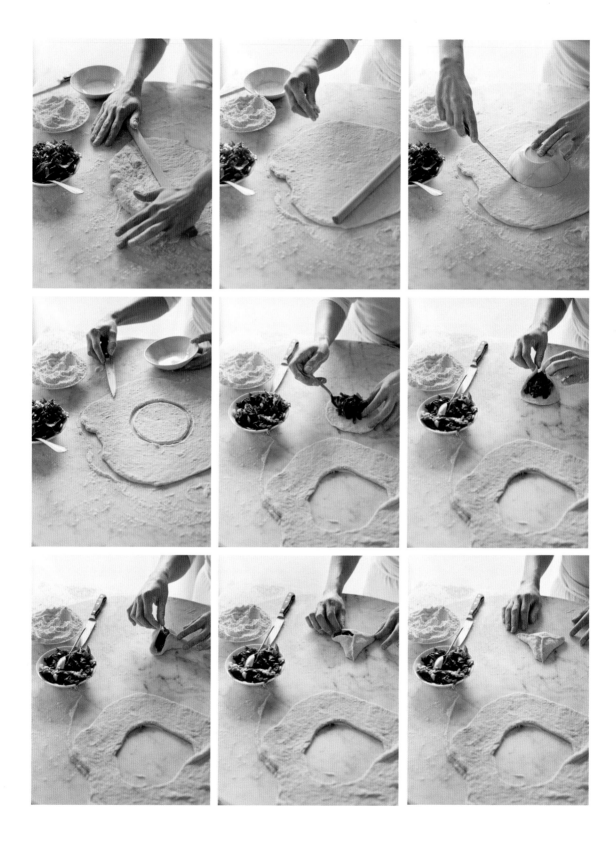

In a small sauté pan, melt the remaining 2 tablespoons butter over medium-low heat, add the pine nuts, and toast, tossing continuously, until the pine nuts turn light golden brown and crisp on the outside, and give off a nutty aroma. Turn off the heat, add the pine nuts to the meat mixture, and toss to incorporate. Set the meat filling aside to cool while you roll out the dough.

Place 1 pound of dough at a time in the center of the floured surface and lightly sprinkle with flour. Place the dough into the palms of your hands and tuck it under itself using your fingertips. Then, stretch the dough out into a smooth, flat, round and place onto the floured surface and, using a thin rolling pin, roll it out until it is smooth and about 16 to 18 inches in diameter and ¼ inch thick.

Cut dough into circles: Using the rim of a small bowl, cut out medium-size rounds, approximately 5 inches in diameter, from the dough. Place the dough rounds on a lightly floured surface area while you cut the remaining rounds from the dough. You should have eight 5-inch rounds of dough. Repeat with the other pound of dough to make a total of sixteen 5-inch rounds.

Cut into circles. Right before you stuff the turnovers, make the spinach filling by combining all the ingredients in a mixing bowl and tossing to combine thoroughly.

To stuff the turnovers: Take 4 to 5 tablespoons of either stuffing and place in the center of each dough round. Take the two sides of the dough and bring them together in the center to completely enclose the filling. Using your fingertips, tightly pinch the edges together to seal. Then, lift the last flap of dough up and over to meet the center point, and pinch together to seal, creating a triangular shape. Make sure the turnovers are well sealed. (see photos)

Lightly brush two large baking sheets with olive oil and place all of the spinach turnovers on one pan and all of the meat turnovers on the other pan (if making both). Place the baking sheets in the center and top racks of the preheated oven and bake for 15 to 20 minutes until the turnovers are crisp and light golden brown. Turn off the heat and remove the turnovers from the oven.

Immediately brush each turnover with olive oil, coating the top and sides.

Serve hot, warm, or at room temperature.

NOTE You will need a rolling pin, an Arabic one if possible (see page 281) and a small bowl, 5 inches in diameter.

VARIATION ❖ Replace the finely ground lamb with lean 80/20 percent ground beef.

سمبوسك

Sambousek
baked lebanese dumplings

From reading this chapter, you can definitely tell that we Lebanese have a love for meat-stuffed breads and pastries. While my Lahmeh b Ajin, Fatayer, *and* Sfiha *are all absolutely delicious in their different ways,* Sambousek *are by far the simplest meat-filled goodie, and oh-so-tasty, too! With few ingredients and no extra spices or specialty items, these oval-shaped dumplings are a cinch to make, and you won't regret it.*

While you'll often find Sambousek fried, I go for the healthier route and bake them in the oven instead until golden brown. ⁜ **MAKES THIRTY 3-INCH DUMPLINGS**

¼ cup unbleached, all-purpose flour (for the work surface)

1 pound Ajin (page 198), at room temperature

¼ cup extra-virgin olive oil

LAMB FILLING

½ pound finely ground lamb

1 small onion, finely minced

1 small bunch fresh flat-leaf parsley leaves, finely minced

½ teaspoon sea salt

½ teaspoon freshly ground black pepper

Preheat the oven to 450°F.

Lightly flour a large work surface or a clean countertop or cutting board. Place the dough in the center of the floured surface and sprinkle lightly with flour.

Place the dough into the palms of your hands and tuck it under itself using your fingertips. Then, stretch the dough out into a smooth, flat round and place onto the flour surface and roll it out until it is about 16 to 18 inches in diameter and ¼ inch thick. Be sure to release any small air pockets in the dough and make sure it is very smooth with no holes.

Using the rim of a small bowl or glass, cut out 30 small rounds from the dough, 3 inches in diameter, leaving behind as little excess dough as possible. Place the dough rounds on a lightly floured surface area while you cut rounds from the remaining dough scraps.

Make the lamb filling: In a large mixing bowl, combine all the ingredients for the lamb filling. Thoroughly mix the ingredients together with your hands then knead it together to form a smooth, creamy, and moist mixture.

Place about ½ tablespoon of the meat mixture into the center of each dough round. Fold the dough over once to enclose the meat mixture and tightly pinch the edges together so they are completely sealed.

Lightly brush two large baking sheets with olive oil. Arrange the dumplings in vertical rows on the prepared sheets, making sure to leave some space between each dumpling. Transfer the baking sheets to the center and top racks of the preheated oven and bake for about 15 minutes until the Sambousek are golden brown.

Once the dumplings are cooked, immediately remove them from the oven and lightly brush all over with olive oil. Transfer to a serving dish and serve immediately.

NOTE You will need a rolling pin, preferably a thin Arabic one (see page 281), and a small bowl or glass, 3 inches in diameter.

Sfiha Baalbakiyeh

meat pastries from ba'albek

Ba'albek, a town in Lebanon's Bekaa Valley known as Heliopolis in ancient times, is home to some of the best preserved and largest Roman ruins in Lebanon, including the Temple of Bacchus and The Stone of the South. In addition to some of the country's most breathtaking antiquities, this majestic city is also home to Sfiha, mini, meat-filled square pastries baked in a traditional clay tanour oven. While my version uses a conventional oven, the slightly spicy tahini-laced lamb filling is true to the original Sfiha recipe and different than the other meat pies in this chapter. Serve as a snack, as part of your mezza, or alongside a main meal—just make sure you make a lot, because there will surely be none left! I like to serve them with Khayer b Laban (Cucumber-Mint-Yogurt Sauce, page 169) and Khyar wa Banadoura (Cucumber, Tomato, and Fresh Herb Salad, page 33), but they are just as good eaten plain, piping hot from the oven!

✤ MAKES TWENTY FOUR TO THIRTY 4-INCH PASTRIES

2 pounds Ajin (page 198), at room temperature

¼ cup unbleached, all-purpose flour, for the work surface and dough

¼ cup extra-virgin olive oil

LAMB FILLING

1 pound finely ground lamb

1 medium yellow onion, finely minced

1 small bunch fresh flat-leaf parsley leaves, finely minced

1 small bunch fresh mint leaves, finely minced

1 long hot red pepper, seeded and finely minced

1 large ripe tomato, seeded and finely minced

2 tablespoons tahini (sesame seed paste, see page 280)

2 tablespoons pomegranate molasses (see page 280)

1 teaspoon sea salt

½ teaspoon freshly ground black pepper

1 teaspoon ground allspice

1 tablespoon freshly squeezed lemon juice

1 cup pine nuts

Preheat the oven to 450°F.

Lightly flour a large work surface or cutting board, place the dough in the center of the board, and lightly sprinkle it with flour. Using a dough cutter or sharp knife, cut the dough in two equal halves.

Place one dough half into the palms of your hands and tuck it under itself. Then, stretch it out into a smooth, flat round, and roll it out on the work surface until it is 16 to 18 inches in diameter and about ¼ inch thick. Be sure to release any small air pockets in the dough.

continued

Using the rim of a small bowl or glass, cut out small rounds, 4 inches in diameter, cutting as many as you can and leaving as little excess dough as possible. Place the rounds of dough onto a lightly floured surface and set aside while you repeat with the remaining dough half.

Then, make the sfiha filling: Combine the meat, onions, parsley, mint, hot red pepper, and tomato in a large mixing bowl. Add the tahini and pomegranate molasses to the mixture and season it with salt, pepper, and allspice. Finally, add the lemon juice and thoroughly mix the ingredients together with your hands, until they are well incorporated and a smooth, pastelike consistency.

Take 1½ to 2 tablespoons of the meat mixture and place it into the center of each dough round. Take two corners of the dough and tightly pinch the edges together. Then, take the other two corners and do the same so that you form a small square with an opening in the center. Securely squeeze all four seams together so that the meat mixture does not escape. Finish by placing ¼ teaspoon of untoasted pine nuts on top of the meat.

Lightly brush two large baking sheets with olive oil. Place half the sfiha on each baking sheet, making sure there is space between each meat pie. Transfer the baking sheets to the top and bottom racks of the preheated oven and bake the sfiha for about 15 minutes, or until the meat is cooked through and the pine nuts are golden and toasted. The dough will be crisp and browned.

Turn off the heat and immediately remove from the oven. Brush each pastry with olive oil on the top and sides, and serve piping hot.

NOTE You will need a rolling pin, preferably a thin Arabic one (see page 281), and a small round bowl or glass, 4 inches in diameter.

VARIATION ❊ If you prefer, you can use 80/20 percent lean ground beef.

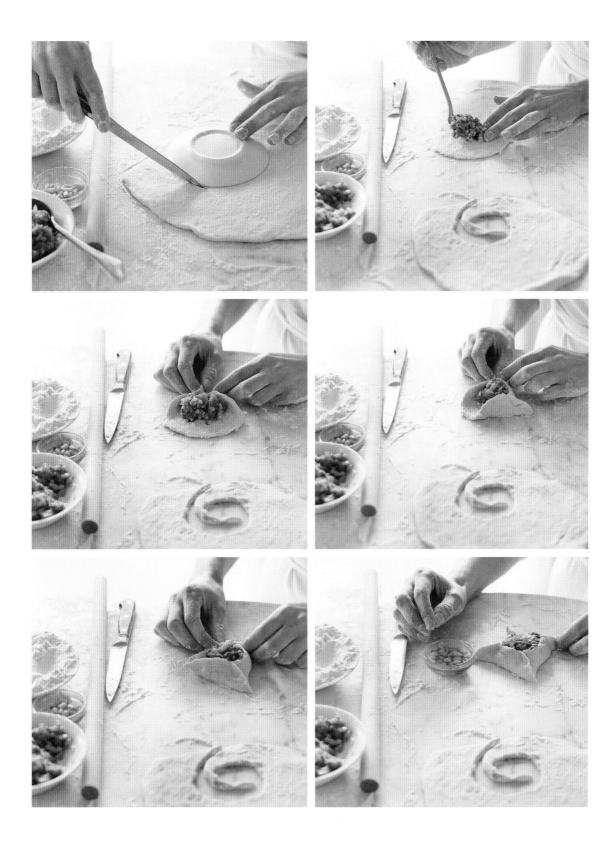

Lahmeh b Ajin
individual lamb pies

From savory dough pastries and pies to countless varieties of bread and mouthwatering sweet treats, the Lebanese are known widely for our baked goods.

Of all our many meat pastries, Lahmeh b Ajin *is by far the most popular and well-known. You may have heard of Lahmajun, which is the same delicious dish just spelled differently. Round dough pies are topped with a very savory mixture of ground lamb, fresh herbs and spices, and a hint of sweetness from one of our favorite ingredients: pomegranate molasses. Topped with pine nuts and baked until piping hot, these slightly spicy personal meat pies are totally irresistible.* ✣ **MAKES EIGHT 9-INCH LAMB PIES**

2 pounds Ajin (page 198), at room temperature

¼ cup unbleached, all-purpose flour, for the work surface and dough

¼ cup extra-virgin olive oil

LAMB FILLING

1½ pounds finely ground lamb

1 medium yellow onion, finely diced

1 small bunch fresh flat-leaf parsley leaves, finely minced

2 tablespoons pomegranate molasses (Dibis Rahman, see page 280)

1 teaspoon sea salt

1 teaspoon freshly ground black pepper

1 teaspoon ground allspice

1 cup pine nuts

8 small lemon wedges, for finishing (optional)

Preheat the oven to 450°F.

Make the pies: Lightly flour a clean work surface or cutting board. Place the ball of dough in the center of the floured surface area and lightly sprinkle with flour on top. Using a dough cutter or sharp knife, cut the dough into two equal halves and then cut each half into quarters for a total of 8 pieces.

Using your fingertips, take each dough segment individually and tuck the dough under itself. Then, stretch it out gently into a very smooth and flat circular shape. Place the dough on the floured surface and smooth it out gently, then roll it until it is about 9 inches in diameter and ¼ inch thick. Repeat with the remaining 7 dough pieces, creating equal-size dough pies. Set the dough pies aside momentarily.

Make the topping for the pies: In a large mixing bowl, combine the ground lamb with the onion and parsley. Pour in the pomegranate molasses and season with salt, pepper, and allspice. Using your hands, thoroughly mix the ingredients together until they are well incorporated. Then, knead the mixture with your fists to achieve a smooth, pastelike consistency.

Lightly brush two large baking sheets with olive oil. Place 2 dough pies on each baking sheet, making sure there is space between them. Place about 4 to 5 tablespoons of the meat mixture onto each dough pie and spread evenly using your hands, so that there is a smooth, thin layer of meat all the way to the edge of the pies. Press the meat filling into the dough, then press in about 1 tablespoon of untoasted pine nuts on the top of each pie.

Bake on the center and top racks of the preheated oven for about 10 to 12 minutes, or until the meat is completely cooked through and browned, and the pies are bubbly and golden brown. When ready, the pie edges should slightly curl and develop a crisp outer crust. Repeat using the rest of the pies and filling.

Serve immediately. If using, squeeze one small wedge of lemon on each pie just before serving.

NOTE You will need a rolling pin (an Arabic one if possible, see page 281).

لبن

Laban
unstrained lebanese yogurt

Laban *simply means "white" in Arabic, and this ever-present Lebanese dairy product has been made since biblical times and probably before. In its unstrained form,* Laban *is silky and shiny, and usually made with cow's milk.* Laban *is used in myriad Lebanese recipes from soups to salads to desserts, and can also be eaten as you would any other yogurt.* ❖ **MAKES 15 CUPS (ALMOST 1 GALLON)**

1 gallon freshly purchased milk (whole, 2 percent, or nonfat skim), at room temperature

5 tablespoons whole-milk plain yogurt, at room temperature (I prefer Dannon)

Pour the milk into a large, heavy-bottomed pot and place over medium heat. Slowly bring it to a steady simmer without stirring and without bringing it to a boil. Watch carefully to prevent boiling or scalding. After 25 to 30 minutes, the milk will foam and start to slowly rise up the sides of the pot, ½ to 1 inch above the original milk level. Once this happens, immediately remove the milk from the heat and let cool.

After the milk has cooled for about 1½ hours, test the temperature, either with a thermometer—it should register 95°F, or by holding your pinky finger in the center of the pot for 10 full seconds—if it is too hot to keep your finger in, the milk hasn't adequately cooled.

Spoon the yogurt into a small bowl and stir until smooth. Slowly ladle in 1 cup of the warm milk, stirring continuously to incorporate the milk into the yogurt completely. Pour this mixture into the center of the pot of milk and slowly stir the warm milk working your way from the bottom to the top of the pot, and all around. Do not scrape the bottom of the pot and do not overstir.

Cover the pot with a lid, and wrap the covered pot with large kitchen towels. Leave the pot at room temperature, undisturbed, for at least 12 and no more than 24 hours.

After the time has elapsed, unwrap the towels and immediately transfer the pot to the refrigerator to chill the laban for at least 6 hours and ideally 12, before eating or using for cooking.

NOTE You will need a cooking thermometer.

———————

taboulie tip! Make sure to purchase and use the milk in the same day; it is highly important that the milk should be very fresh when making laban!

لبنة

Labneh
strained lebanese yogurt

With soft white peaks like the snow-capped tops of Mount Lebanon, Labneh *is a smooth, rich cheeselike yogurt with fewer calories and higher protein than store-bought cream cheese. I love to spread it on warm Khebez Arabi (page 205) and top with olive oil and a sprinkling of crushed red pepper flakes, Zaatar (page 180), or fresh chopped herbs.*

It's made by straining laban, so I typically save half of the laban to eat plain, and reserve half for the Labneh. I generally leave the laban in the refrigerator for at least one to two days so that the flavors can come together, before I strain it. ❖ **MAKES 7 CUPS**

15 cups Laban (unstrained Lebanese yogurt, page 223)

Open the cotton bag or pillowcase as wide as possible and place in a colander over a bowl to catch the dripping liquid. Ladle the laban into the bag, pushing the yogurt down as much as possible. Close the bag, pressing down on it to release as much air as possible. Pull the drawstring tightly and begin to spin the bottom around while holding the top, ultimately twisting the top part of the bag to secure. Place the bag into the colander over the bowl, and transfer to the refrigerator to drain for a full day. Throughout the day, periodically pour the milk liquid (whey) out so that it doesn't overflow.

After one full day, the majority of the whey will have drained, and your Labneh yogurt will have a thicker, creamy consistency, and be ready to serve or use.

NOTE You will need a cotton, muslin drawstring bag or a clean cotton, standard-size pillowcase.

Labneh b Zeit

labneh with oil and spices

In the U.S., when we think of yogurt, our mind automatically goes to "sweet," with sweet flavors of Greek yogurt, and toppings like fruit, granola, and honey. But, in Lebanese and Middle Eastern cuisines, we spike our yogurt, especially our thicker tangier Labneh, *with savory ingredients like spices, olive oil, sea salt, and herbs. We serve* Labneh b Zeit *with a host of dishes including* Kibbeh Kbekib *(page 123),* Manoush b Zaatar *(page 209), and as part of our mezza spread (see chapter 1).* ❖ **MAKES 6 SERVINGS**

2 cups Labneh (strained Lebanese yogurt, page 225)

¼ cup extra-virgin olive oil

½ teaspoon sea salt

Spread the labneh on a serving dish in a circular pattern, using the back of a silicone spatula to smooth out the yogurt. Then, using the back of a small teaspoon, gently press into the labneh to create small and slightly shallow holes. Drizzle the olive oil around the labneh so it settles in the tiny holes. Sprinkle with sea salt and serve.

LUSCIOUS LEBANESE LABNEH BAR ❖ Drizzle the labneh with extra-virgin olive oil, sprinkle with sea salt (as above), and finish with these tasty toppings:

SPICY LABNEH: Crushed red pepper flakes or Aleppo pepper flakes, paprika, and cayenne.

GARLIC LOVERS LABNEH: Freshly pounded garlic paste blended in labneh; finish with minced fresh mint leaves.

HERB-A-LICIOUS LABNEH: Generously top with minced spring onions, fresh mint, flat-leaf parsley, and chives.

ZESTY ZAATAR: Sprinkle with Zaatar spice (page 180).

JULIE STYLE: Crushed red pepper flakes and freshly ground black pepper.

Jebneh Mchallale
syrian string cheese

Translating literally to "stringy cheese," Jebneh Mchallale *is originally a recipe from Aleppo, Syria. One sunny summer afternoon, I was lucky to learn the preparation of this stretchy, salty, braided cheese from my Aunt Marcelle who hails from Syria. Although she showed me and Mama the preparation of string cheese just once, we were able to absorb the recipe and technique quickly, and we make this cheese often—always thinking of Aunt Marcelle. I have fond childhood memories of peeling and pulling on this very snackable cheese, which is sprinkled with tiny black nigella seeds and flavored with* mahlab, *a sweet spice meaning "blessed seeds."* ✤ **MAKES TEN 6- TO 8-OUNCE STRING CHEESE BRAIDS**

12 tablespoons all-natural canning and
    pickling salt (see page 279)

1 fresh whole egg (uncracked, for testing
    the salt levels, do not use an old egg)

1 tablespoon finely ground mahlab
    (see page 280)

1 tablespoon nigella seeds
    (see page 280)

5 pounds unsalted, full-fat cow's milk
    "fresh curd" mozzarella cheese, at
    room temperature, ½ cup of the
    packing liquid reserved

Pour 8 cups of cold water into a large mixing bowl (preferably glass), and stir in the canning salt to dissolve. The water should be cloudy white. Carefully lower the egg into the water and salt solution; it should immediately sink to the bottom but then rise to float on the surface, indicating that there is enough salt in the water. Set the brine aside momentarily.

Pour the mahlab into one small bowl and the nigella seeds into another small bowl. Then, place one large dinner plate next to the two bowls. Add ¼ teaspoon of the mahlab and ¼ teaspoon of nigella seeds onto the center of the large dinner plate and mix to combine. Set aside.

Open the package of cheese and reserve the packing liquid. If there is no liquid, you can use cold water later. On a clean cutting board, cut the cheese into 2-inch cubes. You should have about 100 cubes.

Pour 4 tablespoons of the cheese liquid, or 4 tablespoons of cold water, into a medium saute pan on low heat. Add 10 to 12 cheese cubes (about one-tenth of the total cubes you have) into the saucepan, breaking it down with a wooden spoon and stirring constantly, until the cheese has completely melted. Then, fold the cheese over itself repeatedly until it comes together in one round mass of pliable, melted cheese.

Then, remove the cheese from the heat, scoop it up, and place it onto the center of the plate. The cheese will be hot, but it needs to be braided while still hot or it will cool and harden.

To make the braids: Press the cheese into the mahlab–nigella seed mixture on both sides, then, using your index finger, poke a hole in the middle (it will resemble a doughnut). Using your fingers, widen the hole, and spread it around the plate. Then, begin to stretch it as far as it will go without tearing, to create a large loop. Bring both ends together and stretch again to create a large double loop, continue to bring both of the ends together and then stretch, at least 7 more times, creating the thin, stretchy strands. After a total of 10 stretches and looping, tightly twist and turn the cheese in opposite directions into a braided ropelike long shape, then loop one end over and then under the other loop to make a knot (see photos opposite).

Immediately place the cheese into previously prepared brine solution so that it is completely submerged. Repeat this process with the remaining cubes, using 10 to 12 cubes each time. Once you are halfway through, discard the cheese liquid from the saucepan and add 4 tablespoons of the remaining unused cheese liquid or water to the pan.

After all of the cheese braids are submerged in the brining solution, allow them to brine for about 1 hour. After the braids have brined in the solution, they are ready to eat. Untangle the braids into long, thin strands and enjoy. Soak longer for saltier cheese. Serve the cheese at room temperature.

NOTE Store the cheese in resealable plastic bags in the refrigerator for up to 1 week. Or freeze in resealable plastic freezer bags for up to 3 months.

SERVING SUGGESTION Serve the cheese at room temperature by unbraiding the cheese, then separate the thin strands and pile high on a plate with Khoudra wa Kabis (page 15) and Ejjeh (page 110) or Bayd b Halyoun (page 109) for breakfast or as part of the Mezza.

———

taboulie tip! Unsalted "fresh-curd" mozzarella cheese is typically available at your local Italian market or specialty food store.

taboulie tip! Syrian string cheese is best enjoyed at room temperature. Be sure to remove it from the refrigerator ahead of time before serving.

لبنة بزيت

Labneh b Zeit Kabis

creamy cheese balls preserved in olive oil

During the autumnal harvest time, we often prepare Labneh b Zeit Kabis, *preserving these balls of creamy cheese in olive oil and packing them away in our pantry with other pickles to eat in the colder months. The laban must be strained for two full days to achieve the perfect labneh, which will be a substantial, thick consistency with a rich, slightly sharp flavor.* Labneh b Zeit, *which means "yogurt in oil," is a great snack to serve to guests, particularly with a sprinkling of sea salt and crushed red pepper flakes, and warm* Khebez Arabi *(page 205). I always serve my* Labneh b Zeit *with warm, meat-stuffed* Kibbeh Kbekib *(page 123).* ✢ **MAKES 16 BALLS**

2 cups labneh (strained Lebanese yogurt, page 225)	1⅓ cups extra-virgin olive oil, plus additional for coating hands
1 teaspoon sea salt	

Using labneh that has been strained for two full days, transfer the labneh from the cheesecloth or muslin bag or pillowcase to a clean bowl. Sprinkle with sea salt and stir thoroughly to incorporate.

Lightly coat the palms of your hands with olive oil and roll 2 tablespoons of the labneh in your hands until it forms a smooth, round, ball. Repeat with the remaining labneh; you should have 16 balls of labneh.

Line a large baking sheet with paper towels or a clean kitchen towel, and place the labneh balls on top in a single layer to drain for 2 hours or until they are dry to the touch.

Place the balls into a 16-ounce sterilized jar on top of one another until you have reached about 4 inches from the top of the jar. Then, pour 1⅓ cups of the olive oil into the jar over the balls until they are completely submerged in the oil, leaving about 2 inches of headspace at the top of the jar.

Store the cheese in the refrigerator for up to 4 weeks.

NOTE You will need one sterilized 16-ounce wide-mouth jar, seal, and lid.

جبن

Jeben
cow's milk arabic basket cheese

Simply translated as "cheese," Jeben *is the Lebanese cheese of choice, and can be served at any meal, whether as part of a simple breakfast with fresh vegetables and* Khebez Arabi *(page 205), or as a component in the mezza selection at lunch or dinnertime. Snow white, semisoft, and slightly chewy, this rich unripened curd cheese is made from fresh cow's milk, and can be left unsalted for desserts and other sweet preparations, or can be lightly salted for savory dishes. My Auntie Mona is always considered "Queen of the Jibneh," and whenever I would stop by her house, she would joyfully announce to me that she had* just *made jeben (always the traditional way, molded in plastic baskets for a wicker-texture on the outside)—my absolute favorite cheese! Over plenty of cheese and lots of conversation, we would pass the afternoons together—an experience I still treasure today. Make some quality time for this incredible homemade cheese, and make sure to use the freshest milk you can—preferably purchased the day of or day before you plan to make the jeben.*

❖ **MAKES FOUR 4-OUNCE BASKET CHEESE ROUNDS, OR ONE 1-POUND LARGE BASKET CHEESE**

1 gallon (16 cups) fresh whole milk, at room temperature (it will take at least 1 to 2 hours to come to room temperature)

1 tablespoon liquid rennet or 1 junket rennet tablet (see page 281), dissolved in ¼ cup cold water

Sea salt

4 tablespoons all-natural canning and pickling salt (see page 279)

Pour the milk into a 6- or 7-quart heavy-bottomed pot and place over low heat for 5 to 7 minutes just until it is warm, between 95° and 100°F. Remove from the heat and cool at room temperature.

With long, circular movements around the circumference of the pot, stir in the liquid rennet gently. Then, allow the milk to cool and set, uncovered, at room temperature for about 4 hours, until it registers between 80 and 85°F. The milk should appear firm and will form a curd block in the center of the pot with a thin, watery layer of liquid whey surrounding its outer edges. Using your fingers, gently break up the milk solids by swishing and swirling your fingers through the curds in a circular motion, separating it from the whey into small pebblelike pieces that resemble cottage cheese. Do not stir, squeeze, or whisk the curds.

At this point, return the pot to the stovetop over low heat and gently warm, uncovered, for about 5 minutes; the temperature should read between 95° and 100°F, and the milk should be tepid. The whey will start to separate from the curds and the liquid will become slightly pale yellow. Once the 5 minutes has elapsed, immediately turn off the heat.

continued

Line a large stainless steel strainer with a drawstring cotton bag or pillowcase (see note below). Place bag in the sink. Open the bag as wide as possible and ladle the cheese into the bag, lifting the bag a few times to release air. Move quickly, so that the cheese does not become cold. Press down on the bag, using the palms of your hands, and push as much liquid as possible out of the cheese. Then, using your hands, collect about 1 cup of the cheese curds and mold them into a round shape until smooth on all sides. Squeeze the cheese between the palms of your hands to release as much liquid as possible, creating a 2-inch-thick cheese round. Place the cheese under a clean portion of the bag and repeat with remaining curds; you should have 4 equal-size cheese rounds. Place heavy plates or other objects on top of the cloth bag and weigh the cheese down for 3 to 6 hours to remove excess liquid, flipping cheese over halfway through, until it is somewhat firm to the touch.

Depending on your use, you can leave the cheese unsalted, or salt to taste. You can also brine the cheese, which will keep it fresh, by boiling the canning salt with 2 cups of water, then allowing it to cool completely. Once the brine is cool, transfer the cheese into a 16-ounce wide-mouth sterilized canning jar and submerge entirely in the brine, leaving 2 inches at the top of the jar. Tightly seal the jar and keep refrigerated for up to 1 week.

NOTE You will need a cooking thermometer, one 16-ounce wide-mouth sterilized canning jar, 1 clean cotton muslin drawstring bag or a clean cotton standard-size pillowcase. This recipe can be easily doubled.

Shanklish

spreadable cheese balls with olive oil and spices

Spicy and sharp, Shanklish is a staple cheese in Lebanon and Syria formed into balls and coated in olive oil and red pepper flakes. Stored in glass container jars, it is crumbled and drizzled with olive oil, sprinkled with additional spices, and served with warm Khebez Arabi *(page 205),* Kabis Zaytoun, *cracked green olives (page 184), and fresh vegetables. I prefer to eat my* Shanklish *within a week of preparing it, but it can also be dry aged for up to 1 month. The best I've ever tried was made by Layla Zeina, a close family friend and the chef-owner of a wonderful Lebanese café in my birth town of Utica, New York. This recipe pays tribute to lovely Layla, who generously shared some of her tips and tricks with me for my own recipe.*

❖ **MAKES EIGHT 2½-INCH CHEESE BALLS**

15 cups laban (unstrained lebanese yogurt, page 225)

3 teaspoons sea salt

1 teaspoon Aleppo pepper flakes (see page 279)

1 teaspoon crushed red pepper flakes

In a large 6- or 8-quart heavy-bottomed pot, stir the laban and 2 cups of cold water together until smooth. Turn the heat to low and slowly bring the mixture to a bubbling near boil, about 30 minutes. The laban mixture will separate into liquid and solid, and the curds will be small and scrambled. When the temperature reads 160°F, remove from the heat.

Stir in 2 teaspoons of the salt in slow, long, circular strokes, starting at the outer edges of the pot and working your way in. Allow the laban mixture to cool and curdle for 30 to 45 minutes. You will see larger cottage cheese–like curds underneath the thin whey liquid at the top; the temperature should register 100°F. Cover the pot and set it aside to cool overnight at room temperature.

The following day, remove the lid from the pot and line a large clean, sterilized metal strainer with the muslin cloth bag or pillowcase and place in the sink. Open the bag as wide as possible and pour the yogurt curds in, lifting the bag a few times to release any air and excess liquid. Press down on the bag with the palms of your hands to help drain as much liquid as possible. Once the curds have released as much liquid as possible, pull the bag's drawstring tightly, and start spinning the bottom around while you hold the top. Twist the top part around itself to secure, place the bag into the strainer over a catch bowl, and refrigerate for 24 hours. Throughout this straining, periodically pour the liquid from the bottom catch bowl so that it does not overflow.

After 1 full day, the majority of the liquid will have drained out, leaving you with a thick, dry cheese. Open the bag and scoop the cheese into a large mixing bowl. Season with the remaining 1 teaspoon salt, the Aleppo pepper, and crushed red pepper flakes, and thoroughly stir the curds together so that the seasoning is evenly incorporated. Return the bag to the colander over the catch bowl, and return the cheese to the bag, and transfer to the refrigerator to drain for another 24 hours. After the second day of draining, the cheese will resemble thick cottage cheese–like curds. Remove the spiced curd mixture from the refrigerator and transfer to a mixing bowl.

Scoop 5 tablespoons of the spiced curds and shape it into a small ball, about 2½ inches in diameter, using the palms of your hands. Repeat with the remaining curds; you should have 4 balls. This is the cheese in its freshest form, which is ready to serve or store in the refrigerator in a tightly sealed jar for up to 1 week.

If you would like to age the shanklish, for a sharper flavor, place the balls in a single layer on paper towel– or cloth–lined baking sheets and cover lightly and store in a cool, dry place to age and mature. You can age the cheese anywhere from 1 week to 1 month; the longer the shanklish ages, the stronger and sharper the taste will be, and a layer of mold will form on the outside. After the aging has finished, scrape the mold from the balls and submerge them in olive oil. Roll in Zaatar (page 180) or in spices to taste. Store in sterilized jars to preserve for up to 1 month in the refrigerator.

NOTE You will need a cooking thermometer, clean cotton muslin drawstring bag or a clean cotton standard-size pillowcase, 2 sterilized 16-ounce jars, seals, and lids.

SERVING SUGGESTION When ready to serve, simply crumble on a serving plate using the back of a fork, generously drizzle with extra-virgin olive oil, add more spices to taste, and serve for breakfast with Bayd b Lahem (page 113) or Bayd b Batenjen (page 114) or as part of the Mezza with warm pocket bread, Khebez Arabi (page 205), Zaytoun olives (page 184), and Khoudra wa Kabis (page 15). Our national drink of Lebanon Arak (page 272) also typically accompanies this spicy cheese.

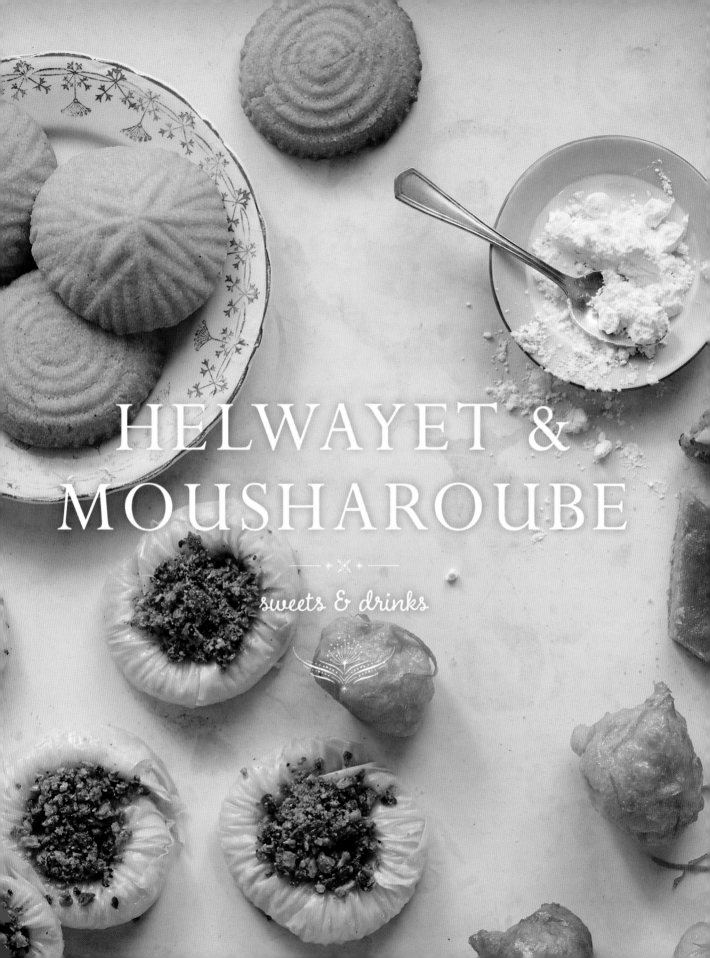

HELWAYET &
MOUSHAROUBE

sweets & drinks

DELICIOUSLY DECADENT AND DELIRIOUSLY DIVINE, LEBANESE SIGNA-
ture sweets are some of my absolute favorite things to make, whether on my show
or at home with my family. From my beloved Baklawa for beginners, to the more
advanced, pistachio-filled phyllo nests Eish al Bolbol, there is a dessert for everyone
and for every occasion. Tripoli, Lebanon, is known for its incredible sweets, and
many of these recipes are my versions of classics from this sugary haven. Dried fruit
and nut fillings, Samneh (clarified butter), and Ater (flavored syrups), are some of
the most important ingredients in Lebanese desserts, and I have included in-depth
recipes for each. While my sweet treats may appear magnificently ornate, they are
much easier than they look, and even easier after some practice!

Though we have a strong culinary culture, we Lebanese are also known for our
incredible beverages, many of which have ancient roots. We serve Ma'a, "water"
out of traditional terra-cotta pitchers so that it is ice cold and refreshing, and our
country is one of the oldest wine production sites in the world. We are known for
our Almaza beer, along with our national aniseed liquor, Arak, which I've included
in this chapter. Served simply with cold water and ice cubes, Arak is bracing and
strong, and the most popular and ubiquitous spirit in Lebanon. But we Lebanese also
take our nonalcoholic beverages very seriously, particularly our cardamom-infused
Ahweh (Old World Arabic Coffee) and Yansoun, an anise seed–steeped tea laced
with cinnamon and honey. As a culture focused on conversation and community, we
never host anyone without offering an inviting beverage or two. Kaskun! Cheers!

Ater

rose water and orange blossom syrups

Ater, *or "syrup," is a very important ingredient in preparing Lebanese sweets. Water, lemon juice, sugar, and either orange blossom water or rose water combine to form a sticky-sweet component that can be used for dipping, pouring, and dousing over our fantastically flavorful desserts. These two ingredients are found in Middle Eastern stores and online (see page 280).*

Temperature is very important when pouring syrups over desserts: room-temperature syrup is always poured over hot pastries and hot syrup is always poured over room-temperature pastries, for maximum infusion into the desserts. These two varieties, Ater b Mazaher (Orange Blossom Syrup) and Ater b Maward (Rose Water Syrup) are used throughout my recipes. I tend to favor the aromatic orange blossom syrup for my Baklawa with walnut filling (page 245), semolina-based sweets, and Knefeh (Lebanese cheesecake). Fragrant rose water syrup is an essential part of my pistachio desserts, like Eish al Bolbol (page 251), Bellawriyeh (page 248), and Rez b Halib (page 267). Trade in either of the flavors, or even combine them together! My Ater keeps for up to 4 weeks in the refrigerator; simply warm in a small saucepan as needed.

☀ **MAKES 3 CUPS (WHICH YOU WILL NEED FOR MY RECIPES)**

6 cups sugar

2½ to 3 tablespoons freshly squeezed lemon juice

2 tablespoons orange blossom water (*mazaher*) or rose water (*maward*) or 1 tablespoon of each if you want to combine them (page 280)

Combine the sugar, lemon juice, and 3 cups of cold water in a medium pot over medium-high heat. Bring to a boil, uncovered, then immediately reduce the heat to low and simmer for 15 to 20 minutes until the syrup begins to thicken. Keep a close eye on the syrup, and make sure it remains clear in color and does not begin to brown or turn yellow.

To test the thickness of the syrup, dip a wooden spoon into the pot; the syrup should visibly coat the spoon. Let the syrup cool slightly on the spoon, then, using your index finger, swipe the syrup and squeeze it between your thumb and finger. It should feel sticky and thick, and once you release your finger and thumb there should be a thin, stringy line of syrup between the two fingers.

Turn off the heat and allow the syrup to cool slightly but remain warm, 5 to 7 minutes.

Once the syrup has cooled, gently stir in the orange blossom water or rose water or 1 tablespoon of each, then taste it; there should be a faint essence of the flavored water. Cover the pot and set aside at room temperature until ready to use. Don't let it cool completely!

NOTE This recipe can be halved easily.

Samneh
clarified butter

Samneh, *pronounced* sem-nee, *means "clarified butter." It is one of my most important baking ingredients, and I refer to it as "liquid gold." Unsalted butter is boiled intensely until the fat turns "transparent as a tear" (in Arabic lore), with impurities rising to the top of the pot and milk solids and salt sinking to the bottom. Samneh should be a bright gorgeous yellow, completely transparent and free of any additional ingredients. Clarified butter has a higher smoke point than regular butter, so I often use it in sautéing and pan-frying. When making clarified butter, make sure to start with high-quality unsalted butter (I love Land O' Lakes) and let the Samneh come to room temperature before using, as it will scald your pastries if it is still hot!*

❖ MAKES 2 CUPS

1 pound (4 sticks) high-quality unsalted
  butter, at room temperature

Put the sticks of butter in a 2-quart pot over medium heat. If the butter is in a large block, slice it into thick cubes. After 5 to 7 minutes, the butter should come to a boil and will start to slightly splatter while frothing and foaming on the surface (the milk solids, water, and salt are separating from the butter). Immediately turn the heat to low and continue to simmer for approximately 10 minutes, occasionally stirring the foam at the top; do not stir any deeper than the surface. You will see tiny honeycomb-like bubbles all over the surface, which will disappear while the sediment sinks to the bottom of the pot. Using a slotted spoon, skim off any white foam at the top of the surface until the butter is completely clear with no specks of milk solids or salt particles visible at the top of the liquid.

Remove the pot from the heat, and allow the white foam at the top of the pot to settle and dissolve, about 2 minutes. Do not stir. Allow the remaining milk solids and salts to settle at the bottom of the pot, then immediately pour the hot butter into a clean mixing bowl, leaving behind the sediment at the bottom of the pot.

Let the clarified butter come to room temperature, but still remain liquid before using. It should be crystal clear and canary yellow.

NOTE This recipe can be easily doubled or tripled. Clarified butter will keep for up to 6 months in the refrigerator or freezer in tightly sealed containers.

قشطة

Ashta
clotted cream

Meaning "cream" in Arabic, Ashta *(or* kashta*) is a luscious clotted cream used as a central component in many Lebanese desserts and as a tasty topping. Traditionally, it is made by boiling raw, whole milk and scooping out the thick cream that forms on the surface. As raw milk is not widely available in many parts of the U.S., I have created a version that combines whole milk and whipping cream. Serve this light and airy clotted cream plain with the accompaniments below, or on any dessert. It's versatile, simple, and delicious.*
✧ MAKES 1 TO 3 CUPS

1 gallon (16 cups) whole milk   1 quart (4 cups) heavy whipping cream

In a large, heavy-bottomed, 8-quart pot, heat the milk and cream over high heat until it is close to boiling, about 30 minutes. The mixture should rise approximately 3 inches above the initial milk level you started with, small bubbles will appear on the surface, and it will look frothy. Once the temperature of the milk is about 200°F, reduce the heat to low and simmer slowly for 30 minutes without stirring.

Remove from the heat and set aside at room temperature for 30 minutes. Place the lid on the pot, wrap with a large kitchen towel and set on the countertop to cool for about 6 hours, then refrigerate for 6 hours more.

Remove the pot from the refrigerator, unwrap, and remove the lid. Run a butter knife along the edges of the pot to loosen the thick layer of cream that has settled at the surface. Using a slotted spoon, scoop the top layer of thick cream off, and use immediately or store in an airtight container in the refrigerator for up to 2 days. Repeat the process to make more cream. You can reuse the liquid up to 3 times.

Serve with the following or use as a topping for desserts.

ASHTA ACCOMPANIMENTS
½ tablespoon granulated sugar or confectioners' sugar (optional)
1 teaspoon Ater (rose water syrup, see page 280)
⅓ cup fresh raspberries
1 teaspoon pistachio nuts, ground into pieces, for sprinkling

NOTE You will need a cooking thermometer.

———————

tabouli tip! Use the leftover liquid for the rice pudding recipe (page 267).

بقلاوة

Baklawa

layered phyllo pastry with walnut filling

When I think of Baklawa, *I'm immediately transported to Christmastime evenings as a child, watching my mother brushing carefully layered, paper-thin phyllo sheets with clarified butter, working like an artist into the wee hours of the morning. These days, I like to make my sweets at night, too; I find it so relaxing and therapeutic, especially when making* Baklawa, *pronounced "bak-lah-wa." You may have encountered this centuries-old dessert before, but most likely the Greek version, which although similar to the Lebanese preparation has some distinct differences. First, we do not use cinnamon, cloves, or nutmeg in our nut filling, and second, while Greek baklava is glazed with honey syrup, we finish ours with orange blossom or rose water syrup. Last, ours is baked light golden brown, whereas Greek baklava is a darker, deeper color. Although my baklawa is a labor of love, it is absolutely and totally worth it, every single chewy, nutty, sticky, flaky bite of it!* ✣ MAKES 40 TO 45 PIECES

40 sheets Athens Fillo Dough (9" x14",
    see page 282), thawed in the box to
    room temperature for about 1 hour"

1 cup Samneh (Clarified Butter, page 243)

3 cups raw, unsalted whole walnuts

½ cup sugar

1 tablespoon orange blossom water
    (see page 280)

3 cups Ater orange blossom syrup
    (see page 242)

In a food processor, grind the nuts and sugar to a grain like consistency. Transfer to a large mixing bowl and stir ¼ cup of the clarified butter and the orange blossom water into the nut mixture, so that all the ingredients are completely incorporated and the texture is somewhat moist.

Remove the phyllo from the box and the plastic wrap inside (reserve the plastic wrap) and carefully unroll onto a smooth, dry surface keeping the plastic wrap underneath the sheets of phyllo. Cover the phyllo with a damp, clean kitchen towel.

Brush the bottom and sides of the 9 x 13-inch baking pan with clarified butter, and lay the first sheet of phyllo on the sheet. Lightly smooth the phyllo sheet with the palms of your hands. Brush lightly with clarified butter, and repeat with 12 more phyllo sheets, placing each on top, then buttering from the edges of the sheet and working your way to the center, to cover the entire bottom surface of the sheet. Make sure not to press down on the phyllo sheets with your pastry brush.

continued

Evenly spread half of the walnut filling on top of the thirteenth phyllo sheet, and lightly smooth the filling out with the back of a silicone spatula so that the filling evenly covers the entire surface area of the pan. Lightly butter another sheet of phyllo dough on both sides and place on top of the walnut filling. Layer and butter 13 more sheets of phyllo (only on one side, as before.)

Spread the remaining walnut filling on top of the stack of phyllo sheets, evenly distributing it without pressing down, as before. Then, lightly butter another sheet of phyllo on both sides and place on top of the walnut filling. Layer and butter the remaining 14 sheets of phyllo dough (only on one side, as before), making sure that the final sheet of phyllo dough is as smooth as possible and generously buttered on top.

Preheat the oven to 350°F.

To achieve the traditional diamond shape baklawa: Using the non-sharp side of the knife, score a straight vertical line down the center, creating two equal halves. Then, still using the non-sharp side of the knife, lightly score 2 vertical lines on each side of each half, so that you have 6 vertical rows. Then, starting in the bottom left corner and working your way to the top right corner, diagonally score rows about 1½ inch apart from each other, creating diamonds throughout the baklawa. Using the sharp side of the knife, cut into the baklawa, starting with the vertical rows, then the diagonal rows—make sure to cut up and down and not run your knife through the traces, as you will tear the pastry sheets. Drizzle any remaining clarified butter on top.

Bake baklawa in the center of the preheated oven for 40 to 45 minutes until the pastry is light golden brown. Remove from oven and cool for 5 to 7 minutes, then douse with Ater (page 280).

Let rest for 2 to 3 hours before cutting and serving.

NOTE You will need a pastry brush and 9 x 13-inch baking pan.

بلورية

Bellawriyeh

layered shredded phyllo dough with pistachio-walnut filling

Bellawriyeh *is one of my quickest and easiest sweets; mouthwatering sticky phyllo pastry squares stuffed with flavorful pistachio-walnut filling and finished with rose water and orange blossom syrup. I love the chewy, crunchy texture and decadent combination of orange blossom–rose water syrup with the mixed nuts. Although* Bellawriyeh *is traditionally prepared only with pistachios, Mama and I fell in love with the combination of nuts—if you prefer just pistachios, omit the walnuts altogether.* ❖ **MAKES THIRTY 2-INCH SQUARES**

1 pound Athens Shredded Fillo Dough
   (kataifi, see page 282), thawed in the
   box at room temperature for 1 hour

2 cups raw, shelled, unsalted whole
   pistachios

2 cups raw, unsalted whole walnuts

1 cup sugar

½ cup warm Samneh (Clarified Butter,
   page 243)

1 tablespoon rose water (see page 280)

1 tablespoon orange blossom water

3 cups Ater rose water and orange
   blossom syrup (see page 242)

Preheat the oven to 375°F.

Bring 6 cups of water to a rolling boil in a large pot, and place a double boiler, steamer basket, or heatproof bowl over the pot of boiling water. Reduce the heat to low and maintain a steady simmer.

Remove the phyllo (kataifi) from the box and sealed bag, and separate the dough into two equal parts over a large baking sheet, making sure not to tear through the shredded strands. Place each half of the kataifi, one at a time, in the bowl or steamer basket and steam for 2 to 4 minutes, tossing the dough with tongs occasionally just until the kataifi is soft, pliable, and moist. Remove the dough with tongs and set aside on a separate baking sheet.

Pour 2 tablespoons of the warm clarified butter over each half (4 tablespoons total) and gently toss with tongs to coat the kataifi completely. Set aside.

Grind the pistachios, walnuts, and sugar in a food processor into a coarse, chunky consistency and transfer to a large mixing bowl. Pour 2 tablespoons of the clarified butter over the mixture in addition to 1 tablespoon of rose water and 1 tablespoon of orange blossom water. Stir to incorporate all the ingredients—the mixture should be moist—and set aside.

Butter the bottom and sides of a 9 x 13-inch baking pan with 2 tablespoons of clarified butter. Completely cover the bottom and corners of the buttered pan with one half of the kataifi, firmly pressing into it with the palms of your hands so that it sticks together and is flattened into one solid piece. Then, pour the nut mixture into the center of the kataifi and spread it in an even

single layer using the back of a silicone spatula or spoon. Now, cover the nut mixture with the remaining half of kataifi, firmly pressing it down with your palms to completely cover the nuts. To finish, drizzle the remaining 2 tablespoons clarified butter over the top.

Place a piece of parchment paper over the pastry dough, and place a baking pan or heavy plates on top of the parchment to weigh it down. Refrigerate for at least 2 hours or overnight until it sets and becomes very cold.

Once the kataifi mixture has adequately chilled, preheat the oven to 350°F.

Remove the pan from the refrigerator, remove the weights, and peel off the parchment paper. Place the pan on the center rack of the preheated oven and bake for 30 to 35 minutes until light golden white in color, and not at all browned.

Remove from the oven and glaze with the rose water and orange blossom syrup until all of the syrup is soaked in and the top is glistening.

Allow the Bellawriyeh to completely cool before serving, 2 to 3 hours. Then, slice into small, even squares; you should have 30.

Store at room temperature if serving within a week, or refrigerate for up to 14 days.

NOTE You will need a pastry brush, two 9 x 13-inch baking pans (or 1 baking pan and two heavy plates to use as weights).

Eish al BolBol

shredded phyllo dough nests with pistachio filling

Meaning "the nightingale's nest" in Arabic, Eish al BolBol *is one of the most ornate and sumptuous Lebanese desserts. Shredded phyllo dough is shaped into small birds' nests, then filled with vibrant green pistachios resembling bird eggs, and coated with aromatic rose water syrup. This dessert is one of my mother's favorite to make. I've simplified the steps to make it easy.* ❖ **MAKES 20 PHYLLO NESTS**

10 sheets Athens Fillo Dough (9" x14" see page 282), thawed in the box to room temperature for 1 hour

2 cups raw, unsalted, shelled pistachios

½ cup sugar

1 cup Samneh (Clarified Butter, page 243), warm

2 teaspoons rose water (see page 280)

2 cups rose water syrup (see page 280)

Preheat the oven to 350°F.

To make the pistachio filling, combine the nuts and sugar in a food processor and coarsely grind into small pebblelike pieces. Transfer the mixture to a small mixing bowl, and add 2 tablespoons of the clarified butter and the rose water. Stir the ingredients together so they are completely incorporated and somewhat moist.

Remove 10 sheets of the phyllo dough from the plastic wrapping and box, and unroll the sheets onto a smooth, dry surface keeping the plastic wrapping underneath. Rewrap the rest and refrigerate for future use. Using a small, sharp knife, slice the sheets in half horizontally to create two sections of 10 sheets; 20 sheets in total. Cover the phyllo sheets with a damp, clean kitchen towel.

Dip the pastry brush in the remaining clarified butter and lightly grease the bottoms of two 12 x 17-inch baking sheets. Take a piece of phyllo dough, working with one at a time, and lay it in front of you on a diagonal. Lightly brush the entire sheet with butter placing the rolling pin in the bottom corner of the dough. Roll the dough around the rolling pin firmly, leaving about ½ inch at the top end corner. Brush the top end corner with butter again, then roll up to seal.

Slowly slide one hand down the rolling pin to gently scrunch the dough sheet into an accordion-like shape. Once you get three-quarters of the way down the pin, stop, and slide it off the end using your other hand. Then, take both ends of the accordion-shaped sheet and gently stretch them out, then wrap them around, while retaining the rippled texture. Bring both ends together and then tuck one end under the other to enclose. Place the nests onto the buttered baking sheets, spacing them evenly apart and lightly brush the sides of each with clarified butter. You should have 20 nests. (see photos following page)

continued

Fill each nest with about 1 tablespoon of the ground pistachio mixture and add a couple of drops of clarified butter on top of the filling. Bake each batch on the center rack of the preheated oven for 10 to 12 minutes until the nests are light golden. Remove from the oven and let cool on the baking sheets for 2 to 3 minutes, then drizzle each nest with 1 tablespoon of rose water syrup. Allow to set for a few minutes before serving.

NOTE You will need a pastry brush, two 12 x 17-inch baking sheets, a clean kitchen towel, and a thin rolling pin (see page 281) or use the end of a long, thin wooden spoon.

Harissa

*baked semolina and yogurt sweets
with almonds and orange blossom syrup*

Harissa is my absolute favorite sweet treat to make and *to eat. I adore the soft, pillow texture and glistening golden-yellow appearance, not to mention the sweet, fragrant, orange blossom—laced flavor. Using fresh* Laban *yogurt (page 223) and ground semolina, or smeed, this signature sweet is found throughout Lebanon, often with different names and spellings like* Namoura, Hista Il Louz, *and* Hareeseh. *My recipe is completely authentic and traditional, and sumptuous.* ❖ MAKES 40 TO 45 SWEETS

1 ¼ cups Laban (page 223) or full-fat
    plain yogurt, at room temperature;
    I prefer Dannon

1 teaspoon baking powder

¼ teaspoon baking soda

5½ cups semolina grain fine (see
    page 279), at room temperature

1 cup sugar

1 ¼ cup Samneh (Clarified Butter,
    page 243), warm

2 tablespoons tahini (see page 280),
    at room temperature

⅓ cup almonds, whole, unsalted and
    blanched

3 cups Atar orange blossom syrup
    (see page 242), hot

Preheat the oven to 375°F.

In a medium bowl, vigorously whisk the laban with the baking powder and baking soda until silky smooth. Set aside to rest and rise for 5 to 7 minutes; it should double its size with the appearance of small bubbles on the surface.

While the laban is rising, combine the semolina grain and sugar in a large mixing bowl and create a well in the center. Pour the clarified butter into the well and thoroughly mix the semolina and butter, using your hands, until the two are completely incorporated.

Create another well in the center of the semolina-butter mixture and pour the Laban mixture and orange blossom water into the well. Using your hands, incorporate the laban into the semolina mixture so that they are completely combined and create a moist, shiny, and somewhat squishy dough. If the dough feels too dry, add a little bit of laban, and if too wet, add a little bit of semolina.

Lightly grease the bottom and sides of a 9 x 13-inch baking pan with a very thin layer of tahini. Gather all of the semolina dough and spread it out evenly in the pan, making sure the entire surface area is covered. Then, lightly press down on the dough with the palm of your hands so that it is level and smooth; the dough should be about 2 inches thick.

To create the diamond shapes, using the non-sharp side of a small knife, score (indent, do not cut completely through the dough) a vertical line dividing the dough into two halves. Then, create two vertical lines within each half, 1½ to 2 inches apart; you should have 6 even rows. Then, starting at the bottom left corner, diagonally score across the vertical lines, reaching the opposite corner (top right), creating lines about ½ inch apart. This will create about 40 to 45 diamond shapes.

Once the dough is scored, place one almond in the center of each sweet diamond and lightly tap it down. Do not push the almond deep into the dough, it should just be settled on the surface.

Bake in the center of the preheated oven for 40 to 45 minutes until the semolina is light golden brown rotating the pan halfway through baking.

Once baked, remove the Harissa from the oven and set aside for 2 to 3 minutes, then coat entirely with hot Atar orange blossom syrup, one cup at a time to throughly soak into the sweet before ladling the next cup for a maximum absorption. The Harissa should still be hot at this point. Set aside to cool completely before cutting.

After the Harissa has completely cooled, carefully cut the diamond shapes through completely following the scored lines you made earlier. Serve at room temperature or store in an airtight container.

NOTE You will need a 9 x 13-inch baking pan.

————————

taboulie tip! For best results be sure that the Laban (yogurt), semolina, and baking ingredients are at room temperature, and the butter is warm.

كنافة

Knefeh

lebanese-style cheesecake

Throughout Lebanon and the entire Middle East, the Lebanese city of Tripoli is known for its incredible desserts and sweet treats. Knefeh, a creamy dreamy Lebanese cheesecake, is one of the most luscious and luxurious desserts out there, made from super-flaky shredded phyllo dough called kataifi, thick homemade semolina-laced cream, and a final dousing of hot orange blossom syrup. With many spellings including kunafeh, konafah, kenafeh, *this fantastic cheesecake is indulgent, super-flavorful, and quite simple to make!* ✣ MAKES ONE 9 X 13-INCH OBLONG OR 9-INCH ROUND CHEESECAKE

1 pound Athens Shredded Fillo Dough (kataifi, see page 282), thawed at room temperature in the box for 1 hour

½ cup warm Samneh (Clarified Butter, page 243)

4 cups heavy cream

1 cup fine semolina grain (see page 279)

3 tablespoons sugar

3 cups Ater orange blossom syrup (see page 242), hot

Preheat the oven to 375°F.

Bring 6 cups of water to a rolling boil in a latge pot, and place a double boiler, steamer basket, or heatproof bowl over the pot of boiling water. Reduce the heat to low and maintain a steady simmer.

Remove the phyllo dough (kataifi) from the box and sealed bag, and separate the dough into two equal parts over a large baking sheet, making sure not to tear through the shredded strands. Place each half of the kataifi, one at a time, in the bowl or steamer basket and steam for 2 to 4 minutes, tossing the dough with tongs occasionally just until the kataifi is soft, pliable, and moist. Remove the dough with tongs and set aside on a separate baking sheet.

Pour 2 tablespoons of the warm clarified butter over each half (4 tablespoons total) and gently toss with tongs to coat the kataifi completely. Set aside.

Heat the heavy cream and semolina and sugar in a medium pot over high heat. Whisk the ingredients together so that the semolina dissolves into the cream, and the mixture begins to thicken and bubble, about 15 minutes. Remove from the heat and set aside momentarily.

Thoroughly coat a 9 x 13-inch rectangular or 9-inch round baking dish with 2 tablespoons of clarified butter and spread half of the softened kataifi onto the bottom of the pan in one even layer. Using your palms, firmly press down on the kataifi so that it sticks together, forming one solid mass. Then, pour the cream mixture into the center of the dough and smooth it out to the corners with a silicone spatula or spoon, so that the cream completely covers the kataifi. Place the remaining kataifi over the cream, pressing it out with the palms of your hands, so that the cream is entirely covered with the kataifi. Drizzle the top layer with the remaining 2 tablespoons clarified butter and bake on the center rack of the preheated oven for 30 to 35 minutes. When the cheesecake is light golden brown on top, set aside to cool for 5 to 7 minutes, then pour ladles of the hot Atar orange blossom syrup over the Lebanese cheesecake.

Allow to set for a few minutes before slicing and serving hot.

عوامات

Awamat
orange blossom syrup-glazed doughnuts

Derived from the Arabic awama, *which means "to float," Awamat are a delight to eat and almost as fun to make. My Sitto made these every year to celebrate the New Year and Epiphany, a Christian feast on January 6, as eating fried dough is said to bring good luck and best wishes for the year to come. Perfectly fried to a light golden brown, these scrumptious, sticky spheres are crunchy on the outside and pillowy-soft inside. Made from sifted pastry flour and yeast, Awamat are one of the most popular sweets throughout Lebanon and the Middle East, piled high in ornate arrangements and served with luscious homemade syrups. I particularly love punching the dough with my fists just before frying; it's just so satisfying and fun.*

❖ **MAKES 50 DOUGHNUTS**

3 teaspoons dry yeast (powder or solid)

1 teaspoon unbleached, all-purpose flour

1 teaspoon sugar

4 cups pastry flour, sifted

¼ teaspoon sea salt

6 to 8 cups canola oil, for frying

3 cups Ater orange blossom syrup
  (see page 242)

1 orange, peeled into strands

Dissolve the yeast, all-purpose flour, and sugar in 2 tablespoons of lukewarm water. Stir together with a fork and set aside to rise for 5 to 7 minutes; the mixture will double in size and small bubbles will appear on the surface.

Then, in a large mixing bowl, sift the pastry flour and salt. Create a well in the center of the flour and pour in 3 cups of cold bottled springwater and the yeast mixture. Mix the ingredients together so they are completely incorporated, then whisk vigorously until the consistency is smooth, soft, and moist—similar to pancake batter.

Cover the dough with plastic wrap, and place a clean kitchen towel over it. Set aside at room temperature to rise for approximately 2 hours (if the weather is warm) and overnight (if the weather is cold.)

When there is about 15 minutes left in the rising time, prepare the Ater orange blossom syrup (see page 242) so that it is still hot when the doughnuts are fried.

Once the dough has risen, carefully remove the towel and plastic wrap as the dough will be very sticky. The dough should have doubled in volume and be filled with tiny air bubbles throughout. Using your fists, punch the dough to release all of the tiny air bubbles.

continued

Line a baking sheet with paper towels and set near the stove. Bring the oil to a high frying temperature, about 350°F in an 8-quart, heavy-bottomed pot over high heat. Once the oil is hot, begin to fry the dough, working in batches of five to seven doughnuts at a time. Using a tablespoon or small ice cream scoop, scoop about 1 tablespoon of the dough and carefully release it into the hot oil. If you use a spoon, use another spoon to scrape the dough into oil with space between each one so that they do not stick to one another. Once the dough rises to the surface, turn it over gently so it cooks on all sides. In between batches, check to make sure you are maintaining an oil temperature of 350°F. Once the doughnuts are light golden brown, remove from the oil with a handheld strainer or slotted spoon and transfer to the paper towel–lined baking sheet.

While the doughnuts are still warm, submerge them in the hot syrup, working in batches and tossing to make sure they are completely coated. Remove from the syrup and set aside on a serving platter, sprinkle with orange strands.

Serve immediately.

جمعه

Maamoul

patterned semolina cookies with three fillings

Maamoul *are a signature holiday cookie that are as fun to make as they are to eat! Though these shortbread pastries are available year-round in Lebanon, they are prepared in extra-large quantities during holidays like Easter, Christmas, and Good Friday. These melt-in-your-mouth butter cookies are shaped with a signature Julie Taboulie* Taabeh, *or* Maamoul *mold (see page 281), and stuffed with walnut, date, or pistachio filling, and then dusted with confectioners' sugar. Although they are far more beautiful using the mold, they can also be shaped and decorated using the tines of a fork.*

I have included my three fillings, and I usually make all three, but feel free to make all of them or just one or two! ❖ **MAKES 24 COOKIES**

COOKIE DOUGH

1 teaspoon yeast (dry or solid)

1 teaspoon unbleached, all purpose flour

3 cups fine semolina grain (see page 279)

⅓ cup granulated sugar, plus 1 teaspoon

1 teaspoon finely ground mahlab (St. Lucie Cherry Spice, see page 280)

1½ cups Samneh (Clarified Butter, page 243), warm

1 tablespoon orange blossom water, (see page 280), at room temperature

1 tablespoon rose water (see page 280), at room temperature

WALNUT FILLING

1 cup raw, unsalted walnuts

⅓ cup granulated sugar

1 tablespoon Samneh (Clarified Butter, page 243), warm

1 tablespoon orange blossom water

DATE FILLING

1 cup fresh whole dates, pitted

1 teaspoon finely ground mahlab (St. Lucie Cherry Spice, see page 280)

2 tablespoons Samneh (Clarified Butter, page 243), warm

PISTACHIO FILLING

1 cup unsalted, shelled pistachios

⅓ cup granulated sugar

1 tablespoon Samneh (Clarified Butter, page 243), warm

1 tablespoon rose water

Granulated sugar (for date-filled cookies), or confectioners' sugar, for sprinkling

Preheat the oven to 350°F.

First, make the fillings: To make the walnut filling, combine the walnuts and sugar in a food processor and grind to a coarse meal consistency. Transfer to a small mixing bowl and stir in the clarified butter and orange blossom water. Set aside.

continued

To make the date filling: Combine the dates, mahlab, and clarified butter in a food professor and grind until a smooth soft paste forms. Transfer to a small mixing bowl and set aside.

To make the pistachio filling: Grind the pistachios and sugar in a food processor into a coarse meal. Transfer to a small mixing bowl and stir in the clarified butter and rose water. Set aside.

Make the cookie dough: In a small bowl, combine the yeast, flour, and 1 teaspoon of sugar and ⅓ cup of lukewarm water. Stir together, then set aside and allow the yeast to proof for 5 to 7 minutes until the mixture doubles in size, and becomes foamy with small bubbles.

While the yeast is proofing, combine the semolina, sugar, and mahlab in a large mixing bowl and mix together with your hands, breaking up any small clumps of semolina or sugar. Create a well in the center of the bowl and pour the warm clarified butter into the well. Thoroughly mix together so that the semolina grains are completely coated with butter. Create another well and pour in the yeast mixture along with the orange blossom and rose waters and thoroughly mix together until a soft and pliable dough forms that is moist to the touch.

Form the maamoul: Scoop about 2½ tablespoons of the dough into the palms of your hands, and mold it into a small round bowl. Poke the middle of the dough ball with your index finger and rotate the dough ball around in your other hand as you deepen and widen the hole you have created. Make sure not to break through the bottom of the ball or tear the side walls.

Take 1 tablespoon of walnut, date, or pistachio filling and place in the small hole, making sure not to overstuff the dough. Enclose the filling by gently folding the surrounding dough over the top of the hole, and pinch the edges together on top. Smooth out a seam into the dough with your fingertips so that it is entirely enclosed. Now, place the dough, seam side up, into the maamoul mold, and gently press the ball into the mold to imprint the design onto the dough. Make sure the dough does not hang over the edge of the mold, as this will create a lip we do not want. Make sure the dough does not stick to the mold, and strike the top edge of the mold onto a hard surface to release the dough.

Place the cookies on two 12 x 17-inch ungreased baking sheets, leaving space between each pastry.

Bake the maamoul in the center of the preheated oven for 12 minutes until they are very light golden yellow. Let them cool on the baking sheet for at least 15 minutes. If you wish to sprinkle granulated sugar on the walnut or date maamoul, they must be slightly warm. The other pistachio maamoul can be sprinkled with confectioners' sugar when they have completely cooled.

Store in an airtight container for up to 2 weeks.

———

taboulie tip! Using the sharp tip of a paring knife, periodically scrape any excess dough from the pattern mold to prevent dough from sticking to the mold.

رز بحليب

Rez b Halib

arabic-style rice pudding

I'm not the biggest fan of traditional Lebanese rice pudding, which I often find soupy and overly rose-flavored. So, I created my own version, which came about during a love affair I was having with arborio rice. Fresh vanilla bean (another of my absolute favorite flavors), arborio rice, and milk make for a creamy-dreamy rice pudding that I finish with a sprinkle of ground pistachios and a light drizzle of Ater *(Rose Water Syrup, see page 242). It's also a perfect dessert to make a day or two in advance, as it needs time to chill in the refrigerator before serving.* ❖ **MAKES 6 SERVINGS**

8 cups (½ gallon) whole milk

½ cup arborio rice

½ vanilla bean pod

⅓ cup sugar

½ cup shelled, unsalted pistachios, ground in a food processor into crumbly pieces

½ cup Ater rose water syrup (see page 242)

In a large, heavy-bottomed pot, combine the milk and rice and place over medium heat, uncovered. While the rice and milk are heating, scrape the seeds from the vanilla bean pod into the milk-rice mixture, using a small, sharp knife. Stir the pod and all the seeds into the mixture stirring occasionally with a wooden spoon, and bring to a rolling boil, 15 to 20 minutes.

Once the rice and milk have boiled, reduce the heat to medium-low and simmer for approximately 20 to 25 minutes, stirring with a wooden spoon to prevent the rice from sticking to the bottom and sides of the pot, and so that a film doesn't form on the top surface.

Once the mixture begins to thicken and small bubbles appear, reduce the heat to low and continue to simmer slowly, stirring constantly for 5 to 10 minutes so the mixture is very creamy and has thickened to the point where it can coat a wooden spoon. Taste the rice; it should be chewy but not mushy. Pour the sugar into the rice mixture, and stir it in until completely dissolved then turn off the heat. The pudding should be medium-thick and very creamy, it should slowly slide off a wooden spoon but not stick to it completely.

Once the pudding has cooked, remove the pot from the heat and remove and discard the pod. Transfer the hot pudding to a serving dish and cover with plastic wrap, pressing the plastic directly onto the surface of the pudding to prevent a skin from forming. Place on the countertop to come to room temperature, then refrigerate for at least one full day prior to serving.

Serve the pudding cold, drizzle each serving with 1 teaspoon of Ater and 1 tablespoon of pistachio nut crumbles, or serve plain.

Knefeh b Toufah wa Sfarjel

lebanese apple and quince cream crumble

Growing up in Upstate New York, apple picking was always one of my absolute favorite fall activities. The wealth of delicious apples grown in the region, along with the stunning scenic views from Route 20 and the gorgeous Finger Lakes made for a wonderful family outing each year. After trying a Honey Crisp apple from one of my favorite local farmers, I was absolutely smitten, and it inspired me to create my Knefeh b Toufah wa Sfarjel, *a creamy, crunchy combination of fragrant quince and sweet Honey Crisp apples. "Quince," or Sfarjel, is a sacred fruit in Lebanese cooking, and after the necessary stewing and cooking (it can't be eaten raw), it turns into the most succulent, fragrant ingredient. Made with sweet semolina cream, and sticky-sweet Ater orange blossom syrup (page 242), this apple-quince crumble is a must-make autumn dessert!*

✳ **MAKES ONE 9 X 13-INCH CRUMBLE**

6 quinces, peeled, cored, and cut into
  ½-inch slices (see 281)

6 tablespoons granulated sugar

Finely grated zest and juice of 2 lemons

6 medium Honey Crisp or other sweet,
  crunchy apple variety, peeled, cored,
  and cut into ½-inch slices

6 tablespoons (¾ stick) unsalted butter,
  chilled and cut into small cubes

SEMOLINA CREAM

1 quart heavy cream

1 cup fine semolina grain (see page 279)

3 tablespoons granulated sugar

CRUMBLE

1 cup unbleached, all-purpose flour

¾ cup granulated sugar

¾ cup light brown sugar, tightly packed

¾ cup old-fashioned rolled oats (not
  quick-cooking)

1 teaspoon ground cinnamon

½ teaspoon ground mahlab (see page
  280, optional)

¾ cup raw, unsalted whole almonds

2 pinches sea salt

12 tablespoons (1½ sticks) unsalted
  butter, cold and cut into small cubes

1½ cups Ater orange blossom syrup (see
  page 242), for serving

Preheat the oven to 375°F.

In a large pan over medium-low heat, combine the quince, 3 tablespoons of the granulated sugar, and the zest and juice from 1 lemon, so that the quince is entirely coated with the other ingredients. Cook for about 12 to 15 minutes, occasionally stirring, until the mixture simmers, and the quince softens and turns bright red. Remove from the heat and set aside.

In a large mixing bowl toss the apple slices with the remaining 3 tablespoons granulated sugar and zest and juice of the remaining lemon. Then, cover the bottom of a 9 x13-inch baking pan with

6 tablespoons of the cold butter cubes and spread the apples on top. Layer the quince slices on top of the apples and set the pan aside.

Make the semolina cream: In a medium pot over medium-high heat, combine the heavy cream, semolina and granulated sugar and whisk together until it comes to a boil. Once the mixture comes to a boil, immediately turn the heat to low and continue to whisk constantly until the mixture thickens, about 15 minutes, making sure the mixture does not burn at the bottom of the pot.

As soon as the cream thickens, pour it over the quince and apples and using a silicone spatula or the back of a spoon spread it evenly over the fruit. Set aside.

Now, make the crumble: In a food processor, combine all of the crumble ingredients so they are entirely incorporated together. Pause periodically, and scrape the bottom and sides of the bowl, then process again a few times so a coarse, crumbly consistency is achieved.

Top the fruit and cream with the crumble mixture, and bake in the center rack of the preheated oven for 30 to 35 minutes until the crumble is light golden brown and bubbly. Remove from the oven, and allow to rest for 10 minutes.

Just before serving, top with Ater orange blossom syrup. Dollop with whipped cream or real vanilla bean ice cream if you wish.

---

taboulie tip! Quince is in season in the early fall months and you can typically find them at your local farmers' markets or online at Melissa's World Variety Produce (see page 283). Look for fresh, fragrant, and highly floral, brightly-colored golden yellow fruit at full maturity.

Ghraybeh

moist butter cookies topped with blanched almonds

Pronounced "gry-bey," Ghraybeh means "to swoon" or "faint" in Arabic, and these super-moist butter cookies will surely have you swooning. Ghraybeh are often prepared for festive occasions, like holidays, communions, bridal showers, and weddings. Clarified butter, semolina, and sugar are combined into a sweet, sticky dough, then formed into diamonds and finished with crunchy blanched almonds. ❖ **MAKES 3 DOZEN COOKIES**

2 cups Samneh (Clarified Butter, page 243), refrigerated until cold and solid

1 tablespoon Crisco

1 cup sugar

1 cup semolina (see page 279)

3½ cups unbleached, all-purpose flour, plus extra for hands

36 blanched whole almonds

Preheat the oven to 325°F.

Using an electric hand or stand mixer, cream the clarified butter and Crisco together on high speed until the mixture is smooth and fluffy and remains cold. Scrape the bottom and sides of the bowl, then add the sugar, and blend until smooth, making sure it is still cold.

Slowly add the semolina and fold into the butter-sugar mixture. Then, sift the flour into the mixture and mix well with your hands until the dough is soft, pliable, slightly sticky, and still cold. If the consistency is very sticky, add flour by the tablespoon.

Lightly flour your fingers, then take about 3 tablespoons of the dough and roll it on a clean, cold surface into a thin rod, about 1 inch round. Using a sharp knife, cut on the diagonal to create diamond shapes approximately 2 inches long; you should have 36 diamond-shaped cookies. Work quickly while the dough is still cold so that it does not begin to crumble. Then, slide the tip of your knife underneath each piece to pick it up and place it onto an ungreased cookie or baking sheet leaving space in between each one. Place 1 blanched almond in the center of each cookie and lightly press it into the dough.

Bake the cookies on the center rack of the preheated oven for 15 minutes, until just slightly golden but still very white.

Remove from the oven and allow to completely cool on the baking sheet 2 to 3 hours before serving or storing. Store in an airtight container at room temperature for up to 2 weeks.

———————

taboulie tip! Do not remove the cookies until completely cooled or they will crumble!

عرق

Arak
lebanese anise liquor aperitif

Pronounced "ah-dut," Arak (also spelled Araq) is the national drink of Lebanon. This smooth and refreshing aperitif is distilled from sweet golden grapes and anise seeds, creating a strong, licorice taste and a colorless appearance that turns milky-white when mixed with water. In its purest form, arak is 100-plus proof, and often referred to as the "milk of lions"! From the tender age of seven, my mother remembers watching her father, my Jiddo (grandfather) harvesting yellow grapes from our family's orchard, and setting up his copper distilling device, his karkeh, right in the middle of the grape vines. Arak is distilled multiple times, then aged for two years before drinking. I have strong childhood memories of seeing my uncles sipping this pungent drink, particularly at summer barbecues and family gatherings. This recipe is for the most basic preparation, and the one we drink most frequently. Cheers, or as we say, Kaskun! (pronounced kes-coon).

✦ **MAKES 1 SERVING**

2 parts Arak, anise liquor (see page 281)

1 part cold water

2 to 3 ice cubes

Pour the arak into a glass, slowly pour the cold water into the glass, and add the ice cubes. Serve immediately.

Ahweh

old world arabic coffee

In Lebanon, coffee is far more than just a hot beverage with caffeine—it's an important part of daily life, conversation, and ritual. Scented with fragrant cardamom, Ahweh *is a rich and thick Arabic coffee always served out of a long-handled metal pot called a* raqwe. *Ahweh begins with high-quality roasted arabica beans, ground very finely and then boiled with water and cardamom pods or powder. Always served in delicate demitasse cups, it has an enchanting smell, and signals the start of a social gathering. No meal is complete without a strong cup, and instead of wine at U.S. girls' nights, we come together for hot demitasses of* Ahweh. *Among groups of Lebanese women, it is a tradition to "read the cups," by flipping them over after the coffee has been drunk, letting them dry, and flipping them back over to reveal squiggly lines and swirls similar to Arabic text. One person "reads" each person's cup, interpreting fortunes for each. Today, I hear from many female fans that the "reading of the cups" was the best part of* Ahweh! ❖ **MAKES 6 SERVINGS**

1 heaping tablespoon finely ground
    arabica beans

9 cardamom pods

Granulated white sugar

½ teaspoon finely ground cardamom
    (optional)

Pour 1½ cups cold water into a *rawke*, or small coffee pot, and bring to a rolling boil over medium-high heat. Remove from the heat and gently stir in the finely ground coffee until it is incorporated in the water. Add 3 whole cardamom pods, then return the pot to the stovetop and place over low heat. Hold the handle of the pot with one hand, and vigorously stir the foam on the surface for about 1 minute, until the foam dissipates. Bring the coffee almost to boiling, allow it to rise, and just before it boils over, quickly remove it from the heat. Allow to rest for 2 to 3 minutes and pour slowly (to avoid unsettling the sediment at the bottom of the pot) into small espresso cups. Sweeten to taste with sugar, and add 1 cardamom pod per cup.

يانسون

Yansoun

anise-steeped tea

Yansoun, *literally translates to "anise." This light, licorice-steeped tea is soothing to my soul and spirit—even hearing the word* Yansoun *soothes me immediately.* Yansoun *is a very healing tea, often used for upset stomachs or baby's colic, and frequently enjoyed before bed to ensure a restful night's sleep. The flavor is fragrant without being overpowering, and the anise adds a slightly spicy sweetness to every sip. I love to sweeten it with orange blossom honey, but feel free to use any raw or clover honey.* ✣ **MAKES 6 SERVINGS**

3 teaspoons anise seeds

1 whole cinnamon stick

3 tablespoons orange blossom or clover honey, plus more to taste

In a large teakettle or regular pot, combine 6 cups of cold water, the anise seeds, and cinnamon stick. Bring to a boil over medium-high heat, then reduce the heat to low and simmer for 5 to 7 minutes. Remove from the heat, stir in the honey, and allow to steep for another 2 to 3 minutes.

Pour the tea into cups through a fine-mesh sieve, pouring in a thin stream so the seeds remain at the bottom of the pot. Sweeten with additional honey to taste. Serve immediately.

LEBANESE PANTRY

Grains and Starches

BULGUR WHEAT ⬩ Bulgur wheat, a quick-cooking form of whole wheat is a frequent ingredient in Lebanese cuisine. There are four distinct grind sizes, and I most often use #1 (fine) and #2 (medium). Bulgur is available in Middle Eastern markets and also from a variety of companies including Bob's Red Mill (found in Whole Foods) and on Amazon.com.

CANNING AND PICKLING SALT ⬩ Used for many of my pickles, this coarse salt is available at many larger grocery stores (Morton's has a version) and on amazon.com.

CHICKPEAS (GARBANZO BEANS) ⬩ I prefer to use dried chickpeas over canned chickpeas in my recipes—the flavor (no canned taste) and texture are much better, there is no salt added in the dried version, and there are fewer preservatives. Dried chickpeas are widely available in grocery stores, Middle Eastern stores, and on amazon.com.

FARINA ⬩ Farina, or *fark*, is a cereal grain made from semolina. Make sure not to get the quick-cooking version. It can be found in many grocery stores, Middle Eastern stores, and on amazon.com.

FREEKEH ⬩ Freekeh is fire-roasted baby wheat. It is a Middle Eastern ancient grain found at Middle Eastern and Mediterranean specialty food stores and on amazon.com. I love the slightly smoky flavor and toothsome texture.

MOGHRABIEH ⬩ These large grains, also known as "Lebanese couscous," are slightly toothsome and often cooked with broth or stock. They can be found on amazon.com and in Middle Eastern Specialty Stores.

PARDINA LENTILS ⬩ These brownish-green lentils are my favorite variety to use, and are slightly smaller than other lentils. They are very affordable, and can be purchased on amazon.com and at many grocery and specialty stores.

PHYLLO DOUGH AND SHREDDED PHYLLO DOUGH KATAIFI ⬩ This flaky, paper-thin pastry can be found in the frozen foods aisle in packages of sheets. The shredded version, "kataifi," can be found on amazon.com—I recommend the Apollo brand.

SEMOLINA ⬩ Not to be confused with "semolina flour," this is the coarse-cut grain of yellow durum wheat and can be found in Middle Eastern stores or on amazon.com.

VERMICELLI NOODLE NESTS ⬩ Vermicelli noodles, particularly broken into pieces, are a very common component in Lebanese rice dishes. You can find them in the Asian or pasta sections of grocery stores, or on amazon.com.

Spices, Spreads, and Condiments

ALEPPO PEPPER ⬩ This moderately hot, slightly fruity spice is used in many of my recipes, and is sold at many specialty stores, grocery stores, and online at penzeys.com and amazon.com.

HOT PEPPER–INFUSED OLIVE OIL ✤ While spicy olive oil is easy to make yourself (simply infuse hot peppers in extra-virgin oil for 2 to 3 weeks), it's also widely available in gourmet, specialty stores and at amazon.com.

MAHLAB (ST LUCIE CHERRY SPICE) ✤ Made from cherry pits, this aromatic spice is used both in sweet and savory dishes. It can be found in some specialty stores and at penzeys.com and amazon.com.

MASTIC ✤ This resin from the mastic tree is neither a spice nor an herb, but has a fresh, piney taste and scent. It can be found in some specialty stores and at amazon.com.

NIGELLA SEEDS ✤ These pungent black seeds are often used in Indian and other Middle Eastern cuisines. They can be found at specialty grocery stores, Indian and Middle Eastern stores, penzeys.com, and amazon.com.

ORANGE BLOSSOM WATER ✤ Distilled from bitter-orange blossoms, this delicate item is used in many of my desserts, sometimes alone and sometimes in a syrup. It can be found at Middle Eastern specialty stores and on amazon.com.

POMEGRANATE MOLASSES ✤ This sweet, tangy condiment known as *Dibis Rahman* in Arabic is used in a number of recipes including dressings, sauces, and meat dishes. Pomegranate molasses is available in Middle Eastern markets, specialty stores, and on amazon.com and worldmarket.com.

ROSE WATER ✤ This highly fragrant flavored water is used in many Middle Eastern and Indian desserts, and also as a skin product. It can be found in Middle Eastern and Indian specialty stores and on amazon.com. Make sure to purchase the variety made for cooking!

SUMAC SPICE ✤ Sumac is one of my most frequently used spices, and has a tangy lemony flavor. Ground sumac is sold in Middle Eastern stores, some grocery stores, and at penzeys.com, thespicehouse.com, and on amazon.com.

TAHINI (SESAME SEED PASTE) ✤ Nutty and creamy, tahini is a common ingredient in many Middle Eastern cuisines, and is used widely in Lebanese dishes. Tahini is sold in many grocery stores nationwide, Middle Eastern stores, and on amazon.com. Tahini is best out of a bottle, not a can, and there should be a clear separation between the oil at the top and the paste below.

Vegetables and Fruits

COOSA SQUASH ✤ This light green, thin-skinned summer squash is native to Lebanon and used throughout our cuisine. Whether stuffed, sautéed, or grilled, it's one of my favorites because of its tender texture and sweet flavor. It is often sold at farmers' markets, certain grocery stores, and farm stands and is harvested in the summer months.

EGGPLANTS ✤ **Sicilian** • This variety of eggplant is small, round, and generally a mixture of white and light purple. Smooth and silky, with a high-glossy sheen, this thin skinned eggplant with small seeds that are minimal, can be found in many farmers' markets and select grocery stores. I love its sweet flavor and smooth, silky texture. **Italian** • The regular variety of small eggplant found in grocery stores is the Italian eggplant, long, and dark purple. Make sure to select eggplants that do not have darkened or bruised skin. **Indian** • The Indian eggplant variety looks like a rounder, very tiny version of Italian eggplant, with dark purplish skin and a slightly oblong shape. You can find Indian eggplant at farmers' markets or select grocery stores.

FRESH GRAPE LEAVES ✤ In my recipes, I always use fresh grape leaves, as opposed to the jarred, preserved version. Fresh grape leaves are often at Middle Eastern and Greek stores, but if you cannot find the fresh ones, you can use the jarred leaves.

FRESH OLIVES ✤ For my Zaytoun (cracked, cured olives), I start with fresh olives, which can be a bit tricky to find. Fresh olives are generally harvested between September and November, and can be found online at greatolives.com and chaffinfamilyorchards. com, among others.

LONG HOT PEPPERS ✤ Available in both bright green and red colors, although more commonly green, these are the long, spicy peppers that are often cured in Italian cuisine. You can find these spicy peppers in many grocery stores and farmers' markets.

SWEET HOT PEPPERS ✤ These peppers are generally smaller and rounder than other hot peppers and add a sweet yet spicy kick to dishes. Please purchase the fresh variety, if you can, which are available in many grocery stores and farmers' markets.

PERSIAN CUCUMBERS ✤ These smaller (4 to 6 inches long, on average) cucumbers have smooth, thin skin, are mostly seedless, and sweeter than many of their larger counterparts. They are the only variety of cucumber I use. They are available in many grocery stores nationwide. If you cannot find them, an English cucumber can often suffice.

PURSLANE ✤ This edible succulent, often considered a weed, is one of my favorite ingredients in salads and other cold dishes. Extremely healthy, it can be found in farmers' markets and some specialty stores. If you can't find purslane, feel free to substitute watercress or spinach.

QUINCE ✤ Similar in appearance to a pear, this bright yellow fruit can be found in the fall months at specialty grocery stores and farmers' markets. Inedible when raw, it becomes sweet and tender when stewed in liquid.

Additional Ingredients

ARAK ✤ Arak is the national liquor of Lebanon, and is made with grapes and flavored with anise. Arak is available at many liquor stores and online at zeetequila.com.

RENNET ✤ Rennet is a product packed with enzymes to aid with cheese making. Available at cheesemaking.com and kalustyans.com.

Kitchen Equipment

ARABIC ROLLING PIN ✤ The Arabic rolling pin is much thinner than the Western version and is often carved with designs or initials. I sell my Julie Taboulie Arabic Rolling pins online at JulieTaboulie.com.

MAAMOUL MOLD ✤ This wooden cookie mold is used to create shapes in my Maamoul pastries. I have designed my own version, and it is available at JulieTaboulie.com.

MORTAR AND PESTLE ✤ Known as a *jidan* in Arabic, this piece of equipment consisting of a ceramic or marble bowl (mortar) with a club-like object has been used in kitchens since ancient times. I use the jidan constantly, for crushing spices, and most often grinding garlic into a smooth paste. Mortar and pestles are widely available at kitchen stores and online, including amazon.com, williamssonoma.com, and bedbathandbeyond.com.

ZUCCHINI CORER ✤ In my stuffed coosa squash recipes, I use this tool to remove the inside flesh. It is widely available in many cooking stores and home stores and at amazon.com.

RESOURCES

A superior selection of the freshest and finest Lebanese, Middle Eastern, and Mediterranean specialty food products and sources out there. A go-to guide of where to buy online and in-store.

Since starting my show I have tasted, tested, and perfected my authentic recipes trying countless brands and full lines of specialty foods, Lebanese, Middle Eastern, and Mediterranean products on the market until I found the perfect ones for each and every one of my recipes. Achieving my traditional, tried and true recipes that are "Julie Taboulie tested and Mama approved" all starts with cooking, baking, and sweet-making using the freshest and finest quality of ingredients that you can find. Thankfully, I have already found them for you. I have selected some of my go-to sources and top product picks for you to create your very own fool-proof pantry just like the one that I have at home. After all, my food philosophy is "fresh is best!"

AL WADI ALAKHDAR
Offers a full line of leading Lebanese and Middle Eastern specialty food products available at select specialty food import stores across the country. They also have all-natural orange blossom water and rose water essences available. alwadi-alakdar.com

ATHENS FOODS
The world's largest and leading producer of Fillo dough and Fillo products. I prefer this brand to make all of my sweets, desserts, and pastries that call for Phyllo Dough. The Athens and Apollo Fillo brand are my top picks for Fillo (Phyllo) Dough, both the thin, flat sheets and the shredded dough called Kataifi. Athens Fillo is the #1 brand in supermarkets sold across the country, and is also available at wholesale clubs, specialty import stores, found in either the refrigerator or frozen food sections. Make sure to properly store and thaw the dough before use. athensfoods.com

BAROODY IMPORTS
This is one of the largest brands and wholesalers of the finest full line of leading Lebanese and Middle Eastern products in America. From dried beans and legumes (chickpeas, fava, and lentils) to grains (bulgur, barley, freekeh, and farro), semolina and farina, spices and seasonings, and my favorite tahini brand Beirut. Although they are a wholesaler, the majority of their products can be found at specialty import stores or at some of the online sources that I have provided in this directory. baroodyimports.com

BOB'S RED MILL
Full line of fresh and fabulous whole-grain and gluten-free foods. Featuring gluten-free flours and grains such as quinoa, millet, amaranth, and more. Also, ancient Middle Eastern grains like bulgur, barley, freekeh, and farro are also available as well as dried chickpeas (garbanzo beans), fava beans, and lentils. bobsredmill.com ⁖ 1.800.349.2173

BUY LEBANESE
An exclusive online source of leading Lebanese brands and Middle Eastern products shipped directly from Lebanon to the World. buylebanese.com

CORTAS
This is my top pick for fragrant flower essences of rose water and orange blossom water. I also prefer their pomegranate molasses product. The Cortas brand of products are affordable and available at their retail store at www.Shamra.com and items can typically be found at specialty import stores or some of the online sources that I have provided in this directory. usacortas.com

HASHEMS NUTS & COFFEE GALLERY
Dearborn, Michigan–based Middle Eastern Foods company specializing in Turkish coffee, roasted nuts and seeds, spices, and an array of authentic Arabic foods. hashems.com ⁖ 1.313.581.3212

JULIE TABOULIE
Julie Taboulie's Lebanese Kitchen online shop is your number one source for specialty Lebanese kitchen tools. JulieTaboulie.com

KALUSTYAN'S
A New York City landmark for the finest specialty foods since 1944. Offering a fresh and full line of Lebanese, Middle Eastern, and International ingredients for all of your cooking, baking, dessert, sweet, and cheese-making needs. This is the most comprehensive source and finest selection of specialty products. Kalustyans.com ❖ 1.212.685.3451 or 1.800.352.3451

KING ARTHUR FLOUR
America's Best Loved Flour, King Arthur Flour offers a superior selection of signature all-purpose, whole wheat, white whole wheat, bread, cake, self-rising and sprouted flours. Along with the highest-quality organic, gluten-free and specialty flours, grains, meals and mixes. Try it once. Trust it always. kingarthurflour.com ❖ 1.800.827.6836

MELISSA'S PRODUCE
Featuring fantastic fresh fruits, vegetables, herbs, and more that are available seasonally. Hard-to-find specialty fresh fruits and vegetables that I call for in my Lebanese cooking such as Quince, Pomegranate, Turkish figs, Indian eggplant, Persian (mini-seedless) cucumbers, Kousa squash, and Zucchini Squash Blossoms are all available. melissas.com ❖ 1.800.588.0151

MYMOUNE
Meaning "my preserve" in Arabic, is a gourmet award-winning line of Lebanese flower waters, jams and preserves, syrups, seasonings, and spices that are all-natural. No colorants, artificial flavors, additives, or preservatives. Made with love, the traditional Lebanese way. mymoune.com

NUTS.COM
Offering premium products of the very finest and freshest nuts, flavorful dried fruits, seeds and spices, coffees and teas, along with chocolates, candies, and sweets. Also all-natural, organic, raw, roasted, gluten-free, sugar-free, kosher, specialty diet, superfoods, and healthy snacks of the highest quality available. nuts.com ❖ 1.800.558.6887

OLIVE HARVEST
Premium quality Lebanese extra-virgin olive oil that is grown, harvested, and produced in the famous fertile lands of the Koura region of Northern Lebanon then imported to the United States. oliveharvest.com ❖ 1.978.261.5119

PENZEYS
Specializing in superior quality spices, seasonings, herbs, essences, and extracts. penzeys.com ❖ 1.800.741.7787

SAHADI'S
A Brooklyn-based Middle Eastern specialty foods family-run market since 1895 on Atlantic Avenue for over sixty years and still going stronger than ever today! Sahadi Fine Foods specializes in staple grocery, pantry items, a famous bulk food section along with prepared foods plus cheeses, coffee and teas, oils and olives, nuts, seeds, and sweets. sahadis.com ❖ 1.718.624.4550

SAMIR'S
A Syracuse, New York, famous international food fixture since 1981 on Genesee Street is my specialty food sanctuary! Samir's Imported Foods stocks a superior selection of Lebanese, Middle Eastern, and Mediterranean products in the heart of Upstate New York. 1.315.422.1850

SPICE ISLANDS
Specializing in an extensive selection of spices and seasonings, herbs and extracts of the highest quality as well as an organic and gourmet line of spices. www.spiceislands.com ❖ 1.800.247.5251

ZIYAD
High-quality line of authentic Lebanese, Middle Eastern, and Mediterranean specialty food staple ingredients, pantry items, and products that are available at most major supermarkets across the country in the international food sections or ethnic aisles as well as specialty food import stores. www.ziyad.com ❖ 1.815.552.6018 or 1.815.552.6039

ACKNOWLEDGMENTS

I believe that one dream can light the world, and my dream (unbeknownst to me) was to be the "ambassador" for Lebanese cuisine and culture in America. I suppose that it is no coincidence that my childhood nickname became my brand/stage name, and I am graciously grateful that God dreamed this dream for me that would become my destiny.

As a first-generation and full-blooded Lebanese-American born to an immigrant Catholic Lebanese family I was immersed in learning, making, and sharing Lebanese cuisine and culture all of my life. Lebanon lives in my heart, soul, and spirit. I set out to share our warm and welcoming ways, heartfelt hospitality, fresh and flavorful foods, generosity and giving nature, resilient spirit, and positivity of the people that are so proud to be Lebanese, and most of all the beautiful and breathtaking land of Lebanon that I love so much. I do not live in Lebanon but Lebanon lives in me. My cookbook is my love letter to Lebanon, to my Mother, to my Sitto (grandmother), and to my whole loving Lebanese family. Ana Bahebkoun, I love all of you!

My heartfelt thanks to Our Lady of Lebanon, Saint Harissa, our beautiful blessed Mother Mary for supporting and seeing me through, I send all of my love to you. To my special sanctuary, The Basilica and National Shrine of Our Lady Lebanon in Youngstown, Ohio, for always bringing me peace, positivity, and prayers. To my whole large, loyal, and loving Lebanese community in my birthplace city, Utica, New York, and to my church St. Louis Gonzaga, Father John, Deacon Paul, the St. Mary's Guild, and the annual Taste of Lebanon! I would like to thank God, Jesus, Saint Anthony, Saint Joseph, Saint Sharbel, Saint Rocco, and all of my special Saints that shed their shining light upon me and uplift me from the inside out.

My dream of writing my debut Lebanese cookbook would not be created or completed without my amazing Mother, Hind Sageer VanDusen, for joining me on this journey from day one, nearly ten years ago, and never wavering or leaving my side, standing by me, supporting me, smiling at me, and most of all giving me the strength to see this special project through. Thanks so much for allowing me to become a sponge. For sharing all of your wisdom, words, wonderful ways in the kitchen, patiently teaching me how to cook correctly and the "Lebanese way." Your tips, tricks, and techniques, secrets and special Sitto stories, I shall hold close to my heart. I could have never done this without you. With all of my heart, soul and spirit, I am truly thankful and graciously grateful to you for all of my days. This will live within me and last with me a lifetime. To my generous grandmother, my special Sitto, Josephine Nassour Rawda for courageously sending my Mother to this country and for founding our "fresh is best" food philosophy so many centuries ago in the old country, I wish I could cook for you today. Along with all of my family still living in Lebanon today, my aunts, uncles, and cousins I miss you much with all my heart.

To my guardian angel in heaven, my father, Edward B. Sageer, I think about you every day and I know that you are dancing up in heaven celebrating with me. To my dearest other father here on earth, Richard L. VanDusen, for always being there for me no matter what and taste-testing, too!

To my sweetest sister, Selma, you make my heart smile and when I see hearts I see you. I always appreciate your two-sense to my vegetarian recipes and spicy sense of humor. You are my best friend. To my older brothers, Freddy and Eddie Jr. (a.k.a. bodyguards!) for being proud of me, protecting me, and providing me with the courage to always stay true to myself and to stand up strongly for what I believe in, you both are my backbone. You are the best brothers in the whole wide world. It's real nice and we really did it! To my beautiful and bright nieces, Sophie Honey and Lola, for being the light in my life, and for loving lemon, zaatar, and manoush (a.k.a. Lebanese pizza) so much! You both bring joy to my world and I love you to the moon and back, and to their beautiful mother Jami, for raising such smart, talented, and thoughtful young girls.

Julie Taboulie wouldn't exist today without the man that gave me my nickname, my Uncle Dominick! You are like another father to me, thank you for helping to raise me into the proud Lebanese woman that I am today. To his lovely wife, my Auntie Layla, for always offering your sound advice and for beautifully handwriting the absolutely amazing Arabic script for the chapter and recipe names in my book, it is beautiful, just like you! To their children, my first cousins, Odel and Danielle, I thank you both for always being there with supportive smiles. To my Auntie Mona, words cannot express the way you make me feel when I hear your vibrant voice, see your smiling face, or feel your warm embrace. You have been like a Godmother to me. Yalla, Yalla, Yalla already I hear you say…I'm hurrying up Auntie! To my Aunt Marcelle, you have always been such a strong matriarch in our family, and for this, I am forever grateful, and for sacredly sharing your Syrian string cheese method with me. I shall always cherish that special day together and I will always think of you. To the Rawda, Sageer, VanDusen, Karrat, and Karam families for being my family first and foremost and for your friendships.

Sometimes the stars align and kismet occurs which is faithfully what happened when I talked to my angel agent, Sharon Bowers. Thank you for believing in me, my brand, and this book from our very first phone call; this cookbook wouldn't be made possible without you. My endless thankfulness to you for your gentle guidance, gumption, and gusto to get this to our happy home of St. Martin's Press. To my lovely writer, Leah Bhabha, for editing my headnotes, recipes, and remarks so fluently and for always keeping my voice on the page so vibrantly. Your patience is much appreciated always. Here's to our mutual love of pickles!

To my happy home of St. Martin's Press! I am so proud to be one of your authors and publish my first cookbook together with you and your highly talented and tenacious team. My utmost thanks to my senior editor, BJ Berti, you are like a breath of fresh air, and I cannot thank you enough for seeing something special in my story, in me, and in my recipes, right from the start, and for shaping this manuscript into the special and beautiful book that it is today. Michelle McMillian, Courtney Littler, and Vicki Lame for recognizing my authenticity. For the delightful design by Jan Derevjanik, your creative direction is as delicious as my recipes. Brant Janeway, Erica Martiano, and the entire marketing and sales team for making this happen. Bravo to all of you and all that you do in getting behind this book in the store, on the shelves, and online. St. Martin's Press you mean the world to me.

To American Public Television for providing such a pioneering and premiere platform to present my cooking shows and for successfully distributing and supporting my series nationwide to public television stations. Special thanks to Tom Davison, Judy Barlow, Hilary Finkel Buxton, Erin Bowles, Lauren Mills, Erin Djerf, Colette Greenstein, Jamie Haines, Dawn Anderson, Cynthia Fenneman, and her entire talented team at APT. To Create TV,

Chris Funkhouser, WNET New York and WGBH Boston in association with NETA and PBS and the sensational staff for "creating," launching, and growing such a strong and successful television channel to share my show with American audiences. Special thanks to all of my loyal and loving viewers who watch my show so religiously, I send smiles to all of you, your families, and friends that share and spread the word of my wonderful program with the world.

My series would not be possible without Visit Syracuse. Special thanks to the valued visionary David Holder, clever Carol Eaton, and powerhouse Nikita Jankowski for making it possible for me to "do my thing" so successfully with your sponsorship and support. I am so humbled and honored to call Syracuse, New York, my home. To my copilot, my director, Brian Anelli, for all of your natural talents that you bring to the table, you are invaluable. To "Team Taboulie" and crew for crafting such a colorful and creative cooking show series from unscripted to the screen so seamlessly. Debra George for always being the calm in the storm, your quiet strength, listening so intently, your loyalty, for being such a steady sound board, and for always being there any time of day, and for your great taste of all my vegetarian dishes.

My series would also not be possible without my kitchen sponsors who carefully created, crafted, designed, and developed my Lebanese kitchen for the show. Candlelight Cabinetry, KichenAid, MacKenzie-Childs, and to my local Syracuse sponsors Kitchen Express, Tile & Stone, Vallar's Tile and Marble, VP by Innovations, and especially my interior designer, Dava Schmidt plus all of the countless construction and crew, I can't thank you enough. Cazenovia Cutblock for providing the custom crafted cutting boards for my show, my book, and my brand, I am blessed to be working with you. In your founder's famous words…it's

sick! Melissa's produce, thank you for providing the freshest produce possible for our show, cookbook, and special events…Melissa's truly is "the freshest ideas in produce."

Ahem, to the amazing Alexandra Grablewski for your kind friendship and for taking such fabulous photos of my food. Over the four-week shoot of my cookbook somewhere between Baba Ghanouj and Baklawa, we became family. You will always hold a special place in my heart and in our family. You are naturally gifted and I am grateful for your sharing your gift in this book. I poured my heart, soul, and spirit into the cooking of this book and you had the foresight to bring my food to full life and capture my soul on each plate. Therefore, my food and these photos have feeling and that is because of how you translated them through your lens.

Last but not least I am leaving off where I began ten years ago with the one simple mission statement "to teach people how to make Lebanese cuisine." My many thanks to all of my "people" particularly Jean Forster and my very first cooking class students in Marcellus, New York, and to Carol Johnson at the Marcellus Free Library for giving the go-ahead and allowing me to teach the community. To meeting Carrie Lazarus so serendipitously that one sunny summer afternoon on the sidewalks of Skaneateles, New York, and bringing me on your morning talk show "Bridge Street" for my very first "Cooking with Julie Taboulie" live cooking segment! I'll always remember my very first sponsors Peter Guinta & Sons Produce, Mediterranean Specialty Foods, and Samir's in Syracuse, New York, thank you for supporting me right from the start to help me to get to where I am today, you are all truly treasured.

Finally, God bless my glorious land of Lebanon. Ana Bahebak Ya Lebnan, I love you Lebanon!

INDEX